The Technique and Practice of Object Relations Family Therapy

The Technique and Practice of Object Relations Family Therapy

Samuel Slipp, M.D.

Jason Aronson Inc.
Northvale, New Jersey
London

Library of Congress Cataloging-in-Publication Data

Slipp, Samuel.
   The technique and practice of object relations family therapy.

   Includes bibliographies and index.
   1. Family psychotherapy.   2. Object relations
(Psychoanalysis)   I. Title.   [DNLM: 1. Family Therapy—
methods.   2. Object Attachment. WM 430.5.F2 S633t]
RC488.5.S574   1988   616.89′156   87-33463
ISBN 0-87668-996-9

To My Families:

**My Mother and Father, Ida and William,
and My Sister, Belle**

My Wife, Sandra, and My Daughter, Elena

Contents

Part II. Family Patterns in Various Psychopathologies

Part III. Family Therapy Approaches

Part IV. Object Relations Techniques in Family Therapy

Preface

This book extends the clinical application of object relations family therapy, which I pioneered in the United States. It uses the integration of psychoanalysis and family therapy developed in my previous book *Object Relations: A Dynamic Bridge Between Individual and Family Treatment*.

The book is divided into four sections: Integration of Individual and Family Theory and Practice, Family Patterns in Various Psychopathologies, Family Therapy Approaches, and Object Relations Techniques in Family Therapy. A review of theory and other family approaches is presented to serve as a foundation for understanding the framework and technique of object relations family therapy. The book is clinically oriented, with examples of case material to demonstrate how the therapist actually works in practice with the family.

Chapter 1 presents a historical overview of the field of family therapy and the three revolutions in psychotherapy. These are the intrapsychic, interpersonal, and family-as-a-whole approaches, which respectively represent one-person, two-person, and systemic psychologies. Dynamic family therapy and object relations family therapy are defined and described.

Chapter 2 reviews in a very broad fashion the evolution of psychoanalysis. This chapter is especially important for those family therapists unfamiliar with psychoanalytic theory, and for those who are knowledgeable but desire a refresher. Some of the contributions of Sigmund Freud, Sandor Ferenczi, Melanie Klein, Ronald Fairbairn, Michael Balint, Donald Winnicott, Heinz Hartmann, Erik Erikson, Edith Jacobson, Heinz Kohut, and Otto Kernberg are presented.

Chapter 3 covers the contributions of Freud and Wilfred Bion to psychoanalytic group psychology. It also reviews its application by Henry Dicks and others to family therapy, as well as comparing my work with the work of Bion.

Chapter 4 describes the evolution of systemic family therapy from the work of Gregory Bateson to its development by Salvador Minuchin and Mara Selvini-Palazzoli. Its contributions and problems are described.

Chapter 5 reviews my typology, in which specific family transactional patterns are related to specific forms of psychopathology in the identified patient. These pathologies include schizophrenia, hysterical/borderline conditions, depression, and the overinvolved delinquent. Combinations and variations of these transactional patterns are presented, as well as a reconciliation of the findings of early childhood arrest with family dynamics noted in late childhood for the borderline patient.

Chapter 6 discusses family transactional patterns for narcissistic personality disorders. Subtypes of the emotional orphan and the Solomon child are presented, and case examples of each are given.

Chapter 7 goes through the process of deciding on the choice of treatment: individual or family therapy, and if family therapy is selected, which type. Ethnicity is also discussed.

Chapter 8 reviews the problems of working with people from various socioeconomic levels. It presents some of the special problems of working in treatment with families from the lowest socioeconomic level.

Chapter 9 evaluates the problems of an eclectic approach and discusses the methods and goals of various forms of marital and family therapy. Curative factors in psychotherapy are reviewed.

Chapter 10 goes through the process of evaluating a family for treatment and presents a case example of the evaluation process and beginning phase of treatment.

Chapter 11 presents the distinct techniques of object relations family therapy appropriate to the beginning and middle phases of treatment. There is also a case example comparing Bowenian, structural, strategic, and object relations interventions.

Chapter 12 is a continuous case of a couple's therapy, demonstrating working with the systemic and interpersonal levels at the beginning and middle phases of treatment. Interpretation of projective identification is demonstrated.

Chapter 13 reviews the complementary projective identifications in a couple in which one member has a borderline personality disorder and the other a narcissistic personality disorder. A case example is provided to demonstrate therapeutic interventions.

Chapter 14 covers the criteria and the process of terminating treatment.

The book further develops the application of my family typology to the treatment process in object relations family therapy. It provides specific guidelines for a therapeutic framework and some intervention techniques that foster symptom relief and structural change.

Acknowledgments

I wish to express my deep appreciation to my publisher, Jason Aronson, who has been not only a source of encouragement and support but also a stimulus, enabling me to think through many of the ideas developed in this book. At moments of difficulty, his bright and cheerful spirit was an inspiration. I wish to thank my editor, Joan Langs, for her constant faith in my work, for her patience, and for her own diligent work with me in strengthening the manuscript. Her insightful and knowledgeable suggestions were of tremendous help. I also wish to thank Lynn Friendly for her conscientiousness in typing the manuscript.

The intellectual interchange with the members of the Family Therapy Program of the Washington School of Psychiatry was a source of stimulation and support. I appreciated the collegial relationships with David and Jill Scharff (who coined the term *object relations family therapy*), and to Roger Shapiro, Robert Winer, and John Zinner.

I also wish to thank the faculty of the Psychoanalytic Division of the New York Medical College for the opportunity to teach object relations theory, in addition to my work in family therapy, to the psychoanalytic candidates.

Most of all, the love and understanding of my wife Sandra, and my daughter Elena, were a constant source of strength in pursuing the challenging task of completing this book.

Introduction

There are several important clinical questions that this book addresses concerning the field of family therapy. How can the understanding arising from systemic forms of family therapy be integrated with psychodynamic concepts? What is object relations family therapy? What are the special techniques of object relations family therapy, and in what stages of treatment can they be used?

The evolution of family therapy has gone in several directions, with systemic approaches relying heavily on technique without an underlying clinical theory, and psychoanalytic approaches being strong in theory but having few specific family therapeutic techniques. Bringing the insights of these approaches together seems an obvious solution. Object relations theory is used to provide a clinical foundation that explains how therapeutic change in families can be effected by systemic forms of family therapy. This tends to demystify why changes in certain structures or functions of family interaction produce changes in individual family members. The theoretical understanding coming from general systems theory is similarly applied to object relations family therapy to enrich its therapeutic repertoire. The new insights concern how the current family system as a whole influences each of the members. It sensitizes the therapist to note and change the circular feedback cycles of communication that is so important for therapeutic progress.

However, systemic family therapy cannot be directly applied to object relations family therapy. First of all, the methods and goals of treatment are different. The therapist in systemic family therapy assumes a directive and more distant stance toward the family, which would be disruptive to the therapeutic framework the object relations family therapist attempts to establish. Second, the treatment techniques of systemic family therapy do not adhere to general systems theory, but rely on linear causality. The goal, therefore, is to employ these systemic insights to treatment in a way that is more consistent with general systems theory.

Another problem has been the lack of any diagnostic system of family interaction. To correct this lack, a typology is presented in which specific forms of family transactions are connected to specific forms of psychopathology in the identified patient. My previous work has covered the areas of schizophrenia, depression, hysterical/borderline conditions, and the overinvolved delinquent. This is reviewed and further extended to include the family transactions related to narcissistic personality disorders. The typology is not presented as being the sole cause of these disorders but is found to be related to their development when specific family patterns occur. This does not exclude genetic vulnerability and other significant contributory causes.

The Technique and Practice of Object Relations Family Therapy

I

Integration of Individual and Family Theory and Practice

1

Object Relations Family Therapy

DEVELOPMENTS IN THE FIELD

This book employs object relations theory with a focus upon three main goals. The first is to present the theories and techniques of object relations family therapy, a form of family therapy that incorporates systemic and psychodynamic features and that facilitates a high degree of autonomy and intimacy. The second goal is to provide a Rosetta stone for understanding how other existing approaches in family therapy work to bring about change. Finally, the book offers a theory that bridges the chasm that has developed between family therapy and individual psychodynamic therapy. The application of this unifying theory is a means of healing the wide separation between individual and family therapy so as to enrich them both through cross-fertilization.

Family therapy was born in the 1960s, during which time there was a strong bias against any established theory, with the exception of theories about theory. The result has been that family therapy has evolved into a number of diverse therapeutic approaches, sharing in a common genuflection to general systems theory. General systems theory is used, however, only at a highly abstract level, whereas at the immediate therapeutic level, "old fashioned" linear epistemology is still employed (Slipp 1984, Dell 1986a). Thus there exists an internal paradox in the field of family therapy.

The diverse approaches in family therapy are not held together by any operational clinical theory. Current family therapy approaches focus on individuals, on subsystems of two or more individuals, or on the system as a whole group. To make matters more complicated, some approaches claim sole possession of the only effective techniques for change. This rivalry is reminiscent of the divergencies that existed within the field of group therapy shortly after World War II. At that time there were strong disagreements about which group therapy approach was best. One school advocated working with the individual in the group (Wolf and Schwartz 1962), another focused on interpersonal relations (Yalom 1970), and others dealt with the group as a whole (Foulkes 1948). Today in group therapy, one no longer hears even the faintest echo of those debates; group therapists now consider that each of these three dimensions are important at varying times. In recent years this same progression has been occurring within the field of family therapy, where various therapeutic approaches are beginning to be used in a complementary way.

BRIDGING INDIVIDUAL AND FAMILY THERAPY

Even though there is currently a gradual movement in the direction of integration, the past rupture between individual and family therapy has been so profound that bridging the gap is difficult. Each holds onto a suspiciousness and a readiness to engage in conflicts over ideas and techniques, often looking for flaws to justify their distrust. However, family therapy has made important contributions to the treatment of psychiatric disorders, and as a result many therapists trained in individual dynamic psychotherapy have been attracted to it.

The appeal of a family approach is often diminished when individual therapists attempt to learn how to do family therapy. There are conflicting therapeutic approaches between individual and family therapy, and many family constructs and methods are experienced as alien. This book should be helpful to those individual practitioners and other clinicians who want to extend their therapeutic expertise to family therapy. It reveals that many family therapy concepts and techniques can be understood by using an object relations framework. Psychoanalytic object relations provides an underlying conceptual structure that explains how most family therapy techniques effect change. The book should also be useful to those veteran family therapists who already employ a dynamic orientation or who use a systemic approach, but who cannot integrate them in their work with families. This book bridges both the psychodynamic and systemic approaches, and develops a way of utilizing them together.

THE BEGINNING FAMILY THERAPIST

One motivation for writing this book was to address the situation experienced by many psychodynamically oriented therapists when they enter certain family therapy training programs. There they are dogmatically instructed to discard what they have learned about psychopathology and treatment, so that they can become "born-again" family therapists. Conflicts immediately develop because many family therapy approaches reject the very fundamentals of psychodynamic psychotherapy, such as the importance of past childhood development, intrapsychic dynamics, and the usefulness of listening and interpreting in the effort to bring about change. The family therapy novitiate is taught not to take a neutral or empathic stance, not to be a participant-observer, not to deal with transference and resistance; defenses and drives are out, dreams are taboo, and the existence of unconscious motivation or conflict is altogether denied. Derivatives of these unconscious drives and transferences are not sought out and worked with; only the manifest content level of communication is acknowledged. The new family therapist is expected to take an active and directive stance, yet no cognizance is made of the therapist's own countertransference in taking such an active stance nor of its effect on the patient's transference. The complexity of human interaction, its richness and challenge in treatment, are denied and neglected. This may leave the beginning family therapist with three options: to become a "true believer" and renounce all past heresies; to drop out of training and reject family therapy as a form of treatment that militates against intimacy and complexity; or to remain in training and superficially comply, while being conflicted and cognitively strained and blocked in development.

Some family therapy approaches, to this day, even deny the existence of mental illness within the patient, and see pathology as existing mysteriously only in the transactions between people. This rejection of the medical model of mental illness is at gross variance not only with psychoanalysis, but with all of the scientific knowledge in the general field of psychiatry. It totally ignores the mounting evidence for genetic vulnerability to mental illness, as well as the temperamental differences that children demonstrate from birth onward. Fortunately, this denial of mental illness is now held only by a small fringe group in family therapy and seems to be a holdover from the antipsychiatry movement of the 1960s.

EFFECTING A RAPPROCHEMENT

How do we begin to have a rapprochement between individual and family therapy? At first glance, many of the constructs and methods of family therapy seem irreconcilable with those of individual dynamic psychotherapy. Indeed, one esteemed colleague, John Spiegel, humorously termed the attempt at integrating these two fields "mission impossible." Everything seems different: the language, the epistemology, the treatment, as well as who is the identified patient. We will demonstrate that there is an underlying theoretical core shared by these two approaches when one uses object relations therapy.

In all of the existing family therapy approaches, including those adhering to psychodynamic theory, the person manifesting the overt symptomatology is labeled only as the "identified patient." However, *all* the family members are viewed as patients, with the "identified patient's" pathology considered simply as the observable tip of the iceberg. There exists a wider system of pathology amongst the family members that lies below the surface. Thus the entire family, and not simply the individual with manifest symptoms, is treated. This finding is also true in object relations individual therapy, even going so far as to include the pathology that may become generated between the patient and the therapist.

It is ironic that the field of family therapy, which in many areas has moved so far away from psychoanalysis, was pioneered by individuals who were psychoanalysts or psychodynamically oriented. The earliest research in family therapy was done by such people as Murray Bowen, Henry Dicks, Ted Lidz, John Spiegel, and Lyman Wynne. The first training programs in family therapy were psychoanalytically oriented, being started by Nathan Ackerman in New York City and Virginia Satir in Palo Alto, California. Both the Ackerman Family Institute in New York and the Mental Research Institute, where Satir worked in California, have moved away from a psychoanalytic approach to a strategic one.

In recent years, the pendulum appears to be swinging back to the psychoanalytic perspective in family therapy, and now the Ackerman Family Institute offers an integrative approach. Leading the renaissance in psychoanalytic family therapy at present is the Washington School of Psychiatry, which has a two-year training program and runs a yearly conference on the psychoanalytic object relations approach to family therapy. Other major schools of family therapy, such as those of Bowen and Boszormenyi-Nagy, have their roots in psychoanalytic theory and utilize many aspects of it. These two latter schools stress the importance of insight and self-awareness, as well as tracing down past repetitive patterns of feelings, thoughts, and behavior through two or three generations in families. Bowenian therapists investigate such areas as family projection patterns, levels of self-differentiation, and triangulated relationships. Contextual therapists, following Boszormenyi-Nagy, explore invisible loyalties, exploitative relationships, vulnerabilities, entitlements, and ledgers of justice and injustice through generations of parent–child relationships. These are the outward manifestations in interpersonal relations of defenses and conflicts in the intrapsychic sphere.

Some of the second-generation family therapists who have made contributions to the field, based on psychoanalytic foundations, include Ian Alger, Fred and Bunny Duhl, James Framo,

Leonard Friedman, Henry Grunebaum, David Kantor, Kitty La-
Perriere, Norman Paul, Clifford Sager, Fred Sander, Roger
Shapiro, A. C. Robin Skynner, Helm Stierlin, and John Zinner. A
recent leap forward in the field was made by the publication of the
book *Object Relations Family Therapy* by Jill and David Scharff
(1987).

SYSTEMIC FAMILY THERAPY

How did the movement away from psychoanalytic to systemic
forms of family therapy occur? The theoretical underpinnings of
systemic family therapies come directly from the work of Don
Jackson and his colleagues of the Palo Alto group in the 1950s and
1960s. Jackson and his group considered that looking for current
observable communication or behavior between people was the
only scientifically accurate method of theory building. They
remained on what Ruesch (1956) termed the "first level of
abstraction" in theory development. This level consisted of only
observed sequences of relationships, having external referents that
were reducible to empirical laws. The Palo Alto group avoided
using the higher second or third levels of abstraction for theory
building. On the second level, observed behavior is brought
together by hypothetical constructs to provide more meaning.
These inferences are not wholly reducible to empirical findings.
Most psychoanalytic concepts such as the ego, superego, and id
rely on this level. The third level of abstraction connects these
constructs into a unified theory that provides a consistent pattern.
Examples are the libido theory or object relations theory. The
fourth, and highest, level integrates these theories into a system,
such as general systems theory.

　　　Jackson (1957) and his group denied the validity of the
"mentalistic" constructs employed in psychoanalysis, which were
on the second and third level, because they were not totally
reducible to empirical findings. They jumped from the first to the
fourth level of abstraction, in which systems theory was employed.
An example of this in their work was the concept of family
homeostasis, or a balance of relationships in the family. Never-
theless, in order to make sense of their own particularistic
empirical findings, Jackson also had to resort to second-level

constructs, even though these had low levels of inference. One such construct was viewing the family as a system governed by rules that serve to monitor the observed interactional sequences, so as to preserve homeostasis (Greenberg 1977). Treatment was related to manipulating and changing those first-level interactional sequences considered to be causing and maintaining dysfunctional behavior in the identified patient.

In the past decade, two schools of family therapy that focus on the family system have emerged to gain wide popularity. These are the structural approach developed by Minuchin (1974), and the strategic approach initiated by the Palo Alto group and developed by Selvini-Palazzoli and colleagues (1978). These two systemic approaches focus on the reverberating system of transactions that currently exist in the family and that serve to sustain the pathology in the identified patient. Both approaches consider that changing the here-and-now system will change the individual's personality as well as the psychopathology.

The theoretical underpinnings for these systemic approaches is a revolutionary departure from the past understanding of psychopathology. Using a new epistemology, based on general systems theory, these two approaches consider psychoanalysis to be linear, and condemn it as "old-fashioned." They say their "new" theory is in keeping with twentieth-century thinking. Systemic family therapists perceive the psychoanalytic view of pathology as a direct linear progression from childhood developmental conflict or arrest. They state that psychoanalysis considers it is only as a direct result of *past* experience that the patient distorts current relationships and develops psychopathology. This, the systemic theorists point out, represents "old-fashioned" linear thinking. In systemic thinking, however, a circular process is involved, with the patient's pathology developing and being sustained through circular feedback loops in the *current* system of family relationships.

Although this newer form of circular thinking is a major contribution to the understanding of the maintenance of psychopathology in the patient, it has certain distinct drawbacks that might disqualify it as an all-encompassing theory for psychotherapy. First, the very therapeutic approach utilized by systemic family therapists itself relies on linear thinking, as mentioned above (Dell 1986a). Second, the baggage with which people enter the system from their family of origin tends to shape the current transactional patterns that evolve. This is a form of linear determinism that strongly shapes the particular form the family system will take. For example (as discussed in Chapter 5 describing my typology), if the parents' personalities are severely disturbed, one type of family system which lacks "family constancy" will evolve. If the parents' personalities are within the upper narcissistic or neurotic range, other forms of family systems develop. It is the conflicted internal worlds of the parents that get dumped onto others through projective identification, and that form the raw material for building the family system of transactions. Thus both linear and circular determinism are significant. It is not either/or, but both/and. Essentially, linear determinism influences the *development* of the family system through splitting and projective identification, whereas circular determinism in the current family interaction serves to *maintain* psychopathology.

Instead of linear and circular epistemologies being polarized, they need to be considered as interactive and interdependent. The kind of thinking that labels one approach "old-fashioned" and considers them both mutually exclusive is itself dualistic and linear.[1] Another drawback to working with only the systemic level is that it does not give sufficient significance to individual responsibility—that it sees people as functioning solely due to group forces. It does not deal with the issues of ethical consequences for exploitative or otherwise destructive relationships. Here, contextual family therapy has made the most significant strides.

THREE REVOLUTIONS IN PSYCHOTHERAPY

If we look at the field of psychotherapy in a global perspective, we could mark off three major revolutionary areas in theory and

---

[1]This same argument occurred in philosophy (Janik and Toulmin 1973). The Logical Positivists, such as Mach, believed that a meaningful theory was confirmed only by empirical observations. Later linguistic philosophers, such as Wittgenstein, who based his work on the logical symbolism of Frege and Russell, found that empiricism itself was limited by language. Thus no theory could tell us anything about the world as it is, but could only give us a symbolic description of the world, which we can use. Therefore Newtonian and modern physics were both applicable, since each provided functional meaning.

practice. These are the *intrapsychic,* the *interpersonal,* and the *systemic* perspectives. The intrapsychic orientation was the major contribution of Freud (1905b), who developed his drive theory at around the turn of the century. Drive theory was a *closed* system to explain both normal personality development as well as psychopathology. It stated that the child's inborn sexual and aggressive drives emanated from the part of the personality Freud termed the *id,* and that these drives sought discharge. Internally, it was believed, these drives created unconscious fantasies that distorted how reality was subjectively experienced. The resulting structural conflict between these drives and the parts of the personality Freud termed the *ego* and *superego,* as well as outside reality, was seen as the soil from which psychopathology grew. The parents and siblings were thought of as "objects" of the child's drives, and thus outside reality, as an active and influential force, was not built into Freud's drive theory. Classical psychoanalysis adhered to drive theory, which itself represents a one-person psychology.

The next revolution occurred in the 1940s, with the introduction of the interpersonal perspective.[2] In the United States, the Interpersonal and Cultural schools were developed by Thompson (1964), Sullivan (1953), Horney (1950), and others. The result was a splintering of the psychoanalytic movement into classical and neo-Freudian camps. In England, the object relations group evolved from the work of Klein (1948), and was developed by the British Middle school of Fairbairn (1954), Winnicott (1958), and others. Both these American and English groups rejected drive theory, and developed a *two-person* psychological model emphasizing relationships, particularly between the mother and child. These new interpersonal theories represented an *open* system, with interaction between the child and the environment seen as being responsible for personality development and psychopathology. These theories were considered more scientific than the others,

---

[2]Actually, Freud's original seduction theory was an interpersonal theory. However, Ferenczi (1920, 1932), his follower, stressed the importance of both intrapsychic and interpersonal factors. Ferenczi's thinking found expression in the work of his two analysands. One was Clara Thompson, who with Sullivan was among the founders of the neo-Freudian movement in America. The other was Melanie Klein, whose work influenced British object relations theorists.

since interpersonal interaction and both verbal and nonverbal communication could be directly observed and studied (Kardiner et al. 1959).

In the 1960s, the third revolution involving systemic thinking was developed by the anthropologist Gregory Bateson, along with Don Jackson and others (1956) in the Palo Alto group in California. It was applied to family treatment, and further elaborated by Minuchin (1974) and Selvini-Palazzoli and colleagues (1978). The importance of the current system of transactions between family members was stressed in the development of psychopathology. This was a psychological model that went beyond the one- or two-person model, and involved the *family as a whole*. Family transactions were found to have circular feedback systems of communication that had rules and almost a life of their own. The past was generally ignored and rejected by these systemic groups as representing "old-fashioned" linear thinking, as mentioned earlier. The focus of conflict changed, being no longer between the different schools of psychoanalysis but between systemic therapists and all of psychoanalysis. The challenge of the 1980s and 1990s is to integrate these various perspectives into a systemic whole. For this purpose, object relations theory, with its constructs of splitting and projective identification, will be used.

ORGANIZED COMPLEXITY VERSUS REDUCTIONISM

Theorists, groping to define reality, are often too quick to think that they alone have the one final and absolute truth. This kind of reductionistic thinking eliminates ambiguity and complexity. But instead of a *single* perspective being viewed as containing the complete explanation of human behavior, and the others being rejected, each perspective can be seen as describing a part of reality. Each perspective—the intrapsychic, the interpersonal, and the systemic—needs to be considered as interactive and interdependent with each other. They are in a dynamic equilibrium, so that change in one area influences the others. Reality is not static, as Heisenberg (1958) points out, and in addition there is no such thing as a detached objective observer. The very act of observing also influences what is observed. A reductionist, dualistic orientation needs to be replaced by genuine general systems thinking, which takes into account a hierarchy of interrelated complex systems; it also recognizes the *one-person, two-person,* and *group-as-a-whole* psychological perspectives, as well as social, genetic, and biological factors (Spiegel 1971) and the influence of the observer.

The first five years of life are crucial to laying down the foundation for personality development, as psychoanalysts have clinically noted and as direct infant observational research has validated (Stern 1985). In addition, it is not only the child's *subjective* response to its environment which is determined by its cognitive and emotional development but also how significant others *objectively* relate to the child's developmental needs. Even though sexual and aggressive drives and unconscious fantasies do shape how the environment is subjectively experienced, other factors have a profound influence as well. These include the child's inborn temperament (Thomas and Chess 1980) and its genetic endowment, as well as actual familial, social, and cultural influences.

This interaction of inborn genetic and objective environmental factors is demonstrated in the Finnish adoption twin studies reported by Tienari and colleagues (1984). This study replicated the Danish adoption twin studies, but in addition closely evaluated the family interaction of both biological and adoptive families. In a controlled study of 200 families, Tienari found that when the adoptive parents were disturbed, the children of schizophrenic mothers were indeed at higher risk to develop schizophrenia. However, when the children of schizophrenic mothers were reared in normal or mildly disturbed adoptive families, they were no more likely to be severely disturbed or schizophrenic than were the control children who had no genetic loading. Thus genetic predisposition for schizophrenia was necessary but not sufficient. The interaction of the genetic potential with a disturbed family environment was found to be essential for the development of schizophrenia in young adulthood.

The current system of transactions in the family is extremely important, as suggested by systemic thinkers, but personality cannot be reduced to this level alone. People are more than how they present themselves at a given moment in time. Individuals are the totality of their genetic endowment, their unconscious fantasies, drives, and intrapsychic defenses, all their past interpersonal relations and social forces impinging on them, and their current system of family relations. To deny any one aspect is to do injury to the others. To overlook a person's history denies the uniqueness of that individual. If one reductionistically views a person as only a cog in the wheel of the family system, there is the danger of diminishing and dehumanizing that individual. In such a view, people are not seen as discrete and complex beings but are reduced simplistically to being only members of a group. If one only uses the *group-as-a-whole* psychology, it may tend to dedifferentiate the family members and to foster regressive behavior that minimizes individual identity and responsibility.

We have to recognize that individuals bring to the group or family the unique personalities and problems that developed in their own particular past. This simple linear determinism profoundly influences the present. Putting a label on a theory by calling it "old-fashioned" does not disqualify or eliminate it. Indeed, the very process of labeling is an example of static linear and not interactive thinking. Theory, being limited by language, is good only insofar as it has pragmatic value, according to James (1963) and Wittgenstein (Janik and Toulmin 1973); and to deny an event that occurs, simply because it does not fit one's philosophy, is illusory. In the book *Candide* by Voltaire (1949), Professor Doctor Pangloss perceives everything that occurs as the best in this best of all possible worlds. He holds on to this belief to confirm his theory, despite horrible catastrophes that befall people. It is certainly true that the consequences of people's defensive behavior often do set up a system of transactions that develops a life of its own. This in turn contributes to the repetitive patterns of relationships that result in the circular cycles of interaction that maintain pathology. Instead of polarizing and reducing phenomena to one level, we need to understand their complex interactions and to build bridges between them.

RESISTANCE TO CHANGE

Why has such polarization occurred during these three revolutions in psychotherapy? Why has change so often been accompanied by conflict, dogmatism, and the need to devalue others? For many therapists the resistance to change may stem from their tremendous investment in training and their past experience. Ideological commitment to a given theoretical position is equated with one's professional identity. In addition, identification with a particular group serves as a political, economic, and prestige-invested power base. Those on top strive to safeguard their positions, which determine their social status as well as self-esteem. If their power base rests on identification with a conservative group's theoretical foundation, change is resisted and a conservative viewpoint is upheld. The members of a radical group, because of personal and socioeconomic motivation, may attempt to enlist support for their new ideas by demeaning traditional theory. The result is a power struggle, and a threat to the integrity of both groups with which the members identify.

On a psychological level, members of each group may then close ranks for strength and thereby function as a tight unit to discredit and destroy the other. Bion (1961) has described this "group think" phenomenon as a "basic assumption fight or flight group." The members share a primitive unconscious fantasy that an external enemy is threatening them and needs to be fought or escaped from to ensure survival. The result is an entrenchment of dogmatism, suspiciousness, and the need to attack and diminish the other; it is "we against them." Thus, even though we may wish for a more reasonable process of change and growth in our professional knowledge, primitive emotional group forces and issues related to survival and power tend to predominate. Hopefully, as we use our existing knowledge to analyze our own profession, we might be able to walk and not impetuously rush to the nearest barricade, and perhaps consider along the way not to declare war. With less conflict, and with an increased ability to engage in productive dialogue, progress in the field of psychotherapy would be not only more cooperative but also more rapid. However, given sufficient time, integration of new ideas eventually will be accomplished.

INTEGRATING INDIVIDUAL AND FAMILY THERAPY

The field of family therapy currently consists of a collection of therapeutic techniques, all of them developed by their own clinical masters—intuitively gifted clinicians who were able to assemble a body of adherents. Despite the efficacy of their techniques, there seemed little understanding, besides high-level abstractions, of how their methods produced change. In order to provide greater clarity and precision as to why certain therapeutic maneuvers work, we need an underlying clinical theory that integrates the three perspectives of psychotherapy: the intrapsychic, the interpersonal, and the systemic. It needs to tie in past linear causality with current circular feedback causality. This book discusses how the concepts of splitting and projective identification, derived from object relations theory, can accomplish this goal. It takes into account the need to preserve self-esteem and personality integrity intrapsychically through these defenses, how they are dumped into the interpersonal sphere to influence relationships, and how aspects of others' responses are reinternalized thereby serving as a feedback loop to sustain psychopathology.

Another vacuum in the field of family therapy has been the lack of a diagnostic typology of family patterns related to specific forms of psychopathology. In individual therapy, diagnosis has long been a stronghold that influences the therapeutic procedures applicable to certain forms of psychopathology. My work over the past 25 years has consisted in developing such a typology (Slipp 1984). In it, (1) specific forms of splitting and projective identification are related to (2) specific forms of family interaction, resulting in (3) specific types of role induction, which are associated with (4) specific types of psychopathology in the identified patient.

DYNAMIC FAMILY THERAPY

Dynamic family therapy needs to be differentiated from object relations family therapy. Historically both dynamic and object relations family therapy drew their heritage from Nathan Ackerman (1958), who is considered by many to be the father of all family therapy. Ackerman extended the insights of psychoanalysis into the treatment of the family as a group.

In dynamic family therapy, the therapist maintains a neutral stance that supports his or her anonymity and respects each of the members' autonomy. The frame of treatment is established by encouraging open dialogue and respecting confidentiality, as well as setting up the mechanics of treatment such as the times each week, the length of each session, the fee, and the place.

The therapist avoids taking a problem-solving or directive approach by not giving advice, reassurance, or instruction. This does not mean that the therapist becomes detached, passive, or silent, but rather attends to other material produced in the session. The therapist does not simply focus on the manifest content of communications or on details, but maintains an overall, even, hovering attention in listening. This facilitates making links or connections between present family interactions and past repressed, unconscious relations. The therapist sensitively tries to tune in to *derivatives;* these are encoded ways of communicating, beyond the members' conscious perception, that represent displacements of unconscious fantasies, drives, and transferences. The family members are too threatened to be able to communicate these perceptions consciously and directly. Thus, their feelings about one another and the therapist may, for example, be encoded by talking about outside relationships, instead of those in the here and now inside the treatment room. By the interpretation of these derivatives at the appropriate time, by the tying of these derivatives into current relations and then connecting them to past transferential relationships, unconscious material is brought to the surface to be worked through. Thus the past is linked to the present through interpretation of the transference, particularly the ways it is acted out interpersonally in ongoing family relationships.

Interpretations provide insight into how past repressed relationships from one's family of origin are repeated in the marital family and how they influence the present. The repressed feelings associated with those old relationships are uncovered, and can be worked through by the development of an understanding as to how they manifest themselves repeatedly in current behavior. These past relationships, and their associated feelings, can then be mourned and given up by the family members. In this way the family's current relationships are not contaminated by the past.

To facilitate the acceptance of these interpretations, the therapist needs to empathically join the family as well as to maintain a secure frame (Langs 1976). The therapist sustains the frame of treatment, which enables the patients to be free to express their unconscious feelings and thoughts. They need to feel the therapist will be able to listen, to handle and contain their feelings in order to provide them with the security to proceed in treatment. The treatment setting must be experienced as safe, and the therapist needs to develop what Modell (1976) terms a *holding environment*. This protected and safe therapeutic setting is considered to be analogous to early child development, in which a harmonious preverbal dialogue (Spitz 1965), affective attunement (Stern 1985), or good-enough mothering and holding (Winnicott 1965) are essential for growth.

Creating such a safe holding environment was also found to be the most crucial element for change and growth in the psychotherapy research of Sampson and Weiss (1977). Creating what these researchers called a "condition of safety" diminishes anxiety and defensiveness so as to allow the emergence of repressed unconscious aspects of the personality. In a few of their cases, the patients themselves were able to make their own interpretations without the need for the therapist to intervene. This security furthers the development of trust, so that a therapeutic alliance with the family can occur. The family members can then join collaboratively with the therapist in a process of self-discovery and understanding. Treatment does not become a dominant–submissive power struggle to determine who is in charge, but a cooperative and supportive endeavor to mutually explore underlying issues and dynamics in the family members.

The dynamic family therapist encourages the family to discuss dreams. The dreamer and other family members give their associations to facilitate interpretation of this material. When defenses and resistances impede progress, these are carefully interpreted and worked through to sustain the ongoing treatment process.

The dynamic family therapist attempts to be aware of his or her own reactions to the family. Uncomfortable feelings experienced by the therapist may signal the search for countertransference reactions. These may be anxiety, fear, hostility, withdrawal, boredom, rescue fantasies, or need for control. The therapist's countertransference may be also exhibited in such behavior as taking sides with one member against others; in masochistic or sadistic interaction with certain family members; in dreaming of the family; or, most importantly, through breaches in the frame of treatment such as not collecting fees on time, being late, or missing appointments. Other indicators that may reflect countertransference blocks, or what Kohut (1977) terms *empathic failure,* are the patient's regression, acting out, terminating treatment, or making efforts to correct the therapist. This form of countertransference represents unresolved conflicts arising from the therapist's own background, conflicts that have been termed *subjective counter-transferences.* The therapist's transferring these unresolved conflicts onto the patient has been called a "countertransference neurosis" by Racker (1957).

Langs (1976) notes that some derivative communication from the patient is due not to unconscious transference and drives but to real reactions to the therapist's breaks in the frame that result from countertransference reactions. The patient unconsciously attempts to correct the therapist by this means. The therapist's alertness to the meaning of such derivatives may serve as a self-correction. Similarly, Searles (1975) noted that patients unconsciously attempt to cure their therapists, just as they did their parents to restore them to their appropriate roles. It thus becomes imperative for the therapist to be aware of these derivatives and other indicators of "subjective countertransference," and to attempt to resolve them so that effective treatment is possible.

OBJECT RELATIONS FAMILY THERAPY DEFINED

The object relations family therapist attends to all of these issues and techniques of dynamic family treatment, but also introduces two other essential elements into the process. The first is the attention of the therapist to how internalized object relations are parceled out through projective identification onto family members. This process needs to be interpreted in a sensitive way. The second additional element is attention to how the family's internalized object relations are also evacuated, through projective identification, onto the therapist.

Object relations family therapy, by its very name, deals with shared, unconscious, internalized object relations. It looks for the primitive defenses of splitting and projective identification as the link between intrapsychic and family dynamics. As a consequence of these defenses and their associated affects, an unconscious collusive system between family members develops, which fosters certain behavior and even symptomatology. One or more individuals in the family are subject to unconscious interactional pressure to contain and act out good or bad aspects of the self or object representations of one or both of the parents. This serves to maintain the self-esteem or personality integrity of one or both of the parents as well as the cohesion of the family as a group.

The particular form of this unconscious collusive system of internalized object relations determines the specific type of current interpersonal relationships in the family, and influences the development and maintenance of specific forms of psychopathology in the identified patient. The four forms of these collusive, unconscious object relations and how they manifest themselves in current interpersonal family relations are discussed extensively in Chapter 5, where the typology is described. Chapter 6 presents the combinations of family patterns found in patients suffering from narcissistic personality disorders. How the therapist can become aware of projective identification when it is happening, and can formulate an interpretation of it to the family so as to be effective in producing change, are elaborated upon in later chapters.

The second element introduced in object relations family therapy is a new and different awareness in the use of countertransference. Not all countertransferences are "subjective" and a product of unresolved transferences stemming from the therapist's past. Winnicott's (1965) more global definition of countertransference responses in the therapist is employed here. Some countertransferences are induced because the family dumps their own unconscious internalized object world onto the therapist through the use of projective identification. This has been called an "objective countertransference." Heimann (1950) considers that this type of countertransference can be used "as an instrument of research into the patient's unconscious." Just as the family attempts to shape the responses of its members through projective identification, this same process may be employed toward the therapist. This is usually an unconscious effort to pull in the therapist to go along with the collusive, unconscious object relations that already exist between family members. (This is an explanation of what structural family therapists call being "sucked into the system.") Therefore, therapists' awareness of their own reactions may provide a valuable clue into the nature of these unconscious internalized object relations that are held collusively by family members. The techniques of how this "objective transference" is worked with and interpreted to bring about change are discussed in Chapter 11 and elsewhere in the book.

In summary, the focus of object relations family therapy is not to maintain a distance from family members—as occurs in other forms of family therapy—by therapists assuming the role of detached or controlling observers. Instead, therapists use their own empathy as a form of vicarious introspection (Kohut 1977) in order to enter the subjective inner world of the family members. In addition, therapists allow their own inner world to be entered by the family through their use of projective identification. Therapists in turn then try to monitor their own countertransferential responses that are influenced by and that in turn influence the family. By attempting to sort out their responses as to whether they are due to a "subjective" or an "objective" countertransference, they can achieve greater clarity in the therapeutic relationship. Therapists finding their countertransference to be based on their own distortions can attempt to resolve them through self-analysis. If their reactions seem to be in response to an "objective countertransference," it can be used to understand the shared unconscious system of object relations and to interpret the process of projective identification to the family.

The stance of the therapist with the family is not that of a detached "objective" observer, but one who has the awareness that he or she affects and is affected by the family. There is an acknowledgment of and a working with the mutual interaction of the family and the therapist, as mentioned earlier, through the use of empathy and the "objective countertransference." The "objective countertransference" needs to be contained, metabolized, and sensitively interpreted by the therapist. The responses of the family members can serve as a check to validate the accuracy of the interpretation. The therapist can also monitor the family's responses to the therapeutic interventions by listening for and interpreting derivatives communicated by the family about them. This serves as a further self-corrective feedback loop.

Using these therapeutic procedures comes closer to "modern" circular epistemology than any other form of family therapy. Indeed, as has been noted (Bateson 1972, Gurman 1983, Slipp 1984, Dell 1986, Wynne 1986), systemic forms of family therapy, although adhering to a circular epistemology at a high level of theoretical abstraction, in fact use linear epistemology in their actual therapeutic interventions.

In object relations family therapy there is a dynamic interplay between the intersubjective worlds of therapist and family. The therapist needs to be aware of the family's processes of splitting and projective identification that influence both transferences and countertransferences toward each other and the therapist. By imparting new information to the system through interpretations, there is an opportunity to change these reverberating cycles of behavior as well as to alter the structure of individual personalities.

Object relations family therapy allows for the greatest degree of closeness between the family and the therapist. The therapist, while maintaining autonomy, is able to empathically experience and understand each of the family members. Thus, at a concrete level, object relations family therapy serves as a model to unlearn old distant and controlling interaction, and to learn how to be both an authentic individual as well as an integrated member of the family group. It provides a framework within which individual boundaries and autonomy are respected and confirmed, along with sensitivity to one another in the family. An extreme of either one of these positions leads to either narcissistic distancing or overly close symbiotic relatedness. Object relations family therapy fosters the kind of meaningful shared intimacy with respect for one another's individuality that the philosopher Martin Buber (1958) so aptly described as the "I–Thou Relationship."

2

Object Relations Theory

ONE-PERSON AND TWO-PERSON PSYCHOLOGIES

The development of a *two-person psychology* in object relations theory is reviewed in this chapter, and its evolution from the *one-person psychology* of classical psychoanalysis is explored. I trace the gradual stages in the development of object relations by various theorists, and conclude with Kernberg's efforts to integrate object relations theory with classical psychoanalysis. Although object relations theory grew out of the British psychoanalytic movement, many of its ideas have marked similarities to those of the neo-Freudian movement in the United States. They both share a common lineage, stemming from one of Freud's closest colleagues, Ferenczi (1920, 1932b), who emphasized the importance of environmental as well as intrapsychic factors.

Clearly, a single chapter cannot offer a comprehensive review of the evolution of psychoanalytic theory from Freud to the present time, but can offer only a very broad perspective. The purpose of this chapter is to help those not familiar with more recent developments in psychoanalytic thinking, or to refresh those already acquainted with them.

The only psychoanalytic theory with which many people are

familiar is the drive (or libido) theory. Indeed, this has been the case for numerous writers in the family therapy literature, who do not seem acquainted with the further developments in psychoanalysis since the publication of Freud's original works around the turn of the century. A great deal of the criticism by family therapy theorists stems from this lack of knowledge of current psychoanalytic theory. By analogy, it would be as if the final and definitive statements about family therapy were made by Nathan Ackerman twenty years ago, and there had been no further developments. Even Freud changed his theories, shifting from an id psychology that focused on tracking libidinal drives, to an ego psychology that dealt with the individual's adaptation of these drives to environmental demands. Also, a certain segment of the psychoanalytic movement, consisting of the British object relations group, the neo-Freudians, and the self psychologists, have questioned the validity of or rejected drive theory. However, many psychoanalysts use the theory, even though they may also work within other theoretical orientations.

INTEGRATING DRIVE THEORY

The position taken here is that sexual and aggressive drives clearly play a crucial role, but are not the primary force for personality development. The child does not develop simply because of inborn instinctual forces, but organizes its early affect states, within the context of human relationships, to form drives.[1] Drive theory, a one-person psychology, needs to be integrated with those psychologies that take into account two persons, as well as group-as-a-whole functioning.

This process of integration has already begun within the classical psychoanalytic movement. It was Jacobson (1964) who first combined both one- and two-person psychologies in her contribution to psychoanalytic theory. She saw sexual and aggres-

---

[1]There has been criticism of Strachey's translation of Freud from German to English in that Freud himself differentiated *instincts,* which were biological and inborn, from *drives,* which were psychological and acquired through experience.

sive drives as important, but developing simultaneously with object relations, particularly within the mother–child relationship. Building on Jacobson's contribution, Kernberg (1975, 1976) furthered this effort to develop a modern unitary psychoanalytic theory. Kernberg's work uses general systems theory to integrate drive theory, structural theory, and ego psychology (one-person psychology) with object relations theory (a two-person psychology). My own work (Slipp 1981) follows this same vein and also includes familial interaction, a system-as-a-whole psychology.

The term *object relations,* although universally applied to a two-person psychology, originated from Freud's one-person psychology, the libido (drive) theory. The libido theory was concerned with both inborn sexual drives and aggressive drives that arose from the id. The aim of these drives was to seek gratification, and they were directed toward an object. The object was a person, but could be an idea, or even something inanimate that the person valued, or what Freud termed *cathected with libidinal energy.* During the oedipal period a boy's sexual drive, according to Freud, aims at gratification from the mother, who is the object, whereas his aggressive drive aims at eliminating the father (another object) from competition.

Psychopathology arose from intrapsychic structural conflict involving these drives, and this structural conflict could take a number of forms. In *superego conflict,* a drive may come into opposition to the values already internalized in the superego. In *ego conflict,* part of the ego may identify with an object, who is also the target of aggression. In *reality conflict,* the reaction of an object to a drive may be experienced as potentially dangerous. In *instinctual conflict,* the person may experience both aggressive and libidinal drives toward the same object. Some of the ego defenses used to deal with aggression might be, for example, displacement to another object, restriction of aims, sublimation, or fusion with libido, as in sadomasochistic relations. One drive may also be used as a defense against another, such as aggression against the self or others to cover repressed sexual excitement.

According to classical theory, ego strength depends upon the individual's ability to neutralize aggression, while non-neutralized aggressive drives contribute to ego weakness. Thus, Freud's one-person system of psychology has its emphasis on intrapsychic processes, with the parents and siblings seen as objects of the child's drives. This is a linear and not an interactive relationship. The use of the word *object* in object relations is a direct carryover from the libido theory, used by psychoanalytic theorists as they gradually evolved their newer two-person psychology.

The significance of the term *object* is quite different in object relations theory, however, since it is not only the intrapsychic structure that is focused upon. Also, instead of a linear relationship, there is a *circular* process. The child's subjective experience of actual interpersonal interaction is internalized into the intrapsychic sphere. Then this internalized representation is projected externally into the interpersonal sphere to determine the child's perception. Finally the interpersonal interaction is reinternalized to sustain the integrity of the individual's inner personality. In object relations family therapy, these concepts are extended even further. There are unconscious internalized object relations that are shared in the family to form a collusive system that shapes personality and psychopathology in the members as well (Slipp 1984). This I termed the *symbiotic survival pattern,* and I have delineated in my typology which forms of shared internalized object relations in the family are associated with which forms of psychopathology.

THE EVOLUTION OF PSYCHOANALYSIS

Freud's (1905b) *drive* theory was a closed system that relied on the principle of the constancy of energy in physics. The child was considered to be born with a fixed amount of instinctual energy, with no further input of energy from the environment. These biological instincts were subdivided into sexual and aggressive drives, which could be shifted around the body, invested (cathected) in others (objects) or in the self, or transformed (bound, neutralized, etc.). If one area became invested with libidinal energy, another area would become impoverished.

Freud's (1915) earliest description of the personality was his *topographic* theory, which divided the psyche into conscious and unconscious portions. Freud (1923) later added three other subdivisions in his *structural* theory—the id, the superego, and the ego. The *id* contained the unconscious instinctual drives just described; the *superego* was formed by the internalization of the parents' values, prohibitions, and ideals; and the *ego,* which contained the mechanisms of defense, mediated between the drives in the id and the prohibitions in the superego, as well as outside reality. In the id the pleasure principle and the primary process reigned, whereas in the ego the reality principle and the secondary processes were paramount.

The developmental schema that Freud (1940) formulated to describe the formation and growth of the personality consisted of a sequence of psychosexual phases of libidinal maturation. These are the *oral* (birth to 1 or 1½ years of age), with its erotic and sadistic subdivisions; the *anal* (1 to 3 years of age), with its sadistic and retentive subdivisions; the *phallic* (2½ to 6 years of age); the *latency* period (5 to 7 years of age), with an apparent diminution of drives; and the *genital* (6 years of age and onward), in which sexual and affectionate feelings are integrated. Freud considered that the child was *autoerotic,* under the influence of these instinctual drives, and did not make attachments to others until the end of the phallic phase.

The discovery of infantile sexuality was considered by Freud as one of his major contributions to psychology. Freud described the *Oedipus complex* in boys as a universal phenomenon, in which the mother is desired as a sexual object. She becomes the object of the boy's sexual aim, and the father is seen as a rival. This complex occurs during the phallic phase of development, and is the central phenomenon of childhood sexuality. The threat of castration by the father was considered by Freud as responsible for the destruction of this phallic phase of development, and repression of the Oedipus complex. This is facilitated by the boy's seeing the female genitals, so that reality reinforces the fantasy of castration. The boy's ego turns away from the mother as the object of his cathexis, and he then identifies with the father. The father, and not the mother, was seen by Freud as the first attachment figure.

The father's authority is internalized by the boy and forms the core of his superego, as the Oedipus complex becomes resolved. The superego prohibitions thus secure the ego against the sexual drives from the id. These sexual drives then become partly desexualized and sublimated, their aim is inhibited, and they form the feelings of affection. This process preserves the boy from the fear of castration and brings on the latency period which is characterized by repression of sexuality. In the female child, the Oedipus complex toward the father is relinquished, as her wish for a penis, and for a child from the father, does not become gratified. The daughter then identifies with her mother.

According to Freud, it was the inborn instinctual drives, in relationship to these phases of development, that gave rise to unconscious fantasies which in turn distorted the perception of reality for the child. When the son, during the Oedipal period, had sexual feeling for the mother, he would distort his perception of the father because of his own aggressive and competitive feelings toward him. Thus the father would be perceived as hostile, competitive, and threatening, even if in reality he was benign and gentle. When an instinctual drive arising from the id came into conflict with the superego, which contained the internalized parental prohibitions, the ego would attempt to deal with it through its defense mechanisms. The ego did this, according to Freud (1923), out of fear that it might lose the love and protection from the superego, which would then result in castration or death. If the structural conflict persisted into adulthood, symptoms developed that corresponded to the point at which this fixation in the psychosexual development had occurred. Freud's work rested largely on intrapsychic processes and reactions to others; but it gave little recognition to how others actually dealt with the person.

Object relations theory can be traced to Freud's (1923) notion that the ego and the superego were formed intrapsychically by internalized object relations. However, the founder of object relations theory is generally considered to be Ferenczi (1920). Ferenczi noted that severe psychopathology resulted from arrested development of the child and not from structural conflict (between the id, ego, superego, and reality), as Freud had noted with neurotic patients. Ferenczi (1932a) recognized that early maternal deprivation was pathogenic for the child. Thus Ferenczi focused on the dyadic relationship of *mother and child*. Similarly in Ferenczi's (1920) "active" treatment approach, he emphasized the need for the analyst to correct this interpersonal deprivation by maintaining an empathic connection with the patient. Currently, other analysts change the parameters in psychoanalytic treatment when working with preoedipally arrested (borderline and narcissistic) patients. This is particularly true for Kohut (1977) and those following his school of self psychology, who stress the need for empathic connection to provide narcissistic supplies (mirroring) to those patients with "disorders of the self."

Freud's theories tend to be more cognitive and objective, Ferenczi's more emotional and humanistic. While Freud's work emphasized the son's relation to the father, Ferenczi focused on the mother–child interaction. The first psychoanalyst to bring the insights of Freud and Ferenczi together to develop the first systematic object relations theory was Melanie Klein (1948). She had been analyzed by Ferenczi[2] and later by Abraham, thus being exposed to both Hungarian and Austro-German psychoanalytic thinking respectively. When Klein developed her theoretical approach, a split in the British psychoanalytic movement occurred, although not as complete a division as developed in the United States. As did her American counterparts in the neo-Freudian movement, Klein rejected Freud's drive theory. There was a polarization between classical psychoanalysts, who maintained adherence to drive theory, which is a one-person intrapsychic theory, and object relations and neo-Freudian psychoanalysts, who focused on a two-person interpersonal approach.

MELANIE KLEIN

Up until 1934, Melanie Klein (1934) employed the drive and structural theories of Freud. After that time she formulated her own concepts of child development and personality formation. She rejected drive theory and proposed that the motivating force for personality development was not the need of the infant to discharge or control instincts, but the need to relate to the *mother*. She considered that the infant even at birth has sufficient ego to

---

[2]Clara Thompson was also analyzed by Ferenczi, and when she returned to the United States, she shared this experience with Harry Stack Sullivan. Both Thompson and Sullivan were major founders, along with others, of the neo-Freudian movement.

use unconscious fantasy as a way of adapting to its environment. According to Klein, instincts were represented and experienced as fantasy. She further differed from Freud in that she believed the superego began developing within the first year of life, and that the Oedipus complex occurred much earlier than 5 years of age.[3] In fact, Klein reversed Freud's developmental timetable. Whereas Freud saw the resolution of the Oedipus complex as consolidating the superego formation, Klein considered that the superego developed first and promoted the Oedipus complex.

Klein divided infant development into the *paranoid-schizoid* position, which lasted until about 6 months of age, and the *depressive* position, which persisted until about 30 months. During the paranoid-schizoid position, the infant relates to the mother as a part object — that is, her breasts, face, hands — and only later, during the depressive period, as a whole object. When the child is frustrated during the paranoid-schizoid position, it experiences its rage against the breast and wishes to attack and destroy it. Klein postulated that the source of this oral aggression was an inborn death instinct, a construct taken from Freud (1920) but which she used differently. Klein considered that the death instinct's outward manifestation was hatred, greed, and envy. The infant psychologically splits the breast, and perceives it as all good or all bad. This is done to get rid of, or evacuate, the painful feelings by projecting them onto the breast, while retaining the good feelings toward the breast. The bad breast is then perceived as a persecutory object, and also becomes internalized into the infant's psyche as a destroyed and destroying part object. Then the child fears that the bad internalized part object (the persecutory breast) will annihilate the good part object, with which the ego

---

[3]Emde (1987) notes from direct infant observational studies that the infant uses "social referencing," turning to the mother to regulate behavior, for example, to explore an object if the mother smiles or to avoid it if she shows fear. By the end of the first year of life, there is "positive affect sharing," where the child looks to significant others to share accomplishments. The child learns "reciprocity," or how to take turns, by the end of the first year, and "empathic" helping behavior by the second year. At 2 years of age the child will restrain its impulsivity in the parent's presence, and by 3 without it. Thus the superego or moral development of the child starts within the first year of life as Klein noted, and prohibitions are internalized by the third year of life.

identifies to form the core of the self. Klein speculated that the internalized persecutory bad breast becomes the forerunner of the persecutory part of the superego, whereas the internalized good, loving breast forms the ego ideal of the superego.

Splitting thus not only serves an emotional function, but is a primitive way in which the infant begins to discriminate and differentiate its experiences with its environment. Klein also saw splitting as the forerunner of the defense of repression. With further development, the infant's ego is better able to identify with the good idealized internal object and is less fearful of its own aggression. The child is then able to give up its need for omnipotent control, and gives over its power to the object. Finally, then, the object can be experienced not as a part object, but as a separate and whole object. With this development the infant enters the depressive position, which corresponds to Mahler's (1964) separation–individuation phase.

The infant, during the depressive position, now experiences depressive anxiety as it becomes aware of its separateness and helplessness. The major fear now is not that its rage will destroy the internalized good breast and the ego, but that its rage will destroy the internal and external whole good object, and suffer abandonment. All loss is perceived as due to the infant's own destructiveness and as punishment for its hatefulness and injury. The infant attempts to undo its guilt and restore the lost object through reparative fantasy and behavior. Therefore, the child desires the mother's real body, not simply because of libidinal desires, but to seek comfort against the terrifying internalized bad objects and to make reparation for the fantasied damage done to the mother. This process of splitting and making reparation toward the mother's body was felt by Klein to lead to the development of the Oedipus complex. With further development, the child gives up its fear that its own aggression will destroy the object, and becomes aware that it can retain the love for the good object even though feeling aggression toward it. The child can then experience mourning for the loss of good objects, as well as guilt. It is at this point that the child also develops the capacity for abstract symbolic thinking and the ability to link phenomena.

Klein considered that the paranoid-schizoid and depressive positions were not limited to early infancy, but persisted as discrete constellations of object relations and their associated anxieties and defenses throughout life. Klein also formulated what she termed the *manic defense,* which occurred during the depressive position. This is similar to narcissistic defenses, with the child denying the psychic reality of loss of dependency and attempting to control and triumph over the object, while having contempt for (demeaning) it. In summary, Klein's contributions to psychoanalytic theory are her concepts involved with attachment to the mother, the importance of unconscious fantasy, the pregenital positions of development, the role of part and whole internalized object relations, reparation for guilt over aggression, and the primitive defenses of splitting and projective identification (Segal 1964).

Klein's concepts influenced Bion, who was her analysand, in formulating his ideas about basic assumption groups. Her paranoid-schizoid position found expression in Bion's (1961) fight–flight group, and her depressive position manifested itself in his dependency group. These are discussed in the next chapter. Klein's formulations strongly influenced the development of the object relations school by noting the importance of attachment and separation during infancy, and of primitive defenses such as splitting and projective identification. My own work incorporated the child's reparative efforts toward the parents. As I see it, this effort was not limited to guilt over the child's fantasied aggression, but involved completing the parents' personality needs around their aggression, dependency, or self-esteem.

Klein's work is more closely related to classical psychoanalysis in that she retained a one-person psychology by focusing almost exclusively on intrapsychic processes. Aggression in the child, according to Klein, was due to an inborn death instinct, and the child distorted reality due to its own aggressive fantasies and defenses. She did acknowledge that the more the infant was frustrated by external reality, the more sadistic and powerful was the bad internal object and hence the severity of the superego. However, she did not sufficiently take into account the actual influence of others on the child's development. Her intrapsychic orientation found expression in her formulations on child development, superego formation, and psychopathology.

Even though Klein used Freud's death instinct differently

than he formulated it, she retained it as a cornerstone of her theory. Considerable criticism has been leveled against Klein's use of the death instinct, and it is interesting that no other psychoanalytic school adheres to the use of the death instinct at all. Developing in the middle between the Kleinian and classical groups, the British Middle School developed object relations into a two-person psychology. The British Middle School criticized Klein's use of the death instinct, as well as her exclusive focus on intrapsychic fantasy to the denial of actual environmental influences.

I shall now trace the development of a two-person psychology in object relations as it evolved in England, and then compare it to its neo-Freudian counterpart in the United States. Bion (1967), a Kleinian analyst who retained such concepts as the death instinct, differed from Klein by considering that personality development was not simply based upon intrapsychic fantasy, but also upon how the mother actually "contained" the infant's distress. Although this acknowledged the effect of the mother, it remained a one-person psychology. The focus was on the child's response to only one aspect of the interaction with the mother.

RONALD FAIRBAIRN

The next major contribution was by W. R. D. Fairbairn (1952), a member of the British Middle School.[4] Fairbairn not only rejected Freud's constructs of the life and death instincts but the whole idea of libidinal drives stemming from the id. He rejected Freud's structural theory, especially the construct of the id, and developed a structural theory of his own. The child's personality was viewed as developing from experiences with real and not fantasied people. Ego development depended upon the infant being not satisfaction-seeking, but object-seeking. In Fairbairn's theory, energy could not be separated from structure, which was consistent with

---

[4]The Middle School evolved as an independent group between the classical and Kleinian factions of the British Psychoanalytic Society. It was Ernest Jones who prevented the British Psychoanalytic Society from splintering, possibly because he had invited Klein from Berlin, and she analyzed his children.

modern physics and linguistics. He coined the term *libidinal ego* to describe this drive for *attachment* by the "true self," and considered that libidinal energy was not from the id but was part of the ego structure. Similarly, he viewed aggression not as a primary instinct arising from the id, but as a response of the ego to frustration in relationships. Thus gratification or control of biological drives was not primary to Fairbairn's way of thinking; what was crucial to it was the preservation or restoration of the integrity of the "true personal self." This formulation has striking similarity to those of Horney (1950) and Kohut (1977) in the United States.

Fairbairn saw the primitive defense of splitting, first formulated by Klein, as due not to fantasy but as a result of the actual relationship of the parents to the child. In Fairbairn's theory of personality development, a newborn infant starts life with an undifferentiated ego merged with the mother. In order to cope with the inevitable frustrating experiences with mothering, a mental representation of the maternal object is internalized. The undifferentiated ego then splits this internalized object into an *ideal object,* which is satisfying, and represses the frustrating object into the unconscious. This repressed, frustrating object is again split into a *rejecting object,* which contains the mother's denial of the needy self, and an *exciting object,* which contains the mother's need-stimulating or seductive aspects.

According to Fairbairn, the ego itself then becomes split into three components. The *central ego,* which remains conscious and controls object seeking, adapts to the external world and relates to the parent as the *ideal object.* The *antilibidinal ego* is unconscious and relates to the *rejecting object.* It contains the child's repressed rage. The *libidinal ego,* which is also unconscious, relates to the *exciting object,* and contains the repressed feelings of need and longing. Fairbairn considered that the antilibidinal ego, and the associated rejecting object, persecuted and further repressed the libidinal ego, and the exciting object, in order to deny the painful feelings of helplessness and dependency. Essentially the patient internalized the bad, unsatisfying real objects in order to control them as a closed system in the inner world, since they cannot be mastered in the outer world. Thus it is difficult for patients to relinquish these internalized bad objects without anxiety and the dread of depersonalization or death. This is because object loss, even though the object may be bad, is equated with psychological death.

Although Fairbairn rejected Freud's structural theory, his own structural theory, while acknowledging the effects of relationships, still emphasized intrapsychic factors (the three egos and internal objects) and remained essentially a one-person psychology. Also the use of his new terminology, *libidinal ego* and *antilibidinal ego,* seems confusing, especially in view of his rejection of the libido theory. Perhaps *object-seeking self* and *object-avoiding self* might have described this better.

While some analysts have criticized Klein for her preoccupation with the death instinct, other analysts have censured Fairbairn for not sufficiently recognizing the role of the patient's aggression toward others. Just as Klein can be faulted for her exclusive focus on internal fantasy and its distortion of the environment, Fairbairn has been criticized for not giving sufficient import to the infant's subjective experiences that distort their outer reality. Although he does bring in the impact of the environment, Fairbairn seems to place too much emphasis on the effects of objective reality (the frustration of infantile dependency) on personality development. Like Klein, he correlates the degree of splitting and the severity of the internalized bad object with the severity of frustration in parenting; however, unlike her, he sees splitting and the internalization of the bad object as due basically to bad parenting. He does not agree with Klein's view of the infant's developmentally limited perception resulting in the infant's use of splitting as being a normal way of adaptation. Fairbairn thus does not provide a theory to account for normal development with good parenting.

It is interesting that Fairbairn did revise Freud's formulation of the Oedipus complex, considering it as not solely due to infantile sexuality. Fairbairn saw the Oedipus complex as arising intrapsychically from the way the child handled object relations, in particular the process of splitting. During the preoedipal period, splitting occurred in dyadic relationships; that is, one object, the mother, was split into a good and a bad object. However, during the oedipal phase, the process of splitting progressed to involve triadic relationships. Now one whole object of the same sex was seen as rejecting, and the other whole object of the opposite sex was perceived as exciting. This formulation of the Oedipus corresponds to the progression from Klein's paranoid-schizoid position to the depressive one, and to Kernberg's (1976) third to fourth developmental stages. (Kernberg's stages are discussed later.) Kernberg notes that following integration of the opposing good and bad valences, the ego and superego are more established as intrapsychic structures, and there is progression to the use of more mature defenses.

There are distinct differences, however, between Fairbairn and Kernberg. Kernberg (1975, 1976) sees splitting as a primitive defense and a forerunner of repression, whereas Fairbairn sees splitting and regression as operating at the same time. Kernberg's work is more in keeping with the findings of the types of defenses in borderline and narcissistic personality disorders versus neurotic conditions. In addition, Kernberg's developmental schema, built on the work of Jacobson (1964), traces the development of structure in the personality more clearly and provides a nonmechanistic explanation for the neutralization of aggression. My own work also follows that of Jacobson (Slipp 1981) and of Kernberg in terms of viewing good and bad self and object representations. By using such broad definitions as good and bad, one does not need to limit oneself to only the concepts of excitation or rejection, but can give greater scope to the complex interrelationship between the child and others.

MICHAEL BALINT

Balint (1968), a member of the British Middle School, more aptly than Fairbairn described this complex interrelationship of the child and others. In pathology he considered that there was a lack of a dyadic fit between the child's biopsychological needs and the environmental supplies, causing what he termed "the basic fault" during the preoedipal period of development. Balint mentions a variety of factors, stating:

The cause of this early discrepancy may be congenital, i.e., the infant's biopsychological needs may have been too exacting (there are non-viable infants and progressive congenital conditions . . .), or may be environmental, such as care that is insufficient, deficient, haphazard, over-anxious, over-protective, harsh, rigid, grossly inconsistent, incorrectly timed, over-stimulating, or merely un-understanding or indifferent. [1968, p. 22]

Balint disagreed with Fairbairn that the infant was only object seeking. Balint saw the infant as object seeking as well as pleasure seeking, thereby combining object relations with drive and structural theories.

DONALD WINNICOTT

Winnicott (1965), of the British Middle School, proposed the first complete two-person theory of how the actual *interaction between mother and child* facilitated the gradual unfolding of the infant's innate potential for growth and development. In this theory both intrapsychic and interpersonal dynamics are recognized more fully. Winnicott noted that prior to giving birth, the mother has an increased sensitivity to the needs of her baby, which he termed *primary maternal preoccupation.* If the infant receives "good enough mothering" that is both need-satisfying and comforting, the infant's desire for omnipotent control of and fusion with the mother can be gradually given up. The mother's holding of the infant allows the infant to relate to its own body and to separate the "me" from what is "not me" gradually. The infant internalizes and possesses this "good mother function," which serves to organize and integrate the ego. During this process the child can employ a "transitional object," such as a blanket or a teddy bear. Winnicott terms this an external "not me" possession that symbolically maintains the internal fantasy of fusion with the good mother.

When the infant's needs are frustrated, and it subjectively experiences the mother as bad, it responds with aggression. However, if the mother continues to provide a "holding environment" by not retaliating or abandoning the infant, it can give up its omnipotence and separate. Winnicott (1958) noted, however, that if the mother does not provide the security of this "holding function" and is actually unresponsive to the infant's needs for nurturance and security, the infant cannot internalize a comforting good mother, and thus lacks ego integration. For the sake of survival, the infant develops a "false self," one that is compliant.

Many of the concepts of Winnicott are similar to those of others. For example, in the United States, Sullivan (1953) described three forms of "personifications" that influenced what he termed the "self system": The "good me" developed when the mother was gratifying and tender; the "bad me" when she was ungratifying; and the "not me" — a dissociated frightened aspect of the self — developed from trauma or excessive frustration. Similarly, Horney (1950) described the "idealized self-image," which was a defensive, grandiose, and false self, as against a "real self." Also in the United States, Kohut (1977) described a defective self, with insufficient self-cohesion, resulting from the mother's lack of providing sufficient self-enhancing reflections, which he termed *mirroring*. Kernberg (1976) also commented that when the mother was gratifying, she was internalized as the good fused self-object that formed the core of the ego. All these concepts about the self involve interpersonal relations; it is the *self in relationship*.

EGO PSYCHOLOGY

Hartmann (1964) acknowledged interpersonal factors, but retained drive theory by postulating a dual-track theory of personality development. One track involved intrapsychic drive satisfaction, whereas the other dealt with interpersonal adaptation to the environment. In the first track, aggression was now considered as equal to libido. Both of these drives needed to be neutralized to facilitate the development of permanent object relations, and ego and superego structures. Interestingly, ego psychologists made a point of differentiating instincts from drives. They noted that self-preservation in animals is actually due to inborn instincts, while in man survival is due to the ego's mediation of drives with the environment. In the face of danger, these drives can be re-formed and discharged into action. On the other hand, Erikson's (1963) developmental schema for personality development was not based on instinct theory but on modes of *relationships* that determined ego identity. Erikson (1964) considered that man's inborn instincts were, at birth, only fragmentary and plastic as potential drives, and that "tradition and conscience" organized them, during a long period of childhood, into drives.

EDITH JACOBSON

It was Jacobson (1964), however, who integrated both drive theory and environmental forces into her formulations. She was opposed to such concepts as primary masochism and the death instinct, and considered instinctual energy as undifferentiated at birth. Aggressive and libidinal drives developed only under the influence of the mother–child relationship. Thus both the development of the ego and the development of drives evolved hand in hand with object relations. Jacobson also felt that these drives needed to be neutralized to provide the energy for psychic structures.

OTTO KERNBERG

Kernberg (1975, 1976) has made a crucial contribution to integrating psychoanalytic theory and practice into a unitary approach by bringing together object relations theory, drive theory, structural theory, and ego psychology. Kernberg does not polarize biological and social forces into an either/or dichotomy, but considers them together as interactive, using general systems theory. He states that inborn, primitive affect and arousal mechanisms become embedded in a matrix of internalized object relations, which in turn serves as the major organizer of them into biological drives. The child's subjective perception of the mother, in accordance with the pleasure principle, becomes stored in memory as self and object representations along with good or bad affective valences. Libido and aggression are not primary inborn instincts, therefore, but are drives that evolve out of the memory of these good and bad self and object representations and their associated primitive affect states.

Kernberg traces this process through developmental stages. The first stage from birth to 2 months is undifferentiated. The second stage from 2 to 8 months of age involves splitting of the fused self-object representation into good and bad. The fused good self-object, built up by pleasurable experiences with the mother, becomes the nucleus of the self and the organizer of integrative functions of the ego. The third stage from 8 to 36 months involves the separation of the self from object representations. Splitting into good and bad persists, and this is seen as the fixation point for borderline patients. The fourth stage consists of integration of these opposing good and bad emotional valences, so that these separate self and object representations are each both good and bad. This integration provides an explanation for neutralization of drives that does not rely on mechanistic, nineteenth-century, Newtonian physical concepts. It is at this point that the ego, superego, and id become firmly established as intrapsychic structures, and the defense of splitting is replaced by repression. This is the fixation point for neurotic pathology. In the last stage, internalized object representations are reshaped through actual current experiences with real people. This is similar to my own formulations, stemming from work with families (Slipp 1984).

The more an individual's self-perception corresponds to how others realistically perceive him or her, the more normal that person is considered. This formulation by Kernberg corresponds to that of Sullivan (1953) and Horney (1950). When the person's internal world is integrated to provide trust in the self, the individual is better able to self-regulate his or her narcissistic equilibrium — that is, self-esteem. However, with preneurotic patients, who feel empty inside, continuous external confirmation is necessary to sustain their self-esteem or even self-cohesion and sanity. Here we have the beginnings of systemic thinking in psychoanalysis, which takes into account how intrapsychic processes determine one's perception of relationships, as well as how current external relationships affect intrapsychic processes.

3

Psychoanalytic Group Theory

FREUD ON THE GROUP MIND

Object relations family therapy draws its theoretical underpinnings not only from individual but also from group theory. Freud's interest in groups was first captured by the fascinating phenomenon of the "group mind," in which people seem to lose their individuality and function only as part of a group. Freud (1921) noted that under such circumstances individuals seemed to regress to a primitive mental state, which included inhibition of their intellectual functioning and suspectibility to the emotional contagion of the group. In *Group Psychology and the Analysis of the Ego,* he reviewed the work of Le Bon and McDougall, who considered the "group mind" as an inherited "herd instinct," an archaic heritage from our animal ancestors.

Freud differed, and felt the herd instinct could be further reduced and analyzed psychologically. He believed that the unifying bond of the group was the libidinal attachment of the members to each other and to the leader. Like an object of love, the leader was perceived in an idealized fashion. Each member identified with the leader, who was then internalized in the member's ego ideal, thereby usurping his or her own individual ego and superego functioning. The leader's values overrode those values connected to the group members' internalized parental images, and permitted the group members to suspend their own critical judgment and intellectual functioning. Freud also speculated about the personality characteristics of leadership that made this phenomenon possible. He considered that the leader tended to be a narcissistic individual, who was not attached to others, and who outwardly appeared independent and masterful. He compared the leader to a hypnotist who subjected others to his or her will.

Recent group investigators have taken exception to Freud's generalized formulations concerning all groups. Freud did not take into account democratic groups, in which the will of the majority is taken into account, since he used as his prototype authoritarian groups (Lippitt and White 1958). Also, the two authoritarian groups Freud selected, the church and the army, might foster dependency and obedience, but of a type that is markedly different from the type of regression that occurs in mob psychology.

WILFRED BION

A major psychoanalytic contribution to the understanding of the "group mind" phenomenon was made by Bion (1961). Bion used the constructs of Klein, such as her theories concerning psychotic anxieties, developmental positions, and the primitive defenses of splitting and projective identification. He differed from Freud's view that libido was the binding force for all groups. Instead he agreed with the formulations of Le Bon and McDougall of an inherited herd instinct. Bion considered that humans are herd animals who achieve security and vitality by attachment to and submergence in a group, but that they also need to achieve a sense of independent identity by rejecting the group.

Bion studied groups at the Tavistock Clinic in London, and noted that a normal functioning group employed rational behavior and enlisted the cooperation of its members to accomplish its task. This he termed the *work* group (abbreviated to *W*). However, under certain circumstances when the leader did not fulfill the role expectations of the group members and maintained an abstinent (nondependency-gratifying) position, the group regressed to a more primitive level of functioning and demonstrated irrational behavior. Loss of individual boundaries between members occurred, and the group functioned as a solitary fused unit. The group became preoccupied with group survival, but at the expense of individual needs. Bion found that the members reverted to using omnipotent fantasies to magically achieve their goal, which remained unconscious and thus outside of the members' awareness.

Unlike Freud, who did not differentiate various types of groups, Bion distinguished the normal work group from this more primitive form of group. He then noted that there were three forms of these primitive groups, and that each had a distinct, shared unconscious fantasy amongst the members as to how the group could magically achieve its goal. Bion termed these *basic assumption groups*. In a basic assumption *dependency* group (abbreviated to *baD*), the members looked for an absolute leader or an external diety, whose goodness, strength, and wisdom would provide security. This was essentially a search for the good object. The social prototype of this baD group, which also is a work (W) group, is the church. In the basic assumption *fight–flight* group (abbreviated to *baF*), the shared unconscious belief was that there was an enemy that must be attacked or avoided. This represented the bad object. A social prototype of baF, which also functions as a work group, is an army. In the basic assumption group of *pairing* (abbreviated as *baP*), the collective unconscious fantasy was a messianic hope, in which a child would be born to a couple. This child would be a savior of the group, to resolve feelings of hatred, destructiveness, and despair. A social prototype of baP, which is also a work group, is the aristocracy.

BION COMPARED TO FREUD

In comparison to Freud's formulations, it was only in the baP group that Bion considered the libidinal bond to be a significant dynamic, but not in any other basic assumption group. Bion's concept also differed markedly from that of Le Bon, of the leader manipulating group members by his or her strong will, as well as Freud's analogy of the group leader to a hypnotist. Bion (1961) states, "The leader is as much the creature of the basic assumption as any other member of the group, and this, I think, is to be expected if we envisage identification of the individual with the leader as depending not on introjection alone but on a simultaneous process of projective identification (Klein 1946) as well" (p. 177). In this process, Bion considers that the leader in a basic assumption group loses as much of his or her individuality, and holds on to the same unconscious, shared, magical belief, as anyone else in the group.

Then what makes for the choice of such a leader? The leader, according to Bion, is a person whose personality lends itself to extinction and exploitation by the leadership requirements of the particular basic assumption group. For example, a leader with paranoid trends fits in with the baF group, and thereby helps to focus on an external enemy to be scapegoated. Bion states that leaders of these basic assumption groups are seriously disturbed persons, being schizophrenic, malignant hysterics (borderlines), psychopaths with delinquent tendencies, or verbally facile defectives. If the personal qualities of the leader do not fit the requirements of the prevalent basic assumption group, that person is ignored and another person is chosen who does fit the group's requirements.

In critical assessment of Bion's formulations, I disagree with certain points. Bion stated that, although these basic assumptions can alternate from time to time in a group, they do not coexist simultaneously. For example, if dependency needs are frustrated a baF or baP might follow. This is at variance with my family work and the research on the authoritarian personality by Adorno and colleagues (1950), in which both dependency on an idealized object or leader in the group (similar to baD), and scapegoating of a demeaned outsider (similar to baF), have been found to coexist simultaneously. This can be explained as due to the mechanism of splitting. The leader or spouse is split into an all-good, all-powerful object and an all bad, persecutory object which is repressed. The repressed, persecutory, bad object is then displaced onto another person or group, thereby protecting the idealized good object. Thus the group idealizes the leader as omnipotent, one who will protect or rescue them—and the group finds a prejudicial scapegoat to blame.

My second disagreement is with Bion's idea that these basic assumption fantasies serve as a defense against psychotic anxiety as described by Klein. Even though these fantasies are irrational, making them analogous to psychosis seems misleading. Instead these basic assumption fantasies can be viewed as a regression to primitive, magical ways of coping that occur when individuals experience an overwhelming degree of anxiety and helplessness. The baF is comparable to Klein's paranoid-schizoid developmental position, with projection of aggression onto an external object to preserve a good internal object; and the baD is analogous to Klein's depressive position, with reliance on an external, separate, and powerful good object.

APPLICATION TO FAMILY THERAPY

There have been a number of similarities between Bion's thinking and marital therapy. Dicks (1963), also working at the Tavistock Clinic, observed that in many dysfunctional marriages there was a shared unconscious complementarity of beliefs, which held these couples together despite great conflict. Dicks noted that unacceptable parts of each spouse were attributed to the other, and acted out between them. Similar kinds of unconscious collusions in marital disharmony were reported by Framo (1981) and Willi (1984). Unacceptable parts of one spouse were projected into the other and became causes of contention between them. Bowen (1978) also commented on the projection of unacceptable aspects of one spouse into the other, who in turn acted this out. For example, one spouse may be irresponsible and the other overly responsible. Sager (1976) described what he termed the *marital contract*, which is an unconscious collusion that occurs at the beginning of a marriage. Each member is consciously or unconsciously expected to fulfill a particular role for the other.

Certain of Bion's basic assumption group concepts have similarities to the findings of family therapy researchers. In basic assumption groups, Bion noted that language is often stripped of its symbolic function, and not used for rational communication. Bion compared this use of language to that of the psychotic. A somewhat similar finding was noted in the studies of families of schizophrenic patients by Wynne and Singer (1963) and Wynne (1986). Language was used not for communication, but for defensive purposes. In these families there is a lack of an observable shared focus of attention and shared meaning in communication, which these investigators termed *communication deviance* (abbreviated to *CD*). This transactional thought disorder between members of the family was considered by Wynne to shape or maintain the schizophrenic patient's thought disorder.[1] With the families of borderline patients, the CD scores of the parents were intermediate between and overlapped the scores of parents of schizophrenics and those of neurotics.

DIFFERENCES BETWEEN BION'S AND SLIPP'S TYPOLOGY

Even though other investigators of marital and family therapy have reported an unconscious dyadic collusion between the marital pair, it has been noted (Slipp 1969, Zinner and Shapiro 1974) that there is an unconscious collusion involving relations in the family as a whole group. My main contribution was in the development of a typology of family interaction (Slipp 1984). This family typology is remarkably similar to Bion's basic assumption groups, derived from therapy groups of strangers who were neurotic or normal. Just as in Bion's therapy groups at the Tavistock, I also found that families with a severely disturbed

---

[1]The discrepancies in the findings of replicative studies by Hirsch and Leff (1971) and Johnston and Holzman (1979), of CD in schizophrenics' families, is accounted for by the investigators Sass and colleagues (1984). In the group studied by Wynne and Singer, the schizophrenic patients had a high degree of thought disorder, which was not the case for the samples of families in the other two studies. Thus a high degree of CD seemed to correlate directly with a high degree of thought disorder in the patient. In paranoid-schizophrenic patients, there seemed to be a greater degree of evasion noted in the parents' style of speech.

child used the defenses of splitting and projective identification. These families also held onto shared unconscious fantasies that set up a system of collusive object relations.

However, for several reasons, I did not use Bion's terminology. Bion's work was not at the time in the forefront of my thinking. Also, each of Bion's three basic assumption groups, although insightful, can be reduced to its more elemental ingredients that more precisely describe the projection processes occurring in the family. This process consists of which split (the good or bad self or object) is being placed into a child or a spouse through projective identification.

Labeling the entire family as responding to one basic assumption could lead to confusion. I found that due to splitting, families usually had at least two of Bion's basic assumptions operating simultaneously with different subgroups of members. In families with a schizophrenic patient, there was scapegoating of the patient by the parent(s) as the bad object, which is similar to Bion's basic assumption fight–flight group. At the same time, idealization of the spouse as the good object also occurred; thus, in that relationship, a basic assumption dependency coexisted between the parents. In families with a borderline patient, the patient served as a go-between or surrogate spouse for one parent, representing the good split object, which was similar to Bion's basic assumption dependency group. Simultaneously the spouse was demeaned as the bad object by the same parent, so in that relationship a basic assumption fight–flight coexisted as well. In a family with a depressed patient, the child served as the good self to rescue one or both of the parents from anger and despair through its achievement; this family functioned like Bion's basic assumption pairing group. I used the identical term "savior" independently to describe the same process. Here the child, born of the union of the parents, would be expected to gratify the parents' narcissistic needs. But at the same time, one of the parents was demeaned by the other parent as the bad self, while the child was idealized as the good self.

This same complication, of several basic assumptions coexisting, also has other forms of expression in family relationships. For example, very often the parent would project a different split introject into each of two children.[2] One child might receive the bad object projection, and serve as the family scapegoat, while another child would receive the good self projection, and serve as the family savior. Both of these children, in their own way, would protect the stability of the family group by draining off hostility, and the achievements of the savior would enhance the self-esteem of the parents. In other cases, the same child might have these or other combinations of projections placed into himself or herself either simultaneously or at different points in the family life cycle. The child might receive the good object projection, and serve as a go-between, while later receiving the good self-projection, and serve as the family savior.

Another reason for not using Bion's basic assumption terminology in describing collusive object relations in the family is its lack of specificity. This is clearly illustrated in what a number of family therapists have described as the "gruesome twosome." In this instance, the parents join together in a rigidly bounded parental coalition, one in which they are mutually supportive of each other, but which excludes the children. On superficial inspection, since the parents pair together, this might be classified according to Bion's basic assumption of pairing. However, the term *pairing* is misleading; labeling it as baP would be incorrect, as the parents are not seeking confirmation of their self-esteem through the child's functioning as their savior. Instead, according to my typology I classify the "gruesome twosome" as a subtype of the schizophrenic type of object relations. Each parent is projecting the good maternal object into the other to provide mutual confirmation of their self-esteem and identity. (This would be Bion's baD.) Instead of actively scapegoating their children, the parents emotionally abandon them and leave them to fend for themselves with their needs for nurturance ignored.

My final objection to Bion's typology is that it did not contain a fourth group, in which one person acts out anger, guilt, or other negative aspects of the self for another. This is probably one of the most frequent forms of family interactions found in

---

[2]Whether or not a good or bad introject is projected onto a child may be determined by birth order, intelligence, creative ability, appearance, or temperament. Internalized object relations include both good and bad self and objects.

marital and family discord. Even though Bion's basic assumption of fight–flight has some general similarity to projecting unacceptable feelings into an external object, there are also very clear differences. Bion's baF is related to Klein's paranoid-schizoid position, in which one's own overpowering aggression against a parent is projected into another person so as to preserve the internalized good object. The other person is seen as the bad parental object who threatens the survival of the self, and needs to be destroyed or escaped from. In the fourth type of my typology, unacceptable feelings that one person feels guilty about, and that would diminish that person's self-esteem, are split off and projected into another, who is manipulated unconsciously to express them. Then the other can be punished like a mischievous child for expressing the negative side of one's own ambivalence, the bad self. The level of paranoia is much greater in Bion's baF, with the other experienced as the external persecutory object threatening survival. In this fourth type, the person identifies with his or her own persecutory figure internalized in the superego. There is no external threat to survival, nor does the other have to be destroyed or evaded. Instead of the superego punishing the self intrapsychically for having unacceptable feelings, the conflict is *externalized*. The other is needed to express these negative feelings, and then the other can be punished as the bad one.

A FAMILY AVENGER

In order to elaborate on the fourth type of the typology, which is found in the overinvolved delinquent, and in other circumstances where one person acts out the bad self or role of the avenger for another, I present the case of Bill and Nancy. Bill had been divorced and left his son, Henry, in his former wife's custody. With Bill's consent, she moved to another state. Bill was then able to pursue his professional career, and devoted all his energies to becoming a financial success. He paid child support, but had little direct involvement with his son, Henry. He knew his former wife was, as he stated, "a flake." She sounded as if she had an infantile or borderline personality disorder, and did not work or make a constructive life for herself. She lived off her alimony and child support, and had a series of unsatisfactory love affairs with married men. Henry grew up without adequate parental nurturance or guidance.

Henry was not a serious college student, spending Bill's money on a car and trips. He dropped out of college for a while, drifted from one job to another, and still demanded financial support from Bill, which was always forthcoming. It seemed that Henry was acting out his rage and making Bill "pay" for his emotional unavailability by provoking guilt. When Bill married Nancy, he invited Henry to visit. Henry was envious of the luxurious home that his father and Nancy owned, and was rude to Nancy. Bill did not intercede to protect her.

Bill's financial overindulgence increased Henry's greedy demands. The situation peaked when Henry threatened to sue Bill if he did not increase his financial support, buy him a new car, and continue to pay for his return to school. Bill did not become angry. Nancy did not want to have Henry visit their home again because of his abusiveness. Bill then began seeing Henry secretly. When Nancy discovered this, she became upset and angry. Bill could not see anything wrong with his inability to set limits and otherwise deal with his son. Instead he felt that Nancy was keeping him from being a good father. He felt that his first wife had been a neglectful mother, and that now his second wife was interfering with his relationship with Henry. It was, he believed, because of his two wives that Henry had problems. On exploration, Nancy claimed that she had encouraged Bill to see Henry and spend time with him. What made her angry at both of them was Bill's lack of setting boundaries and protecting her from Henry's rudeness, and Bill's subsequent secrecy and lying.

It became clear that Bill had needed to provoke Nancy into being angry at Henry so that he could project the negative aspects of himself into her. Thus he could deny his guilt over being an uncaring and uninvolved father, and his anger and disappointment with Henry's behavior and poor academic performance. He could remain the good one, and Nancy was induced into being the critical or bad one. The projective identification was then interpreted in marital therapy, that he probably felt guilty in agreeing to let his first wife, whom he believed was an incompetent parent, rear Henry. However, it was a conflictual situation for him, since he had needed to devote considerable energy and time to his career. It was therefore difficult for him to deal with his guilt over this, and with his disappointment now in Henry. Thus, in order to avoid becoming unhappy and depressed over this conflict, he unconsciously needed Nancy's help to express the negative side of himself that he could not accept.

The aim of this interpretation of his projective identification into Nancy of the role of avenger was to enable Bill to reown his projection of his own internal conflict, and to work it through intrapsychically. Now his guilt and anger would not be acted out interpersonally, which would have threatened the stability of his second marriage; now he could effectively set limits and guide his son. At no time did Bill experience Nancy as a threat to his survival, as a bad, persecutory, external object. Instead, she served as a container to act out his own unacceptable negative feelings, his bad self, whom he could blame. Thus, he could avoid guilt, not see himself as a bad father, not lose his self-esteem, nor become depressed. Once he owned his conflict, he could deal with his own guilt and was no longer able to be manipulated and punished by the angry and self-defeating behavior of Henry. The working through of this conflict facilitated Bill's ability to integrate his ambivalence, and to then function as a more realistically concerned parent. This was not only beneficial to Henry, but it preserved his marriage to Nancy.

THE SYMBIOTIC SURVIVAL PATTERN

The families I studied that contained severely disturbed young adults were unable to meet not only their children's developmental needs but the parents' needs as well. In this respect these families did not function in what Bion would term a *work group.* The developmental needs of the individual family members were sacrificed for the survival of the family as a group. I have termed this process the *symbiotic survival pattern,* since each family member feels responsible for the self-esteem and survival of the others in the family. This burden of responsibility leaves each member feeling both omnipotent and helpless at the same time.

FAMILY INTERACTION IN NEUROTIC
OR ADJUSTMENT DISORDERS

My original research (Slipp 1969, 1973, 1976, 1977) was restricted to families with young adults suffering from schizophrenia, a hysterical-borderline condition, or depression. Continued clinical work showed that the four discrete patterns of the typology could exist also with normal and neurotic families. These patterns of unconscious collusive object relations were not limited to families containing severely disturbed patients, but had a wider application. In a family with a neurotic patient or someone suffering from an adjustment disorder, these patterns of family object relations seemed to be a regressive adaptation to situations that threatened their self-esteem or security. When such a family felt helpless to protect itself by its usual coping mechanisms, it also regressed to a more primitive mode of adaptation. This regression is similar to what Bion found in his basic assumption groups with relatively healthy individuals. With these more normal families, the regressive adaptation tended to be more time limited and less intensely a matter of survival than with families containing a more disturbed member.

In our work, the family members had preexisting ties and a history together, while in Bion's groups the members were strangers. Yet both groups' members seemed to regress. Bion's explanation is that people are born with a herd instinct, similar to that of other animals. Perhaps, according to this theory, when the neocortex cannot cope with situations that threaten survival, a changeover to more primitive portions of the brain that have specific built-in genetic pathways may occur. In this way, at least group survival is insured, so that the species is perpetuated. This is an interesting speculation to account for people's regression during times of danger to forms of functioning that might be characteristic of early childhood development, or primitive peoples, or animals.

What is highlighted by the studies in psychoanalytic group psychology is that people seem to have less autonomous functioning and to be more susceptible to external group pressure in the here and now than individual psychoanalytic theory had considered. Though individuals with severe psychopathology are more narcissistically vulnerable, even normal individuals seek security and confirmation of their self-esteem and identity through others, especially in groups. The degree to which an individual's sense of security and self-esteem is experienced as threatened thus seems to be determined by the degree of narcissistic vulnerability and the extent of the environmental trauma. The finding that individuals are markedly influenced in their personality functioning by here-and-now group interaction is probably the single most significant discovery in family therapy. This finding is further developed in the next chapter in our review of systemic family therapy.

4

Systemic Family Therapy

GREGORY BATESON AND GENERAL
SYSTEMS THEORY

Two forms of systemic family therapy have achieved prominence in recent years. The first is structural family therapy devised by Minuchin (1974) and his group, and the other is strategic family therapy expanded from the work at the Mental Research Institute by Selvini-Palazzoli and her group (1978) in Milan, Italy. Both systemic approaches are theoretically based on the newer epistemologies of general systems theory and cybernetics, as initially applied to the study of families by Bateson (1972) and his colleagues at the Mental Research Institute in Palo Alto, California. Both focus on the current, ongoing, pathological transactional patterns reverberating between family members, patterns that are held in place by family rules. It is precisely these pathological transactions in the family that are considered to produce symptoms in the "identified patient." The symptom bearer is considered as only the person *identified* as the patient, but the entire family is the patient. Thus the context of the family—that is, its pattern of transactions—is emphasized, and not the symptoms within the patient.

In their treatment approach, both structural and strategic

family therapy are directive, which Bateson (1972) strongly felt was not congruent with the newer epistemologies upon which they are based. To be more precise, this was because both of these approaches perceived the therapist as being in charge, and having the power to control interaction and institute change. The therapist was seen as outside and relatively unaffected by the system and relying on *linear* thinking for his or her actual therapeutic interventions. This finding was noted by Dell (1986a), Gurman (1983), Slipp (1984), and Wynne (1986).

Both of these systemic forms of family therapy are short-term treatment approaches, with the strategic being the briefer, lasting from one to ten sessions. (This contract can be renewed for another ten sessions.) Structural family therapy generally has the family meet with the therapist on a weekly basis, while strategic family therapy has meetings every other week, monthly, or at longer intervals. Structural family therapy derives much of its underpinnings from small group dynamics of social psychology, attempting to analyze and to restructure the component elements of the family group. On the other hand, the strategic form is more related to philosophical theory, especially concerning linguistics and semiotics, and focuses more on the family as a whole. Both systemic approaches employ the mechanism of "reframing" as a therapeutic technique. Reframing is derived from semiotics, in which the meaning of the symptom is redefined from indicating one thing to indicating another. During this process, the patient is taken out of the scapegoated, sick, or bad role of "identified patient," and the symptom redefined into interpersonal terms, often serving an altruistic or good function for the family.

Both these systemic forms of family therapy employ the concept that feedback occurs in the family in order to maintain pathological transactions. The structural group, however, actively attempts to intervene and change the subgroups and break up rigid transactional patterns held in place by negative (deviation-reducing) feedback loops. The strategic group attempts to change the pathologic transactions (vicious cycles) that stem from the erroneous efforts of the members at solving a problem. These are held in place by positive (deviation-amplifying) feedback loops. In terms of the therapeutic stance, the structural therapist is closer to the individual dynamic therapist. Engagement is enhanced by "joining" the family system where it is and assuming a role of participant-observer, being both in and outside the field. The strategic therapist, however, remains altogether outside the family system, and offers the family "paradoxical" prescriptions and rituals that go along with the homeostatic balance of the family as a whole. Thus the strategic therapist considers that change is brought about paradoxically, by not making overt efforts to change the family.

STRUCTURAL FAMILY THERAPY

The basic assumptions in structural family therapy are that pathology is not solely intrapsychic, but that individuals influence and are influenced by constantly recurring sequences of interactions with others in the family. Even though the structural family therapist does acknowledge that an individual's personality is formed by past events, the psyche is seen as contained and governed by current interactions with others. Transformation of the present family structure is considered as having the power to change not only overt behavior but also the intrapsychic dynamic of each of the members of the family system, according to Minuchin (1974). The therapist in structural family therapy thus does not explore or interpret the past for the individual members, but joins the family system and uses himself to restructure the existing current family interaction along lines considered more therapeutic.

The structural family therapist takes the position that changing the current, external context of relationships will change the intrapsychic structure of each individual, which denies that the past becomes internalized and relatively stable. This formulation is at odds with the psychodynamic understanding of personality, that even if the present external context is changed, the intrapsychic structure and function will not be altered significantly. This is also in opposition to the "structural determinism" of Maturana (1978), which sees the internal structure of the individual as determining how that individual perceives and reacts to external reality. Dell (1986) points out that individuals are unable to undergo what Maturana terms "instructive interaction." For example, each patient, according to his or her own structure, will respond differently to a therapist's intervention.

To the structural family therapist the past is not relevant, except for its having created the present. Also, the present is considered as having the power to change the past. This is a reversal of emphasis from that of dynamic therapy. The structural therapist sees the external as changing the internal. In dynamic therapy the emphasis is on changing the internal in order to change the external. Similarly, according to Maturana (1978), only those interventions of the therapist that fit the patient's internal structure would be effective in bringing about change. However, the structural family therapist believes that once the negative feedback cycles are changed, the new family transactions become internally self-perpetuating, without the family members' needing to understand their etiology.

One of the major contributions of the structural family therapy school is the method of analysis of the family's structure and function. The family is seen as maintaining its differentiation and ability to perform its functions through its subsystems. These subsystems are divided into *individuals, dyads* (such as husband–wife, spouse–child), *generations* (spouses, siblings), *sex, interests,* and *functions.* Each member belongs to different subsystems with different levels of obligations, rights, and power. Boundaries of the sybsystems need to be *clear* and semipermeable — that is, firm enough to allow a member to function without interference, yet open sufficiently to permit contact with others. If the boundaries are too *diffuse,* the distance between members is too close and differentiation becomes blurred; this results in a decrease of autonomous functioning. Minuchin describes this process as occurring in what he calls *enmeshed* families; I have described the process using the term *symbiotic,* and others have called it "the amorphous we experience" (Boszormenyi-Nagy 1965), "undifferentiated family ego mass" (Bowen 1978), or "pseudomutuality" (Wynne et al. 1958). If the boundaries are too *rigid* and closed, communication between subsystems is reduced, as found in what Minuchin terms *disengaged* families. In such cases there is a reduction in the sense of belonging and of loyalty, and a diminished ability to trust others and to ask for help or support. In structural family theory, the family is seen as a dynamic entity adapting to both developmental stages and stresses by restructuring itself in order to support the growth and developmental needs of its members.

If the boundaries between the subsystems do not remain firm and flexible but become rigid, dysfunctional patterns of interaction occur, leading to psychopathology. Minuchin describes three types of rigid triads that may develop: (1) Stresses in one subsystem (such as husband–wife) become detoured (displaced) into another subsystem (such as father–son), so that harmony apparently remains in the first subsystem. (An example of this, from my typology, could be found in families in which the schizophrenic child is scapegoated by a parent to preserve a spousal relationship.) (2) Each spouse pulls on the child to side with them. (3) Cross-generational coalitions occur—such as between a parent and a child—in which there is formed a rigid boundary against the other parent.

This phenomenological method of analyzing the structure and function of the family is then utilized in the treatment process. The structural family therapist makes a structural map of the family, depicting the various subsystems and the kinds of boundaries (clear, diffuse, or rigid) between them, as well as the power hierarchy, coalitions, and affective involvement (affiliation, overinvolvement, or conflict). From this map, specific goals for treatment of the family are formulated. An example of such a goal might be to reestablish the spousal subsystem so that the child, who has joined in a cross-generational coalition with one parent, can again become part of the sibling subsystem.

To accomplish this goal, the therapist assumes a nonthreatening stance by *joining* the family. This involves accepting and blending in with the family's organization and style, while at the same time remaining an objective observer of the system. This would be similar to participant-observation in individual therapy. Two ways to facilitate accommodation of the therapist and family are (1) *tracking,* in which members are encouraged to speak, and are confirmed by being heard by the therapist; and (2) *mimesis,* in which the therapist copies the family's style and affective range of communication. In the latter, the therapist may promote acceptance and give support by even mimicking the family's speech patterns and language or duplicating their physical movements.

For example, if a father takes off his coat, the therapist might take off his coat. If a patient eats a certain sandwich, the therapist might also select the same sandwich and eat it.

As in individual therapy, a therapeutic alliance is established in structural family therapy, which will facilitate the participation of the members of the group and progress in treatment. When this is secure, the therapist then creates interventions to *unbalance* the system. This may be accomplished by joining one subsystem to enhance it with his or her power, and then joining another by supporting the weaker member; by shifting a member from one subsystem to another, by manipulating seating and spatial arrangements, and so on. In this way the boundaries that are too diffuse can be tightened, or those too rigid can be loosened. The power heirarchy can be appropriately reestablished and coalitions disrupted. The goal is, via the therapist's directives and maneuvers, to restructure the family along lines that will preserve members' individuality as well as interdependency, and that will best support their developmental needs for growth. The therapist may challenge the family's perception of reality, provide alternate possibilities, and help develop healthier transactional patterns. This is done by blocking dysfunctional transactions, emphasizing individual differences, bringing out into the open any covert conflict that has been detoured, and helping in the resolution of this conflict once it is overt.

As in strategic family therapy, homework assignments may be given, but here it is usually to a subgroup; for example, getting a parentified child away from a parent–child coalition and into the sibling subsystem. The Structural group thus has many of the characteristics of individual therapy such as engagement and attempting to change structure slowly, to bring underlying conflict to the fore, and to help in its resolution. This is unlike the Strategic group, in which the belief is that at a certain nodal point, a specific prescription to the family is required to enable it to make a quantum leap forward, or else the very opportunity for change is lost.

STRATEGIC FAMILY THERAPY (THE MILAN GROUP)

Strategic family therapy was developed by Selvini-Palazzoli, a psychoanalyst, and her team of psychoanalytically trained therapists (1978), but it is even more removed from individual dynamic psychotherapy than is structural family therapy. It uses the concepts of Bateson and colleagues' (1956) double bind theory and his ecology of the mind (1972), Jackson's (1957) concepts of family homeostasis and rules, as well as Shands' (1971) noting that language promotes linear thinking. Therapeutically it extends the strategic method of Haley (1963) in prescribing a symptom to bring about change in a symptom. The time frame of Palazzoli's Milan group is the here and now; that is, current pathological transactions in dysfunctional families are considered to bring about symptomatic behavior in the identified patient. Although the Milan group does discuss psychoanalytic principles when they formulate a prescription to give to the family, the principles of psychoanalytic therapy do not play any part in the treatment process itself. There is a rejection of the psychoanalytic view as being *linear,* in that it sees one person's behavior as the cause of another's behavior. They point out that, on the contrary, each person both influences and in turn is influenced by the other's behavior, so that there is a circular feedback system established. However, this position is also held by such analysts as Racker (1957) and Langs (1976) who see a circular feedback system based on transference–countertransference relationships in the "bipersonal field."

According to the Milan group, in pathological systems the family develops solutions to problems that are compulsively repeated in accordance with specific rules that maintain the family homeostasis. Symptomatic behavior in the identified patient is considered as a reflection of pathological transactions and rules specific for each pathology. However, the specificity of these pathological transactions has not been developed by the Milan group for various forms of pathology. Most of their work has centered on anorexia nervosa (Selvini-Palazzoli 1974) and schizophrenia (1978). In their study of schizophrenia, they consider the pathological transactions in families are sustained by *paradoxes,* which "can only be undone by *counterparadoxes* in the context of therapy."

The Milan group discusses a hidden symmetrical relationship in schizophrenia that is paradoxical. By symmetrical they mean that even though one spouse in the marriage desperately needs confirmation (mirroring), the other spouse has the same problem.

Each marital partner seeks such confirmation, but neither trusts the other and each partner needs to be in control. To give approval to the other under this circumstance is experienced as submission or domination, and therefore confirmation is withheld. On the other hand, according to the Milan group, to criticize the other partner sustains one's prestige and authority. (Some psychoanalysts might hold a similar formulation, but would emphasize that self-esteem and personal identity are dependent upon the other's validation because of developmental arrest.)

If the symmetrical relationship was expressed in open and direct communication, rejection of the demands of the other might result in escalation of conflict with the possibility of abandonment or violence. Thus the marital partners need to keep this symmetrical relationship hidden. The dominance–submission conflict continues secretly in order to avoid its exposure and the possibility of defeat. Both partners therefore avoid the definition of the relationship by disqualifying their messages. Their communication becomes paradoxical[1]; that is, it is cryptic as issues are sidestepped, subjects are changed abruptly, nonsequiturs are used, amnesia exists, and even disconfirmation occurs. By *disconfirmation,* the Milan group means the occurrence of a message that is neither a confirmation nor a rejection but that implies, "I don't notice you, you are not here, you do not exist." Another even more subtle disconfirmation is, "I'm not really here, I don't exist in the relationship with you."

This understanding of the communication patterns in the family of the schizophrenic patient is one of the major contributions of the Milan group. It clearly fits in with the research by Wynne and Singer (1963) on communication deviance in families of schizophrenics, which found that the transactional thought disorder in the family shapes the thought disorder in the schizo-

---

[1]*Paradoxical* implies a lack of logic—that is, of objectivity. However, the strategic group introduced this term simply to describe the hidden nature of communication. My own preference is to describe how this communication is used. It is employed for defensive or cover-up purposes, and not for transmitting to another one's genuine feelings or thoughts. Dell (1986a) also objects to the use of the term *paradoxical,* especially when it is used by the therapist to describe an intervention, since many of these so-called paradoxical interventions do not lack logic but are quite clear even to the patient.

phrenic patient. Here the Milan group provides a clinical description for the transactional thought disorder in the family of the schizophrenic. This is an important departure from the traditional psychoanalytic view that the thought disorder in schizophrenia is due to a regression to a primitive state of primary process thinking. Instead, as Sass and colleagues (1984) point out, language is used by the schizophrenic for defensive purposes, to alter the description of time, space, and structure, as well as semiotic symbol-referent relationships. Causality is thus obfuscated as an escape from the anxiety of a reality experienced as intolerable. Objective reality is rendered into a timeless present state, subjectivized, and robbed of its threatening nature. This formulation is in keeping with Bion's (1967) concept of the patient's attacks on linking, where causal connections are disrupted, including links between people, thoughts (internal and external), and psychic functioning.

THE MILAN APPROACH: DIFFERENCES AND SIMILARITIES

There are some similarities and differences between my work and the Milan group. I also found in families with a schizophrenic patient that conflict is avoided between the spouses, and that this conflict stems from their exploitative and controlling relationship. Each needs the other to function as a good external mother (or mirroring selfobject) to sustain his or her own self-esteem and identity. This differs from the belief of the Milan group that this sort of pathological transaction is explained on the basis of positive feedback, which escalates conflict. The Milan group does not deal with developmental arrest or intrapsychic deficit, but considers that the pathological feedback cycle occurs from *hubris*. This is a term borrowed from Bateson (1972),[2] which he used to describe the repetition compulsion as described by Freud (1920) in

---

[2]Bateson equates the death instinct of Freud with positive feedback, in which there is a tendency to repeat an unpleasant experience. However, I would disagree; and even though I do not adhere to either the life or death instinct, I would consider that Freud's life instinct, which is innovative and deviation-

Beyond the Pleasure Principle. Hubris is used by Bateson as similar to *ego mastery*—that is, it describes the repetition of something with the hope of succeeding someday. However, hubris is a philosophical-religious term that has a moralistic, judgmental component that implies pride or arrogance. In order to eliminate such a loaded term, ego mastery seems more descriptive of the process.

The Milan group does not address the issue of why the spouses try to control each other in order to force the other to provide personality confirmation. They see the spouses as *not* fragile, but only "showing" fears of intimacy and abandonment. I found not a "show" but an actual arrest of personality development in the parents of many schizophrenic patients, who did have a real fear of both intimacy and abandonment. Because of the parents' developmental arrest, they needed continuous confirmation or mirroring from their spouse to sustain their own self-esteem and self-cohesion.

This problem goes back to the parents' own families of origin, as Bowen (1978) has pointed out in his three-generational hypothesis. The parents were not able to use or did not receive the necessary mirroring during their childhoods to develop self- and object-constancy, and thus to self-regulate their narcissistic equilibrium. Thus the problems from their families of origin are acted out in their marital families, where the control and exploitation of the spouse is necessary for their own narcissistic needs. There results what I have termed a lack of *family constancy* in the marital family; family constancy does not exist when each member feels compelled to support the self-esteem and personality integrity of the other, resulting in a *symbiotic* relationship. To openly express aggression is perceived as destructive to the relationship; and loss of the relationship is experienced unconsciously as abandonment and death.

Even though the Milan group recognizes that childhood experiences influence present behavior, this is considered as linear thinking. But it is from these very childhood experiences that the

---

amplifying, could be equated with positive feedback. The death instinct would then be equated with negative feedback, since it is conservative and deviation-restricting.

basic ingredients are derived, and from which the circular feed-back transactions evolve. This explains some of the phenomena that the Milan group report, such as the parents' need for confirmation, why a "difficult" partner with the same problems is chosen, and why aggression is experienced as so damaging and needs to be avoided through the use of paradoxical communication. The Milan group does acknowledge that the spouses come into the system with the "mistaken" linear belief that they can dominate the system and have power over it, only to be caught up in a paradoxical escalation toward "linear pseudo-power."

However, no "reality" is ever objective; even the circular thinking of general systems theory is subjective (Maturana 1978). This so-called mistaken linear belief is the subjective reality of the spouses. It is also unconscious and associated with fearful emotions that are outside of their awareness. Thus the family system that evolves out of their need to interact defensively is shaped by the individual psychopathology (structure) that each member brings into the field. One can conclude that the problems each spouse *enters* the marriage with derives from *linear* causality, but that the *effect* on the other spouse has *circular* consequences. Instead of abandoning a deterministic viewpoint, it can be considered as having validity—and the responses that influence both sender and receiver in a circular fashion as also having validity. They are interactive and interdependent, and neither one alone is sufficient to understand the total picture of their transactions.

FAMILY THERAPY MILAN STYLE

In terms of treatment, the Milan group reframes the patient's symptoms. The patient is not identified as sick, but as altruistically trying to help the stability of the entire family. They ignore the threatening aspects of the symptom as a protest for change, and note instead the symptom's positive potential to sustain the integrity of the family. Thus the Milan group feel they do not challenge but *confirm* the family's homeostatic balance that insures its survival. In the prescriptions and rituals they expect the family to perform, they ignore causes, reasons, and feelings.

Interventions involve the entire family system, and symptoms and coalitions are portrayed as having the aim of helping the entire family. In this way, what they label as *counterparadox* is used as a lever to bring about change.

The strategic method of family therapy arose out of the need to deal with extremely difficult cases that had failed in other forms of treatment. There was considerable resistance to change in these families. The use of counterparadoxical interventions went along with this oppositionalism and harnessed it in the service of change. Many of these families came from distant parts of Italy, and could be seen only on a weekly or less frequent basis. Change needed to be instituted quickly or the opportunity would indeed be missed. The families also seemed to be relatively unsophisticated and not psychologically minded, many being blue-collar or farm families having an authoritarian power structure. Thus to attempt to establish a close therapeutic alliance with an open dialogue would be quite difficult, if not impossible. Following the medical practice of prescribing rituals or behavior would be more acceptable, and would better correspond to their limited role expectations. The major contribution of the Milan group has been to develop an effective and brief form of therapy with families that would otherwise not be treated at all, or would be considered as treatment failures. The directive techniques, distant stance, and paradoxical interventions that the Milan group developed were suited to the structure of these kinds of families and proved to be effective.

PROBLEMS WITH THE NEWER EPISTEMOLOGY

There now exist some critical problems with the theoretical foundations of both these systemic approaches because of newer thinking in cybernetics. Both of these systemic approaches are based on the concept of *family homeostasis* as developed by Jackson (1957) and others of the Palo Alto group. A number of recent investigators have challenged the very validity of the concept of homeostasis. Dell (1982) favors abandoning this construct, which he considers erroneous, because it separates and polarizes the stability (negative feedback) processes from the change (positive feedback) processes. In its place he would use the concept of *coherence,* which he states "implies a congruent interdependence in functioning, whereby all aspects of the system fit together." Becvar and Becvar (1982) also agree with this position that any functional system is sustained only by a balance between change and stability. Keeney (1983) considers general systems theory, which is the newer epistemology underlying all of family therapy, as an example of simple or lower-level cybernetics. Homeostasis is seen as deriving from two separate processes for change and stability. Keeney noted that systems maintain their stability by the constant interplay and complementarity of positive and negative feedback (morphogenesis and morphostasis), or otherwise the system would self-destruct.

Thus the techniques in structural family therapy, which work primarily with the negative feedback loops and generally ignore the positive feedback, run into trouble theoretically. This is also true of the strategic family therapy approach, which only works with the positive feedback loops. Newer epistemologies consider these two feedback loops as not separate but interdependent; thus one cannot restrict oneself to only one of these forces. Homeostasis is seen not as a stable force, as old theory has it, but as constantly changing.

Dell (1986a) also questions the technique of prescribing paradoxes in strategic family therapy. Supposedly they make sense to the therapist, but appear nonsensical to the patient. Dell challenges both these assumptions, since (1) there is not an adequate understanding of why the paradox is effective, and (2) often these interventions are framed in ways that do make sense to the patient. For example, when a therapist instructs a patient to perform his symptom further (a paradoxical intervention) if a therapeutic effect results, it is not simply determined by the instructive nature of the intervention. Instead it must fit in with the patient's structure. To deny this just feeds the therapist's mystical illusion of grandiosity.

It remains unclear why a paradoxical intervention does seem to work. We have already mentioned the possibility of harnessing the patient's and the family's oppositionalism in the service of change. Haley (1980) suggests that the paradoxical intervention supposedly explodes the system and alters the sequence of events.

Stanton (1984) does not find such a unidimensional explanation to be satisfying. He states that such interventions have a "startle" effect—that is, they shift attention (reframe) and in a sense "jostle" the system. They may also defuse the emotions surrounding a problem by presenting it in a ludicrous light. The ability of the therapist to contain his or her emotions may provide a different perspective for the family, one valuable for its objectivity. Thus the exaggeration draws a sort of caricature that distances the family from the symptom, and enables their better judgment to come to the fore.

Another explanation for the effectiveness of a paradoxical intervention might be that there is a balance between negative and positive feedback in sustaining homeostasis. If the paradoxical intervention enhances the positive feedback, then the negative feedback will come into play to delimit this effect, so as to prevent disequilibrium of the system and its members. An example of this in individual therapy is the "need–fear dilemma" described by Burnham and colleagues (1969) in schizophrenia. A schizophrenic may seek a symbiotic relation in treatment out of a need to sustain his or her personality, but when this is accomplished, there is a threat that it will proceed too far and that the merger will result in a total loss of the self. Thus there is a homeostatic withdrawal and fear of intimacy in order to sustain personality integrity. This finding is experimentally validated by the tachistoscopic laboratory studies of Silverman (1975). Usually the subliminal message of "Mommy and I are One" is ameliorative for symptoms of a wide number of disorders. However, if the message is given to a schizophrenic who is already poorly differentiated, it does not work. Instead, it is defended against to prevent total annihilation of the self.

Thus, there is a built-in homeostatic mechanism within the human personality to prevent self-destruction. This provides an alternate explanation for the effectiveness of paradoxical interventions, which is the antithesis of the Milan group's belief that such interventions do not threaten the homeostasis as they work only with the positive feedback cycles. Instead, by enhancing the positive feedback, paradoxical interventions profoundly threaten the homeostasis and may bring into effect opposing forces to preserve group integrity.

Dell (1986a) further states, "What is needed is a theory that will integrate paradoxes so well with our larger superstructure of theory, that these interventions will no longer appear to us to be even vaguely paradoxical" (p. 224). Such an encompassing theory is developed in the next chapter. In this theory, reframing the identified patient's symptoms as being altruistic and serving the family's cohesion will not be seen as paradoxical, but will actually fit in with this overall theory of family functioning. It is a theory in which there is an interplay between the structure of the individual personalities and the group as a whole. The group as a whole is formed from the structure of the individual personalities, and in turn helps shape the individual personalities, which in turn preserve the group, and so on. It is a theory that takes into account not only the effect of current interaction, but also each participant's structure that had been formed in the past.

II

Family Patterns in Various Psychopathologies

5

An Object Relations Typology

OBJECT RELATIONS AS THE BRIDGE

Object relations theory is a psychoanalytic theory of personality development that does not simply focus on intrapsychic processes. It takes into account the interaction between intrapsychic dynamics and interpersonal relations. Unlike the libido theory, which considers gratification or control of instinctual drives as primary, and objects as only the *aim* of these drives, object relations theory develops an understanding of personality development that is tied in with interpersonal processes. It considers that, from birth onward, individuals need to bond, to form attachments, and to relate to others. Each succeeding developmental stage includes a form of relationship that serves as a positive feedback loop, to enable further intrapsychic development. Object relations theory recognizes both the influence of past interaction on intrapsychic development and the influence of current relationships on personality integrity. It is a two-person psychology and is concerned with the development of the self in relationship to others.

CHILDHOOD DEVELOPMENT

The first attachment the infant makes is to the mother, and through a gradual interactive process, the infant internalizes the mother's functioning. The infant splits the mother into good or bad, depending on whether she is perceived as gratifying or frustrating. This gives rise to internal representations of the mother, connected to pleasurable and unpleasurable affect, and in relation to one's own self-image as both good or bad. The child, through this process of internalization, can take on the role of the good mother in relationship to the self, to comfort and regulate the self. Internalization of the good mother is facilitated through the use of a transitional object, such as a teddy bear or blanket, which serves as a symbolic substitute for the good mother when she is absent. At around three years of age this internalized process becomes stabilized, and the infant can evoke the image of the good mother even when she is absent. The child is then able to sustain a sense of its independent identity and can begin to regulate its self-esteem. This developmental milestone is termed *self and object constancy,* and is part of an overall process of separation and individuation of the child from the mother to establish the child's self as separate and independent.

In Mahler's (1965) schema of infantile development, this progression to object constancy occurs with the resolution of the Rapprochement subphase of the Individuation–Separation phase. In Klein's (1975) formulations, the child progresses from the Schizoid-Paranoid Position to the Depressive Position, whereas in Kernberg's (1975) developmental progression this is Stage 4. The child ceases to use the defense of splitting and is able to integrate its ambivalence, to see the object as both good and bad. The object has been differentiated from the self, with relinquishing of the defense of projective identification, and is seen as a whole and not a part object. With the awareness of its separateness, the child experiences dread in giving up the old part object, even if it is bad. Then the child is able to mourn its loss, experience guilt, and can employ more mature defenses such as repression.

The term *individuation* refers to this process of internalization of the good mothering function, so that people can regulate their own self-esteem and achieve their stable identities through time, relatively independent of others. We use the word "relatively" here because no one is secure enough to become independent of the effects of current relationships, even those who have a separate and solid core of identity. Everyone is interrelated to others and to events in the current environment, and affected by them to varying degrees. Success or failure in one's work and love relations, group and family processes, all influence self-esteem and personality functioning to some degree. However, if there is a stable core of identity, and the ability to self-regulate one's self-esteem, these serve as buffers against the damaging effects of environmental losses, failures, and rejections.

This developmental process may be arrested during childhood due to a genetic deficiency that interferes with the infant's ability to attach to and internalize the mother; or it may be arrested due to problematic mothering, the kind that Winnicott (1965) described as not being "good enough." The person then remains unable to function independently. The arrested development continues into adulthood; these individuals remain narcissistically vulnerable, requiring continuous external confirmation of their worth and identity in their current relationships. This need for mirroring or validation is especially important in family relationships. If the arrest occurs quite early in infancy, the individual as an adult may not even be able to sustain the integrity or cohesion of the self, and a psychotic reaction may result following a loss in a current relationship. If the arrest occurs later, lack of external confirmation may result only in a loss of self-esteem. The lack of confirmation may be due to an actual event such as a loss or a failure; it may result from the individual's subjective perception of a situation. Therefore, it is not a deep mystery why family therapy originated in work with more primitive patients, who are unable to separate and individuate, and who remain excessively vulnerable to their *current* family system of relationships to sustain their self-esteem and identity.

PRIMITIVE DEFENSES USED TO COMPLETE THE SELF

Although normal adults may use primitive defense mechanisms at times, they are predominantly the defenses of individuals with

developmental arrest, such as those with narcissistic and borderline disorders or psychosis. The two main primitive defenses are
splitting, first described by Freud (1938, 1940), and *projective
identification,* first described by Ferenczi (1920). Klein (1948)
further elaborated on these defenses as being part of the normal
developmental process during infancy. Her formulations remained totally within the intrapsychic sphere, however.

Klein considered the underlying basis for these primitive
defenses to be fantasy. Fantasy was the way the infant developed
attachments to others, and it was used to regulate the self. During
this developmental process, the infant used the pleasure principle
to define its subjective experiences with the mother. If the
experiences were pleasurable, the mother was experienced as all
good; if they were unpleasurable, she was all bad. Thus the mother
was "split" into a good or bad object. Through introjection, the
mother became internalized as the object image or representation,
and it was in relation to this that the infant developed its own
self-image. In order to protect this self-image, the infant needed to
preserve the good mother image and to evacuate the bad mother
image through projection onto others. Thus others were experienced, during what Klein termed the *paranoid-schizoid* phase of
development, as persecutory bad objects. This primitive defense
of *splitting,* of seeing oneself and others as all good, and dumping
the all-bad object *externally* into another person, can be viewed as
the forerunner of the more mature defense of repression. In
repression, however, ego boundaries are more intact, and an
unacceptable feeling or thought that would threaten one's self-
esteem is displaced from the ego into one's *own* unconscious.
During normal childhood development, ambivalence is eventually
integrated, so that one's own internal images of self and others are
seen as simultaneously both good and bad. Others are not simply
seen egocentrically as merely need-satisfying part objects, but as
whole individuals having their own separate motivation.

The second primitive defense is *projective identification,*
which is a forerunner of the more mature defense of projection.
Grotstein (1981) and others do not differentiate projective identification from projection, viewing them as a continuum of the
same process. I see them as different, with projection being solely
an intrapsychic defense, and projective identification both an

intrapsychic and interpersonal defense mechanism. One individual evacuates a good or bad, self or object image externally into another person, who then serves as a *container* for this projection. However, the other is induced through verbal and nonverbal communication into thinking, feeling, or behaving in accordance with this projection. Thus there is an attempt to transplant one's own internal split image into another and to manipulate the other to *collude* with it. The other's evoked response is then reinternalized through identification, thereby serving as a negative feedback loop, so that objective reality reinforces the projector's internal world of images.

Intrapsychic contents become *dumped* into the interpersonal sphere and acted out, thereby constituting a *transpersonal defense* as well. In this way, an individual can manipulate others and vicariously live through them to maintain his or her self-esteem and identity. This requires a loose ego boundary between oneself and others, a denial of separateness, and a lack of awareness of others' needs and motivations. Thus instead of true intimacy and sharing, there is a lack of differentiation and an exploitation of the other as a need-satisfying object to complete the self.

THE SYMBIOTIC SURVIVAL PATTERN AND THE FAMILY TYPOLOGY

I began in 1968 by studying the family interaction of outpatients who could not self-regulate their narcissistic equilibrium, and still needed confirmation by others to sustain their self-esteem and ego integrity. The sample consisted of over 125 families coming for help because of a disturbed young adult living at home. Each family member was diagnosed and evaluated by a structured clinical interview and a battery of psychological tests (Slipp 1973).[1] Over 50 percent of these young adults were diagnosed as

---

[1]One of the rating scales was the Rotter I-E Scale, which is correlated with field dependence and independence (Witkin et al. 1954). We hypothesized that patients still dependent on external confirmation might be more field-dependent. The California F Scale for authoritarianism was used as a measure of rigidity and overconformity, and to evaluate the defense of splitting—that is, idealization and

schizophrenic. The family was then seen in family therapy, and regular clinical conferences were held by the staff to discuss individual and family dynamics. It was understood that family dynamics were not necessarily causal, but were contributory, since there is evidence for genetic vulnerability to schizophrenia.

Not only did the patients employ the primitive defenses of splitting and projective identification to sustain their self-esteem and ego integrity, but also the parents did this as well. The resulting collusive network of shared primitive defenses and shared unconscious fantasies I termed the *symbiotic survival pattern* (Slipp 1969, 1973). In this process there was a breakdown of individual boundaries, a disruption of the developmental tasks necessary to meet the members' needs for growth, and an overly close involvement with each other. Each member felt narcissistically vulnerable and at the same time responsible for the others. An aspect of the parent's (or parents') internal object world was placed through projective identification into the child, who served as its container. The child was induced into thinking, feeling, and acting out interpersonally in accordance with the projection. The child's evoked response was then reinternalized by the parent(s) through identification; thereby the parent(s) could live vicariously through the child. Thus internal conflicts and developmental arrests were disowned and displaced from the intrapsychic into the interpersonal field.

This unconscious collusive process not only sustained the personality integrity of one or both of the parents, but preserved the family homeostasis, and the child's self-esteem and identity as well. Extending this research into the study of families with a depressed patient (Slipp 1976) and families with a hysterical or

---

scapegoating. The Rotter I-E Scale results did not correlate with the degree of pathology nor the narcissistic vulnerability of the patient as hypothesized. Thus field dependence and autonomy seemed unrelated. With the California F Scale results, the level of authoritarianism also did not correlate with the degree of psychopathology. It did closely relate to the socioeconomic level of these families as measured by Hollingshead and Redlich's scales (1958). Middle-class families were less authoritarian, while blue-collar and welfare families were more authoritarian. The ability to engage these families in treatments was also better the lower the authoritarian level (Slipp et al. 1974, Kressel and Slipp 1975, Slipp and Kressel 1978).

borderline young adult (Slipp 1977), I correlated specific forms of splitting and projective identification used in the family interaction with specific forms of psychopathology in the child. (See Fig. 5-1.)

FAMILY TRANSACTIONS IN SCHIZOPHRENIA

In schizophrenia and borderline conditions, one or both of the parents have not internalized the good preoedipal mother so as to be able to self-regulate their self-esteem and identity. The parent(s) remain dependent on external objects, and family relations are anaclitic. The parent(s) attempt to sustain their narcissistic equilibrium by splitting in order to avoid the threat of loss of the spouse, who is experienced transferentially as the all-good mother object. In schizophrenia, the parent(s) fear that open expression of aggression will destroy the marital relationship, so the spouse is idealized and sustained as the *good preoedipal mother* (O+). Aggression is denied toward the spouse and split off and displaced into the child, who is seen as the demanding *bad maternal object* (O−). The child is therefore induced into the role of family "scapegoat." The child internalizes and functions as a container for this negative introject, thereby developing a negative self-identity. There is a shared family fantasy that aggression is destructive, which serves to reinforce the child's own omnipotent destructive fantasies and to interfere with the development of self and object constancy. Thus the child feels worthless, is unable to defend itself, being fearful that its own aggression will destroy the object and the self to which it is merged internally.

One variant of this interaction is that in which the child is not actively scapegoated but ignored and thereby suffers narcissistic injury. This pattern is also described by Lidz and colleagues (1957) as the "marital skew" of families with a schizophrenic patient. In this subtype there is almost a *folie à deux,* with each spouse functioning as a good preoedial mother for the other, and being nurturant and supportive only within the spousal subsystem — even though one spouse may be severely disturbed. Some therapists, applying Bion's basic assumptions to these families, have labeled this marital skewing erroneously as "pairing," because

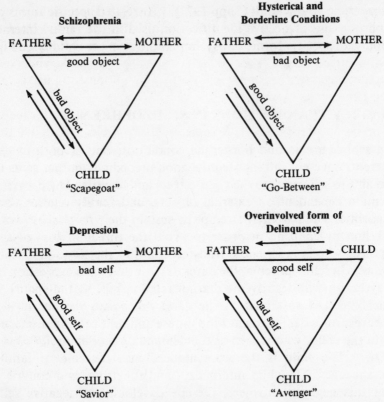

Fig. 5-1. Categorization of family interaction. The father is indicated as the initiator of splitting and projective identification in all four patterns for purposes of simplicity. The mother may just as well be the initiator, except in hysterical and borderline conditions in which the child is female. Projective identification is used as the intrapsychic and interpersonal defense mechanism that induces others to act out the internalized self or object image. The child serves as a container for the parent's projective identification, and a negative feedback cycle is thus established that (1) maintains the personality integrity of the parent(s), (2) maintains the family homeostasis, or balance of defenses, and (3) sustains developmental fixation in the patient. In all these instances the child is made responsible for the self-esteem and, in schizophrenia and borderline conditions, the survival of the parent(s), thereby establishing a symbiotic survival pattern. In one type of delinquency, splitting and projective identification of the bad self into one child and the good self into another child occurs.

Reprinted from *Object Relations: A Dynamic Bridge Between Individual and Family Treatment* by S. Slipp, New York: Jason Aronson.

superficially it is a dyad. In baP, as defined by Bion (1961), the parents would try to gain gratification through their child's achievement, which was not the case here.[2] The real function of each spouse for the other in this case is to gratify dependency needs for one another, while ignoring the developmental needs of their offspring.

The bad object is subtly projected onto the child, who feels he or she is worthless or a burden that the parents are unable to handle. Thus, the child may experience itself as a bad and demanding person, and feel responsible for the parents' emotional abandonment. This is made even worse when there is an overt family myth that the child's demanding behavior may cause the physical or emotional breakdown or death of a parent. Thus the child feels not only that it is bad and is responsible for its neglect, but guilty over the possibility that its rage over the abandonment will damage the parent as well.

The systemic interaction between the spouses that appears to generate a good deal of underlying aggression and conflict seems to be the mutually exploitative relationship between them. Each spouse, because of narcissistic needs, attempts to control the other so as to function as the good preoedipal mother, to provide confirmation (mirroring) of their own self-esteem and identity. If the other spouse makes demands or frustrates mirroring, he or she is seen as a bad mother $(O-)$. Each feels coerced to give approval to the other, which is experienced unconsciously as submission to the bad mother and a loss of the self. On the other hand, to express hostility openly to the spouse is to risk abandonment, which is also experienced as a loss of the self.[3] To deal with this double bind, the parents covertly distance themselves, and communication becomes cryptic to avoid definition of the relationship by disqualifying messages. This *defensive use of language* is

---

[2]Bion's basic assumption of pairing is more closely related to the depressive form of the typology, with the child functioning as savior. This is described later.

[3]This double bind conflict between the parents may become internalized in the schizophrenic patient, as described by Burnham and colleagues (1969) in the need-fear dilemma. The schizophrenic needs a symbiotic relationship that provides continuous gratification in order to preserve self-esteem and identity, yet at the same time fears closeness, because of the possibility of invasion, control, and loss of identity.

described clinically by Selvini-Palazzoli and colleagues (1978), and in the research of Wynne and colleagues (1977) on communication deviance (CD). Language is used not for communication but to cover up conflict, and in CD is characterized by the lack of a shared focus of attention or shared meaning.

FAMILY TRANSACTIONS IN HYSTERIA AND BORDERLINE CONDITIONS

In families with a hysterical or borderline patient, one spouse does not participate in the mutually controlling and exploitative type of marital relationship as found in schizophrenia, which needs continual confirmation by each spouse functioning as the good preoedipal mother (O+) for the other. This nonparticipating spouse has sufficient autonomy not to be exploited simply as a need-satisfying object, and, instead of covertly maintaining autonomy through the defensive use of language, openly rebels and risks rejection. However, this spouse still is not strong enough to assert his or her needs or to be able to physically leave the marriage. Instead, the response is to withdraw emotionally. If the identified patient is a female, the husband demeans the wife as the bad maternal object (O−), and the female child is idealized as the *good preoedipal mother* (O+). The defenses of splitting and projective identification are used by the father. Because of the mother's emotional unavailability, the daughter turns to the father for substitute dependency gratification. Kernberg (1986) similarly noted in borderline conditions that this sequence of events resulted in premature positive oedipal striving toward the father to compensate for deprivation by the mother.

The child serves in the family role of "go-between" (or surrogate spouse) to sustain the parents' openly conflicted relationship. Unconsciously she serves as the good preoedipal mother to gratify the father's narcissistic needs. Since this relationship of the child to the father involves seductive binding and an oedipal triumph over the mother, resolution of the oedipal conflict does not occur. The daughter herself as an adult may then also eroticize relationships and use sexuality to gain narcissistic gratification from others, just as she was emotionally seduced and used by her father. This pattern was first described by Freud (1905a) in the famous case of Dora, and by Lidz (1957) in what he termed *marital schism*. What seems to differentiate the borderline patient from the hysteric? The borderline is seduced and later emotionally abandoned, is used and thrown away as worthless, whereas the hysteric is not abandoned and remains identified with the seductive parent. Stone (1988) considers that this process of being sexually exploited and then discarded as worthless contributes to the borderline's repetitive sexual acting-out, as well as self-destructive suicidal tendencies. The borderline internalizes an image of herself as worthless and discardable. Stone has termed this the "Marilyn Monroe Syndrome." The daughter's self-esteem is further damaged by the father's rejection, since she is thrown back onto her identification with the devalued and demeaned mother, the O−. Although the preponderance of borderline patients are female, and these constituted our study sample, similar dynamics seem true for males.

In both types of family interactions with a young adult schizophrenic or borderline patient, there was found a lack of what I term *family constancy*—in other words, one or both of the parents cannot sustain their self-esteem and self-cohesion without continuous confirmation by some family member actually functioning as an O+. Family relations are *anaclitic,* dominated by the fear of losing the good preoedipal mother. In these families the child not only keeps the family together by adopting the scapegoat or go-between role, but sustains the parents' personality integrity as well.

FAMILY TRANSACTIONS IN DEPRESSION

In families with a depressive patient or an overinvolved form of delinquency, the parents' relationship with each other and the child is not anaclitic as above but *narcissistic*—that is, good or bad aspects of the *self* are put into the child through projective identification. In depression, one of the parents is perceived as a failure. The other, more dominant parent demeans the failed parent as the *bad self*. The *good self* is projected into a child, who is overtly pressured to achieve. The dominant parent can then identify with and live vicariously through the child's success. The child feels compelled to perform as the family *"savior,"* to function as an antidepressant to bolster the dominant parent's self-esteem. (This is the family pattern most similar to that described in Bion's basic assumption group of pairing.)

The child fears failure, which means being rejected; but also the child cannot own its own success, develop confidence, or separate. The dominant parent makes it difficult for the child to do these things. The child's success is not gratified (mirrored) because of this parent's unconscious envy and need to control this source of narcissistic supplies. Often such parents brag to others about the child's success, in order to feed their own narcissism, but do not acknowledge or confirm the child directly. The child's success is either taken for granted, is considered to be not good enough or an accident of fate, or to be due to other outside circumstances. Thus the child receives, besides the overt message to succeed, a covert message to remain weak and dependent, to fail. I have called this no-win dilemma *the double bind on achievement,* since the child cannot win whether he or she succeeds or fails socially.

This interpersonal process gradually becomes internalized in the intrapsychic structure of the depressive. The pressuring, nonconfirming parent is internalized as the ego ideal in the superego, which is so perfectionist that nothing is ever good enough, and the depressive therefore cannot gratify him- or herself. Instead, the patient remains dependent upon external approval and feels dominated and used by others in significant relationships (Arieti 1962). Often these patients play out an oppositional game with others, as described by Bonime (1959). First they comply to the other person's wishes and needs, and then they rebel sufficiently to sustain some autonomy. They do not gratify the other's needs or expectations. Instead, they may even provoke this kind of interaction by stimulating the other person's expectations, so that he or she is dependent on them for performance. Then they can fail, in order to frustrate the other. In this way they passive-aggressively act out their rage to defeat others' exploiting their success—and they do not gratify others, just as they themselves were not gratified. This oppositional game is compulsively repeated, even if it means cutting off one's nose to spite one's face. The game is acted out without conscious awareness by the patient. Thus the depressive can avoid assuming responsibility for his or her unconscious hostility and thereby avoid risking rejection.

This typology of family interaction for depression does not discount that there may be genetic predispositions and other determinants for this disorder. My effort was to isolate those factors in the family that influence individual functioning, and which can be worked with in either family or in individual treatment. For the purpose of scientifically further validating this depressive form of the family typology, it was subjected to further clinical and laboratory research. We found, in working with a number of children of Holocaust survivors, that their family constellations at times seemed to fit this depressive typology. The parents had been cheated of a normal life and opportunity for educational and occupational development because of their internment by the Germans in concentration camps during World War II. They often pressured their children for achievement therefore, in order to live vicariously through them, yet at the same time seemed to experience unconscious envy of their children's having advantages that were denied them.[4] The better-functioning group of children perceived less parental pressure for achievement, and greater gratification, whereas the more poorly functioning group experienced greater parental pressure for achievement, and less gratification (Slipp 1984).

Another study (Slipp and Nissenfeld 1981), of forty-eight nonschizophrenic, neurotically depressed women in an experimentally designed double-blind research project, used Silverman's (1975) laboratory tachistoscopic technique of psychodynamic activation.[5] The maternal symbiosis message, "Mommy and I Are

---

[4]We divided our group of children of Holocaust survivors into well-functioning and poorly functioning groups. Then we devised a Succeed–Fail questionnaire, consisting of thirty attitude items that measured whether or not a parent pressured their children, gratified their children's achievement, and whether or not the patients could gratify themselves. A structured clinical interview was devised, as well as a battery of rating scales, including Cohen's Fear of Success Scale (1974), the Beck Depression Inventory, and the California Personality Inventory.

[5]Subliminal messages of "Mommy and I Are One" (symbiotic), "Destroy Mother" (aggressive), "Succeed for Mother or Father" (exploitative success), or "Succeed for Yourself" (autonomous success) were given to the experimental

One," was found to be the only statistically significant one to reduce depression; however, it was not effective if the mother had been experienced as pressuring and nongratifying (O−) on the Succeed–Fail questionnaire. Thus only merger with the O+ was ameliorative. The "Destroy Mother" subliminal message did not increase depression with this neurotic group, as it had in similar tachistoscopic studies with psychotic depressives. This fact probably indicated a higher amount of aggression in the psychotic subjects, and was in keeping with Karl Abraham's (1911) clinical finding that the psychotic depressive intrapsychically destroys the internalized love object.

Greenberg (1980) and I also conducted a similar double blind tachistoscopic study on 108 high school underachievers. This study used the same maternal symbiosis message, but changed the autonomous success message from "Succeed for Yourself" to "My Success Is OK." I speculated that this previous message had not worked because autonomy for the depressive is equated with rejection and that success needed sanctioning. We felt the same dynamics might be operative with underachievers as with depressives. The various experimental and control groups were exposed to subliminal stimulation four times a week for six weeks. The "Mommy and I Are One" message was most effective with boys who experienced their mothers as gratifying (O+), but not with those boys who perceived their mothers as conflicted over their success (O−). This latter group of students had a high fear of success, a lower self-concept and lower self-mother and self-father differentiation on tests. The "My Success Is OK" message correlated with higher grade scores for girls, especially when the mother was not gratifying (O−) and the father was less conflictual toward achievement (O+). On testing there was a lowering of self-father differentiation following subliminal stimulation, and thus the sanctioning of success was experienced as identifying with a gratifying message from the father. Although these studies are

---

group. A neutral message of "People are Walking" was used for the control group. Before and after exposure to the subliminal messages flashed by the tachistoscope, a variety of scales were administered (the Multiple Affect Adjective Checklist, Thematic Apperception Test, and the Adjective Rating Scale developed by Silverman).

not definitive, they do provide validating experimental evidence for our clinical findings with depressives and their families.

FAMILY TRANSACTIONS IN OVERINVOLVED DELINQUENCY

I have not studied delinquents, yet the clinical findings of Johnson and Szurek (1954) with one form of delinquency seemed to complete the paradigm. This was the overly involved delinquent, who acted out conflicts for the parent(s) against society. This description does not apply to other forms of delinquency, which may result from lack of attachment during childhood, chaotic family functioning, identification with a delinquent peer group, and other factors. In the case of the overly involved delinquent, one of the parents projects his or her own *bad self* into a child, who is induced into acting out the parent's anger. This child then serves in the role of family *"avenger."* Both in cases of depression and of overly involved delinquency, the pressure for personality compliance is less encompassing than in schizophrenia or in borderline conditions, as it is limited to social performance either in accord with or against society.

VARIATIONS AND COMBINATIONS OF PATTERNS

Various combinations of these typological patterns were also found being projected onto one child in the family. Some patients who demonstrated both schizoid and depressive features (schizo-affective disorders) seemed to function as both the family scape-goat and its savior. In other families, the roles of scapegoat and avenger seemed to be played out by one child, who manifested schizoid and psychopathic features. In still other families, these roles might be divided among different children, with one child functioning as the family savior while another child performed the role of its scapegoat. With the progression of time and the influence of intervening events in the family life cycle, these roles could be reassigned or even reversed within the same family. This was also the case when the identified patient became nonsymptomatic due to therapy, and another child was induced through projective identification into being the symptomatic identified patient.

All these patterns could also be clearly delineated as well in families in which the identified patient manifests neurotic symptoms, or problems indicating mild disturbance. Just as Bion was able to evoke regressive behavior in relatively normal stranger groups by maintaining an abstinent leadership position, and frustrating the members' expectations and dependency needs, families that were relatively normal or showed mildly neurotic behavior could also regress and use more primitive defenses when their self-esteem or security was threatened. The typology becomes even more valuable in delineating interactional patterns, since the extent of its usefulness is much broader than first believed. The appearance of these four patterns in both normal and neurotic families seems to depend on the extent of current external frustration or psychic trauma, or to an area of narcissistic vulnerability in the members that is connected to an occurrence in the past that was experienced as traumatic.

RECONCILING EARLY CHILDHOOD AND FAMILY DYNAMICS IN BORDERLINE PERSONALITY DISORDERS

In borderline conditions, the focus presented earlier in this chapter was on the family dynamics found in adolescents and young adults. Clearly the pathological interaction in borderline patients starts much earlier. Most psychoanalytic literature that focuses on intrapsychic dynamics considers that there is an arrest in these cases of both separation and individuation processes of early childhood development (Mahler 1964, 1965). Kernberg (1975) puts the fixation of the borderline patient in his Stage 3, where the Self is differentiated from the Object, but where splitting persists. It is only in Stage 4 that integration of ambivalence occurs, and a self-concept develops that has coherence and continuity. Others are then seen as whole objects who are separately motivated. Because of their developmental failure, borderline patients cannot modulate their tension and are overly dependent on external objects for self-esteem and integration. Because of superego and ego weaknesses the borderline patient cannot tolerate anxiety, is impulsive, and cannot sublimate. Whereas Kernberg leans more toward a hereditary defect, Masterson and Rinsley (1975) emphasize early interpersonal relations between mother and child as influential in causing borderline personality development. They state that these patients demonstrate that they have the full capacity for internalization and integration of objects once their abandonment depression is worked through in treatment.

Masterson and Rinsley believe that during the *rapprochement* subphase of the *separation individuation* phase of development, the mother withdraws her emotional availability as the child makes efforts to separate. They find that the mother, who is usually also borderline, or more severely disturbed in her personality makeup, needs to defend herself against her own abandonment fears by clinging to her infant. Thus the mother's abandonment depression is dumped into the infant, who now also needs to cling to the mother to restore her emotional availability. Separation for the borderline patient is experienced as an abandonment by the good maternal object (O+), and the child needs to cling to bring back this good object.

In the family studies of Edward Shapiro and colleagues (1975, 1977) of adolescent borderline patients and their families, the conflicts in these patients seemed a continuation of this infantile problem with separation. Separation and autonomy of the patient from the family was still perceived as a hateful devaluation of the family, and was punished. The patient's clinging dependency was also criticized by the family as demanding and draining. Shapiro found that the parents themselves had evolved complementary roles, with one being autonomous and the other dependent. The adolescent then became the container, through projective identification, of the disavowed aspect of each parent, and was punished for that. Thus both autonomy and clinging dependency resulted in criticism and emotional withdrawal by the parents.

In such a situation, the parents' marriage can be seen as being between one person with a narcissistic character disorder, who denies dependency and behaves in a self-sufficient manner, and a spouse who is borderline, and serves as a container for the other's dependency needs. The narcissist can deny and externalize his or her conflict and use projective identification to have the borderline spouse express dependent needs. Thus instead of punishing oneself, the borderline spouse is criticized and demeaned for expressing dependent needs. If the adolescent expresses dependent feelings or tries to leave, he or she then becomes the target of aggression.

In the family typology for the female borderline patient, there seems to be a discrepancy between rejection by the mother during childhood and rejection by the father during adolescence. How can these be reconciled, since they also involve different parents? The following sequence of events is suggested. The daughter may have experienced emotional abandonment by her mother during early childhood because of the daughter's efforts to separate and individuate. The mother may not have wanted this separation because of her own neediness and being demeaned by her husband. The daughter then attaches to her father as a mother-surrogate (O+) for nurturance. (Kernberg [1976, 1986] noted that premature oedipal stirrings for the father develop to compensate for deprivation by the mother.) The daughter herself is used by the father as a O+ for his narcissistic needs for admiration. Then again, because of her need to separate, the father abandons the daughter by withdrawal or by turning to another woman, who will function as a "good" maternal object (O+). Therefore, the conflict over being used to gratify another's narcissistic needs and then being abandoned—the same conflict that occurred during infancy with the mother—becomes reenacted during adolescence with the father. This same theme of being used and abandoned, or using others and abandoning (or threatening to abandon) them, becomes a repetitious theme in later relationships with others as well.

6

Narcissistic Personality Disorder and Family Structure

NARCISSISTIC AND BORDERLINE DISORDERS

There has been some controversy in the psychoanalytic literature regarding the nature and genesis of personality disorders. Adler (1980) places narcissistic and borderline personality disorders on a continuum, with narcissistic disorders being less severe. Kohut (1977) describes the borderline personality as due to a "fragmented, unstable self and selfobjects," whereas narcissistic personalities have a "stable, cohesive self and selfobjects." Kohut notes Freud's discovery that the neurotic represents the "guilty man," suffering from repressed oedipal wishes. In narcissistic personality disorders, however, the individual is called by Kohut the "tragic man." The child is deprived of the interaction with its mother to which it is entitled, and which is required for normal development and even survival. The child needs to idealize its parents in order to gain the sense of security and safety that is important for survival (a holding environment); the child also needs to obtain mirroring or validating responses from the parents in order to develop a positive self-image, confidence, and the ability to regulate its own self-esteem.

Kernberg (1986) differs, and states that people with borderline and those with narcissistic personality disorders do have differentiated self and object images, good ego boundaries, and the ability to test reality; in these ways they are unlike those with psychotic disorders. However, both continue to use primitive defenses, their ambivalence is not integrated, and both require external validation to sustain self-esteem. Borderline patients suffer from a weak sense of identity, have not achieved object constancy, and have a tendency to regress and use primary process thinking. Adler and Buie (1979) believe borderline patients lack object permanency and cannot even evoke the image of the mother, whereas narcissistic patients lack object constancy.

Turning to interpersonal relations, the Masterson–Rinsley hypothesis (Rinsley 1985) considers that borderline pathology develops because of a double bind during the rapprochement subphase of the separation-individuation phase of early childhood development; this double bind enjoins the child from further separation and growth through a threat of abandonment. Thus the borderline fears that separation will result in the loss of this unreliable holding introject or self-object. Although this is less well understood for the narcissistic personality, Rinsley states that "in both personalities, major overt or underlying themes of rejection and abandonment, loss of inner controls, split good–bad perceptions and related thinking, impairment of self and sexual identity, pre-eruptive and eruptive rage, and depression and symptomatic behavior reflective of unrequited symbiotic needs are evident" (pp. 318–319). The narcissistic personality has negotiated the individuation process but not that of separation, whereas the borderline personality is arrested in both these processes. Rinsley points out that the sense of the narcissist's dependency and helplessness is overcompensated for by manic and grandiose defenses, in order to inflate poor self-esteem. Such a person often remains cut off and detached from a world experienced as unpredictable and dangerous.

Rinsley notes that the parents' need to eliminate their own bad persecutory self-object representations results in putting it into the child through projective identification. The child in turn internalizes this projection to develop a harsh, sadistic superego and a negative self-identity. Rinsley terms this *adultomorphiza-*

tion, since the child functions as a "quasimaternal container" for the parent — in other words, as a bad maternal object (O −). At the same time, the child is also used by the mother as her own good-enough mother (O +), which fixates the child's infantile grandiosity (grandiose self). The child then has the power to identify with its early, sadistic superego, and by using a manic defense and projective identification can at times put its harsh and sadistic features onto others, who are thereby devalued. Thus Rinsley states the narcissistic person may tend to idealize those seen as potential persecutors and demean others seen as dependent.

Rinsley points out that the mother, who unconsciously experiences her baby as a dangerous persecutory object (O −), may defend against the terror of the baby's demands by giving in to it overindulgently. The mother's submission contributes also to the infant's sense of grandiosity, and to its continued need for mirroring in later relationships. The child does not learn boundaries nor to recognize another as a whole and separate person. According to Rinsley the narcissist's need to save, rescue, or heal one's parents, to reestablish them as providers of needed supplies, is due to manic restitution. I see this also as the induced role that the child is unconsciously compelled to assume, in order to preserve the parents' self-esteem and identity — that is, part of the symbiotic survival pattern in the family. The end result in functioning is the same, whether one considers it as due to intrapsychic manic restitution or to a family interactional pattern, or both.

Elements of both obsessional and depressive character formation are also evident in the narcissistic personality disorder, with emotional distance and a false self-facade. In both the borderline and narcissistic personality disorders there is fear of the possibility of abandonment by the maternal surrogate figure (O +). For the borderline personality there is greater terror, due to the frightening loss of the good holding introject and fragmentation or fusion of the self and object representations, resulting in a micropsychosis. With the narcissistic disorder, which is more stable, there are efforts to control and subjugate others into functioning as the good mother object in order to safeguard the input of narcissistic supplies (mirroring).

FAMILY FACTORS IN NARCISSISTIC DISORDERS

The formulations just discussed explain the lack of self-regulation of narcissistic persons, and their need to control and obtain continued mirroring from another who is seen transferentially as the good object (O +). This also provides an explanation as to why the narcissist idealizes and demeans others. However, these dynamics focus on early childhood development, whereas family studies indicate that pathogenic interaction is not limited simply to that period of time. If there is dumping of the parents' inner worlds and exploitation of the infant for the parents' needs, the process does not suddenly stop when the child reaches 5 or 6 years of age, but continues on into young adulthood. The parents' personalities remain essentially the same through all the child's developmental phases, and the same processes of projective identification continue. When the child becomes an adult, these past familial patterns have become internalized and are reenacted through projection and projective identification in current relationships with others. This repetition compulsion serves as a negative feedback cycle, especially in current family relationships, to sustain psychopathology.

One of the clearest findings, in borderline and narcissistic personality disorders, is the lack of a secure holding environment, which is not limited to the mother but includes *both* of the parents. This results in a lack of trust in others, and the erection of narcissistic defenses. This involvement of both parents seemed to be a necessary condition, as the narcissist, being unable to depend on others, can depend only on him- or herself for survival. The lack of a secure holding environment with regard to both parents was first noted by Karl Abraham (1911) to be a factor in depression, which he called "primal parathymia." The infant experienced feelings of rejection and disappointment from *both* parents during the preoedipal period. The result was a sense of abandonment, rage, oral aggression, helplessness, and then feelings of resignation and hopelessness. These affective states seem to be present to a marked degree in the narcissistic personality disorder as well as in depression.

Rinsley's finding that parents dumped both their bad and good object representations into the patient fits two forms of my typology, the *scapegoat* and the *go-between*. Possibly the varying combinations of being scapegoated (demeaned) or serving as a go-between (idealized) may determine the varying degrees of schizoid versus grandiose-hysterical features in borderline and narcissistic conditions. The combination of these two induced roles in the narcissistic personality disorder preserves the patient from becoming schizophrenic, since the grandiosity seems to counterbalance the negative self-image.

In these families, the child (usually a boy) was seductively bound to a parent (usually the mother), who also scapegoated the child. The child's grandiosity was reinforced by this oedipal triumph, yet at the same time a negative self-identity was formed. This process is repeated in adult life with others who are idealized and/or demeaned. Sexuality is used also by the phallic type of narcissist, for control and as an expression of anger to demean the other person, thereby combining seduction and scapegoating together into a single act. Sexual promiscuity, the Don Juan complex, occurs in this form of narcissistic personality disorder. As in the Greek myth, Narcissus is looking for mirroring and needs an Echo who is submissive, undifferentiated, almost a part of him, and who can repeat the words he needs to hear to feed his grandiose image.

THE EMOTIONAL ORPHAN

Some other parents adhere to their duty in terms of social role function, but are not nurturant and emotionally abandon their children. These parents may have an empty and distant relationship with one another, obtaining their own nurturance from their work or extended family. The husband may go through the role function of being the provider, while the wife does her duty as a housekeeper and mother, but with little emotional investment in her relationship with her husband or children. Other parents join in a "gruesome twosome," functioning as a good maternal object for each other, but being distant and nonnurturant to their children. In either situation, the child feels unimportant and demeaned, the bad object, and internalizes a negative self-identity. There is also simultaneously a person of lesser social or emotional status, such as a maid, sibling, grandparent, teacher, or the like, who values the child as special. Thus the child internalizes separately an accepting good object (O+) and an abandoning bad object (O−), without being able to integrate the two. I term this child the *emotional orphan,* who will feel entitled to be cared for by others as an adult.

CASE EXAMPLE OF THE EMOTIONAL ORPHAN

The following case is that of a young business executive who was coerced into treatment by his wife, under the threat that if he did not get psychiatric help, their marriage would end in divorce. He superficially complied at first, and then later became actively engaged in treatment after he felt that he had been provided with a secure frame and a safe holding environment.

> He stated, "I have always known my parents did a lot of damage to me emotionally, though it could have been worse. It makes it hard for me to get to my feelings, to be open. I put up a protective bubble around myself, and won't let others come close to me. I recall that when I was a small child, I fell off a swing and cut my lip, and was rushed to the hospital by the maid." (The maid was a warm and concerned person, to whom he was special.) "My mother stayed home and continued to play her canasta game. I realized that my mother wasn't there for me. I remember being rushed to the hospital. The maid had a towel under my face and lots of blood soaked into it. It is a terrible realization about your parents when you feel so alone. The bubble I put up was to keep the world out and to keep me from going out into the world. It held me down from being myself. But I did go out and sought gratification from others. I got my stroking from other adults.
>
> I learned how to act, since I needed to be liked by grown-ups. I was the lovely, perfect, model child with adults (a false self), but I couldn't relate to my peers. In fact, it got me into trouble with my peers; they could see through the facade very quickly. My peers saw my insecurity, and it interfered with their acceptance of me.

This became especially worse when I became involved with girls as a teenager. I was more insecure than the girl. I had no one to talk to about my feelings. My father was too busy at work; neither parent was there for me. It was terrible not having any support." (At this point the patient stopped talking and I made a derivative interpretation, asking if his closing up to me paralleled his closing out his parents, not trusting me to be there for him either, feeling that I would not be understanding. He agreed that he was distrustful of me as well.) "I felt my parents were my handicap, and I managed to be successful by working around the handicap. Now I'm feeling myself, and I know the anger is there. It's built up and has become so strong I'm afraid if I let it out I'll lose everything that I've built up. I see a fire-spitting dragon inside me that will destroy everything, without regard for life or property. It's like Godzilla. I'm afraid I'll destroy everything and everybody."

In another session he recounted a recurrent childhood dream. He found himself wandering through the streets, naked and with nobody noticing him. He said, "I felt like nothing, nonexistent, invisible. My main struggle was to know I was something. I had thought as a child my parents were making me independent by having me fend for myself, that it was for my own good. Yet I didn't have a choice, and it made me feel insecure. Now I know that I was rationalizing. They just didn't give the proper time and attention to me. They took the easy way out; they ignored my needs and problems. With my children, if they are upset, I know I have three possibilities open to me: (1) I can blame them by saying "You are doing something wrong"; (2) I can ignore it, like my parents; and (3) I can support them. I can address the problem, try to understand it, comfort them, and try to help. I know that with the first two ways my children will be turned off, but when I support them they will trust me and come to me with their problems and let me help, and they'll feel good about themselves." (The patient had attempted to deny his parents' neglect and to rationalize it, in order to preserve his idealization of them and thus maintain some security as a child. He became aware of his feelings of worth-

lessness and vulnerability. He felt nonexistent to his
parents and unprotected.)

In a much later session this patient reported another dream. "I'm in an airport, and my wife is with me.
I can't find my tennis racket. I then find myself outside
and helpless. I had handed my wife the tickets so she
could get on the plane, and I'm running around looking
for the tennis racket and losing my orientation. When I
feel desperate my obsessiveness gives me the illusion of
serenity and the evenness of things. The desperation I
felt as a child was for love, to be held and taken care of.
I felt panicky and desperate, and unknowingly was
crying out for help. I had no place to go. When I don't
have control I panic. Once when I tried to get to therapy
and I was late, I panicked and almost had an automobile accident. I didn't have my bearings; I felt helpless.
I panic or go inside myself depending on the situation.
If it's something material, where there is a focus or an
end, I'll panic and get obsessive. If it is emotional, I go
inside myself and try to forget or ignore it. I know there
is rage inside; I can feel my blood boil. Sometimes I
experience it physically, like my skin itching, and I
scratch uncontrollably. It lets off some of the rage. I've
itched less lately."

(I inquired, "Were you feeling lost and helpless
with me lately?") "There have been times when I had a
feeling of helplessness; it doesn't reach rage; that rarely
happens anymore. When you are not responding in a
helpful way it does get me angry. Then I feel alone, and
you are sitting right there. It reminds me of my father.
I got so little from him, and I don't expect much from
you. When I pay for service, I expect to be taken care of
(entitlement). When I want my wife to take care of me,
she says that she's not my mother. She feels it is
inappropriate, it's not wifely but motherly. When I got
married, I didn't have the concept that things should be
shared. I expected her to do all the taking care of. She
got little from me, and I did all the taking. Now the
pendulum has swung, and perhaps I do more of the
caretaking now. We were both such needy people when
we married."

(I stated, "I guess you expected both your wife and

me to function as a caretaking mother.) "It was unconscious, although I did question if my wife could be a
good mother." (I asked, "To whom?") "I guess it was to
me and not just to my children. Would she be a good
mother to me? I expected her to take care of me like a
mother takes care of her children. My wife wanted to
get away from her parents, while I felt I had already
run away from my parents and was independent. I felt
she should be a dutiful wife and take care of me. In the
beginning of the marriage, she fell into that role but was
unhappy in it. Now we are working our way back into
the middle where we are sharing. I still feel overwhelmed and panicked when I'm not taken care of, but
also overwhelmed when I do most of the taking care of.
I'm looking for that middle ground. I'm so pleased that
now I am not a robot, but have feelings, try to
understand my wife and children. It's important to me
that the children are around, and we can continue to be
close when they leave. With my parents, they didn't
touch each other; it was empty, whether the children
were there or not."

THE SOLOMON CHILD SYNDROME

Another prominent pattern, in which there is a lack of a protective
holding environment from either parent, is that of the child caught
between divergent expectations and demands from each of the
parents. I term this the *Solomon child syndrome,* since the child is
torn apart between the parents. Each parent demands that the
child be loyal in the conflict with the other parent or risk rejection.
(This pattern is often found in divorcing couples.) Each spouse
needs to be validated and vindicated through the child. Thus each
parent expects the child to function as a savior for him or her, and
not for the other parent.

The role of savior for one parent is diametrically opposite to
that role for the other parent. These conflicting demands on the
child are insensitive to developmental needs, and tear the child
apart in different directions. If the child performs for one parent,
the other parent feels betrayed by the child, who is believed to be
allied with the spouse. Each parent's anger at the spouse is

displaced onto the child, who is scapegoated as an O−. This makes the double bind on achievement even more virulent, since there is also a double bind between the parents as well. The child feels used, controlled, and criticized at each turn, and cannot trust either parent to be nurturant and protective. In the regular double bind on achievement, it is limited to one dominant parent; and often the failed parent, though without power, is warm and nurturant. The end result of each parent exposing the child to two separate and conflicting double binds on achievement results in a more pervasive sense of helplessness and despair. The patient therefore erects a narcissistic defensive structure, the "plastic bubble" of Volkan (1973) or the "cocoon" described by Modell (1976), to defend some semblance of autonomy and personality integrity.

CASE EXAMPLE OF THE SOLOMON CHILD SYNDROME

One patient, a writer, came initially with his wife for marital therapy. He then continued on alone in individual psychotherapy. He recounted coming from a family in which there was considerable conflict between his parents. His father had not emancipated himself from his own mother and demanded that his wife also submit to his mother's tyranny. When his wife refused, the patient's father continued to idealize his mother and to demean his wife. The patient's family became an armed camp, and he found himself caught in the crossfire, attempting to please both parents. Each parent made a divergent demand on the patient's loyalties, and to be on either side required that he perform in ways unacceptable to the other parent. The mother, who came from a cultured middle-class family, insisted that the patient learn to play the violin. The father, who was proud of his athletic ability and masculine prowess, insisted that the patient be a good baseball player.

> The patient stated, "One of the things I remember my father doing alone with me when I was very young was to play catch. He used a hardball, and of course each of us had a padded baseball glove. We did this in the back yard, always on Sunday. During the week he returned

late and tired, and paid little attention to anyone except for meting out arbitrary punishments each night on my mother's private complaints of intransigence and disobedience. What I recall is how hard he threw the ball. I am certain he considered it some kind of toughening experience. My hands were an important issue in their wars, my mother wanting them "soft, protected so that he can play the violin," my father wanting them "hard so he'll be able to take care of himself." (These were subtle ways of putting down the other and the other's family of origin, ways into which the patient became ensnared.) "I wanted only that both of them get what they wanted, and felt responsible in not being able to please either of them." Thus the patient was caught in the middle of his parents' conflict, with conflicting demands made upon him, so that he was damned if he did and damned if he didn't comply to each of their demands for performance.

The patient felt responsible for keeping the family together and sustaining the self-esteem of his parents, since each parent demeaned the other. He recalled the subtlety of his mother's ways of undermining his father, and the violence with which the father degraded the mother in front of the children. He stated, "I superficially complied, but perversely refused to return the proofs they needed from me. At some very early stage, before I was aware of making a decision on the subject, I set up around me an invisible and impenetrable thicket that allowed me to grow into adulthood without ever actually doing a thing anyone wanted of me, even though I always felt yoked. This was a barrier that kept in as well as out. I managed never to disclose a single facet of my real self to anyone or share with a single human being, myself included, a shred of my actual feelings or thoughts. It continued for so long that I am now unaware of who that real self may be or even if there is any such person.

"It is as if when I left their home, I packed up my parents and took them along, my father stuffed inside me and my mother to be implanted in someone else. I accomplished making my own household a replica of their home. I would be simplistic to say that this structuring was inevitable, for the reason that I had no

other model. For even in those days we had radio,
newspapers, movies, and the comics that provided
different versions of what the All American Home was
about. . . . In the first place, I had recruited a willing
and able helpmate, someone who for her own reasons
would participate in establishing the proper tone, and
play this difficult part in all its diverse aspects. Without
her I could not, or perhaps would not, have done it. I
needed someone who would stay the distance, adapt to
the training, and grow to become submissively aggressive, like my mother, and in the end respond with
despair to the pressures that developed.

"With everything in place I could attempt to
understand how my father felt by putting myself in the
position he had been in and reenacting his part. I
learned his rages meant that he was probably the most
helpless one of us all. And I tried to understand how my
wife-mother could find no other means for her salvation
than staying—or, rather, how she eventually even derived satisfaction from the role. Later with my wife and
my own firstborn, I replayed this scenario from a
different perspective. I was like an actor who twenty
years later returns to the stage of his youth playing an
older character opposite the same younger part that
earlier launched his career. I felt cheated out of my
firstborn, holding his mother responsible for keeping
him from me with interferences and interventions, that
she defended as protection from those of my alleged
excesses she considered abnormal or inimical to his
survival. I then retreated from both of them, furious
and sullen" (like his father) "at what I considered this
interposition. When all my parents' efforts to drive me
inevitably misfired, their response was to increasingly
enrich the mixture, choking off the air and accelerating
erratically until my engines finally flooded."

Thus what seems to be the most significant factor in this case
is a lack of safe holding by both of the parents. Whether it is due
(1) to being seduced and abandoned as the go-between and
scapegoat, (2) treated like an emotional orphan, or (3) a Solomon
child, the child erects narcissistic defenses since its environment
lacks the necessary nurturance for normal development. The child

is exploited by being induced into the roles of go-between and scapegoat, or the child is compelled to perform divergent savior roles for each of the parents. The child learns to erect distancing barriers and to deny its dependency feelings to avoid feeling controlled and taken over psychologically. This is done to maintain some semblance of integrity, even though one's authentic being is secretly hidden away and masked by a false self. Later in life the narcissist experiences other's requests, even when these are legitimate, as demands, and feels controlled. The normal give and take, the mutuality, of relationships becomes disrupted, because of this fear of being taken over and controlled. Unable to trust others, the narcissist attempts to make up the deficit in nurturing by controlling others to function as good maternal objects.

III

Family Therapy Approaches

7

The Choice of Treatment

INDIVIDUAL OR FAMILY THERAPY

This chapter concentrates on some clinical issues that confront therapists when patients first come to us for help. How do we decide whether to use individual or family therapy as the treatment of choice? If a decision is made that family therapy is indicated, how do we select the approach in family therapy that would be most effective with a particular family?

Clearly the choice of treatment is not simply ours to make, but has to be worked out between the patient and the therapist collaboratively. It has to coincide with the patient's wishes and with the best clinical judgment of the therapist. For example, if the patient comes in requesting marital therapy for conflict resolution with the spouse, the therapist cannot prescribe individual treatment. This would need to be the case even if the therapist recognized that the patient had psychopathology and would benefit more from individual treatment. A therapeutic contract has to be established in which the general goals and form of treatment are mutually agreed upon. Later in therapy when each partner of the couple does not simply project his or her problems onto the other, and begins to own his or her own psychopathology, individual therapy can then become an option to recommend for consideration. It is not uncommon that as clients become more aware of the problems they themselves bring into the relationship, such a change in the form of treatment ultimately is desired by them as well. At that time, the therapeutic contract can be modified, and the treatment modality and goals changed.

The majority of referrals for marital or family therapy to private practitioners come for help with conflict resolution. Many couples avoid conflict and sweep issues under the rug until they trip and fall over the accumulated mountain of covered-up conflict. Others are in a continuous state of war, with criticism over minor issues constantly erupting. Many couples also do not know how to fight cleanly, but hit below the belt. They do not stay with issues over which they disagree, but tend to attack and diminish each other's self-esteem. These personal attacks involve overgeneralizing each other's faults, dredging up past conflicts, and name-calling. For example, one spouse might say, "You're *always* being critical; I *remember even* on our honeymoon, you were beating on me for something, *you bastard.*" The therapist can help the couple to fight constructively, by focusing on the issues and by working together to arrive at a resolution of conflict that involves mutual understanding and compromise.

Families of patients hospitalized for mental and physical illnesses, as well as families who have experienced the death of a member, can benefit from family therapy. In these cases the family therapist can help the family work through feelings of loss and guilt to achieve a new balance of relationships. Working with the families of recovered alcoholics has also been an important therapeutic advance. Some families, whose members have already had individual therapy or who are quite sophisticated about talking about their feelings and thoughts, request family therapy to help improve their communication. This kind of referral will probably become more frequent as individuals grow in their individual therapy, and become aware of the other therapeutic options available to them.

GENERAL GUIDELINES

Are there general guidelines used when deciding upon whether or not family therapy is the treatment of choice when there is not a presenting problem of marital or family conflict? Essentially the guidelines I use most often are the patient's level of differentiation of a stable sense of self, and the patient's involvement with the family. With adult neurotic patients, who use mature defenses such as repression, sublimation, displacement, and so on, and who have separated and moved away from their families, have a stable autonomous identity and a life of their own apart from their families, and are struggling with intrapsychic structural (neurotic) conflicts, individual psychotherapy is indicated. To involve the family would be inappropriate, and the patient would probably drop out of treatment. These patients have separated and individuated; their problems are internalized. To bring in the family would be regressive and antitherapeutic. On the other hand, with those patients who are children or young adults still living with their families, or adults who remain deeply involved with their families, a combination of individual and family therapy might be most effective.

COMBINED THERAPY

If the child is the primary patient, the same therapist can conduct both individual treatment with the child and family so long as confidentiality of the individual sessions is not breached. A contract must be established with the child, that confidentiality will be observed unless the therapist feels it very essential to further discuss in the family session an issue brought up in individual treatment. If this breach of confidentiality is felt to be necessary, the therapist agrees to inform the child first and discuss this in individual therapy before bringing it up in the family session. This prevents the individual therapist from being boxed into a collusion with the child, and being controlled by the same fear that the child has in bringing something out into the open. Clearly not all secrets need to be revealed, but those that are essential in the child's relationship with the family need to be available for discussion.

If the patient is an adult, the combination of individual and marital or family treatment simultaneously by the same therapist becomes complicated and quite difficult to work with because of transferential issues (oedipal and sibling competition), problems of confidentiality, and the breaches in the frame of treatment. If individual treatment is first and followed by marital or family therapy, the other spouse may feel the therapist cannot be impartial. If marital therapy is first, and the therapist continues alone with one spouse, the other spouse may feel rejected and angry. The least complicated solution for adult patients is to recommend separate therapists for individual and marital or family treatments. However, even here, splitting of the transference can occur, with one therapist being seen as the bad one and the other as the good one. These complicating issues are less significant in short-term treatment, but even here the therapist also needs to be sensitive and deal with them.

In summary, for those cases in which the family seems to play a significant role in aggravating or perpetuating the patient's problems, a family therapy approach is most helpful. This is particularly true for less differentiated patients, who use splitting and projective identification, have less autonomy, cannot maintain their own self-esteem and identity, and remain excessively vulnerable to the influence of their families.

WHICH FAMILY APPROACH FOR WHICH FAMILIES

Even though some advocates for a particular form of family therapy might claim that their approach is suitable for all types of families, this is clearly not the case. Each family therapy approach has certain distinct characteristics that may make it more or less suitable for a particular family. No matter how hard a therapist may try, all families cannot be put into the Procrustean bed of one form of family therapy. Each family is different, and these differences need to be evaluated in order to determine which form of family therapy will offer the greatest chance for engagement in treatment, and for bringing about corrective change. The following factors yield some general guidelines to help determine which approach in family therapy might be most appropriate for which type of family. Some family therapists may not agree with these recommendations; however, they come from my own experience while doing research in the engagement process (Slipp et al. 1974, Kressel and Slipp 1975), as well as my outcome studies (Slipp and Kressel 1978, 1979), and the experience gained through working with families clinically for over twenty-five years.

These factors will be divided into three sets of variables that encompass individual, familial, and sociocultural levels. On the *individual* level one needs to assess the general personality characteristics of each of the family members, which would include their type of defensive structures, level of authoritarianism, degree of psychological sophistication, and motivation for treatment. On the *familial* level, the therapist can evaluate the level of psychological functioning between family members. This would include the form of illness in the identified patient, the kind of typology the family fits into, the degree of differentiation of the members, and their need for distance and control. On the *sociocultural* level, one needs to assess the influence of ethnicity and socioeconomic level.

INDIVIDUAL FACTORS

If the individual family members seem to have relatively rigid, obsessional types of defenses, then breaking up negative feedback cycles, as occurs in structural family therapy, is one consideration. If the family members seem to be more expressive and hysterical in their defensive structure, they may be carried away by inappropriate solutions to problems. In these cases, positive feedback cycles may need to be disrupted, as occurs in strategic family therapy.

In our engagement studies (Slipp et al. 1974, Kressel and Slipp 1975) we found that the higher the level of authoritarianism, as measured by the California F Scale, the lower the engagement in treatment. This was particularly true for the fathers in the fifty-one families we studied. In addition, the more serious the form of mental illness in the identified patient, the lower was the engagement rate in family treatment. However, when both parents were low in authoritarianism, even when their child had the most severe form of mental illness, we had a 100 percent engagement rate in treatment. Highly authoritarian families tended to project blame and to be extrapunitive, whereas less authoritarian families were able to be introspective. Thus, how the parents related to one another and to the patient was a stronger determinant for the family's remaining in and using treatment than was the severity of the child's mental illness. This finding is directly related to the research of Leff (1976), which showed that how the parents related to the identified patient, who was schizophrenic, was the most important determinant for prognosis. It even superseded whether the patient took his or her medication. If the family was hostile, critical, and intrusive (described as having "high expressed emotion," or high EE), patients suffered the highest relapse rate. Reducing the amount of time the patient spent with the family to less than thirty-five hours a week, or employing a psychoeducational approach to reduce the level of "expressed emotion," was shown to reduce the relapse rate. Here the family itself can be therapeutic or antitherapeutic in its approach to the patient.

For the most highly authoritarian families, who show high expressed emotion as well as those families that are least sophisticated, a psychoeducational approach may be most appropriate when it is done in a group setting with families of other patients. They would be provided with group support, learn to think psychologically, and, hopefully, reduce their guilt and hostility toward the patient.

In terms of motivation for treatment, our research on engagement found that we had a nearly perfect rate of engagement when both parents were motivated to receive help. In cases in which only one spouse initiated and sought treatment, about one third of the families dropped out of treatment. Special efforts are thus needed to get the less motivated spouse involved in treatment. It was usually the husband who was found to be more resistant to treatment, which resulted in its termination. This finding that the husband's attitude is a pivotal factor in determining whether or not the family remained in treatment was also documented by Shapiro and Budman (1973). Although clinicians in the past have mainly focused on the mother, empirical evidence increasingly indicates that marital stability is more a function of the father's stable, positive personality traits than of the mother's (Barry 1970).

FAMILIAL FACTORS

Various kinds of psychopathology can be treated by various approaches in family therapy, but the family members' needs for distance and control must be taken into consideration. Certain families, because of their high degree of distrust of others or because of ethnic or socioeconomic differences, may require a greater amount of distance between the family and the therapist. This distance is a factor that, as Kanter and Neal (1985) point out, varies with the two systemic approaches in family therapy. Strategic family therapy works at a great distance outside the family, whereas structural family therapy operates at a median distance. I would add that the psychoeducational approach probably allows for the greatest distance, and the behavioral approach next to the greatest, whereas dynamic and object relations approaches operate with the closest space between the family and the therapist. The order of comparative distance between the family and the therapist in various approaches to family treatment, starting from the greatest to the smallest distance, is as follows:

1. Psychoeducational
2. Behavioral
3. Strategic
4. Structural
5. Bowenian
6. Contextual
7. Psychodynamic
8. Object Relations

RECOMMENDATIONS

These are my recommendations in terms of the family's need for distance and control. For the families of chronic schizophrenic patients, who may need the greatest therapeutic distance, the psychoeducational approach in a supportive group setting may be most appropriate. Family members are taught about the causes, symptoms, and psychopharmacology of schizophrenia, and how one person influences another. Intellectual defenses are supported and bolstered, and there is the minimum amount of demand on family members to reveal their intimate feelings and thoughts. Hopefully, their level of expressed emotion will diminish, and they will be more empathic and reduce their demands on the patient because of their greater knowledge.

Brief strategic approaches may be indicated for highly resistant families, who are profoundly distrustful, avoid intimacy, and assume an oppositional stance to treatment, all of which has foiled previous attempts at therapy. Here the therapist adopts the role of a controlling authority who respects the family's need for distance. By means of a paradoxical intervention, the family's distrust and oppositionalism is used in the service of change. The system is thus exploded sufficiently to remove the patient from the scapegoated position. By the therapist reframing the patient's symptoms so they are perceived as altruistically motivated, the family may comply and displace their scapegoating and anger from the patient to the therapist or elsewhere. A behavioral approach is appropriate for other families who are not oppositional but who also need considerable distance.

For families who have relatively moderate difficulty in using verbal communication to express their feelings and thoughts, an approach that focuses on action is often more appropriate. These families would include lower-socioeconomic-class patients, psychosomatic patients who are out of touch with their feelings *(alexithymia),* and certain ethnic groups. Here a middle-range distance that does not rely solely on verbal interchange is needed, as provided by structural family therapy. For white Anglo-Saxon families who have difficulty in being expressive of their feelings, an approach that is also relatively middle-distant and that emphasizes cognition and not emotions is indicated. The Bowenian family therapy approach has been useful here, since it encourages people to become aware of current and past family patterns, but not to express their feelings.

In the case of families who desire and can tolerate more intimacy and openness, the contextual approach of Boszormenyi-Nagy and Spark (1973) as well as dynamic or object relations family therapy are appropriate. However, one need not restrict these approaches only to those families already tolerant of closeness. The therapist can recognize which families need greater control and distance for their security, and can respect this need. Therefore the therapist, at the beginning of treatment, will need to operate at the distance that these families can tolerate. As the family develops more trust, its level of defensiveness will be reduced, and it may become more open and closer to the therapist. Therapy itself can serve as a model for more open and intimate relationships between family members.

ETHNICITY

With certain ethnic groups different forms of family therapy have been recommended by clinicians as most effective. Although the description of an ethnic group involves stereotypic thinking or overgeneralization, and is not always applicable to a specific family, there are certain frequently occurring characteristics of various ethnic groups that the therapist needs to be sensitive to in working therapeutically with these groups. The following are some of the findings of clinicians who have worked extensively with various ethnic groups in family treatment.

McGoldrick (1982) describes Irish-American families as wanting to change, but to do so without exposing their inner, intimate feelings to the therapist. The therapist is seen as similar to a priest, to whom they can come to confess their sins and obtain forgiveness. Because of this, they maintain a polite distance and tend to comply superficially to the therapist's directives, whether real or implied. McGoldrick recommends for these families a problem-solving or behavioral approach that is also relatively structured. Such an approach, she feels, would be more effective than a psychodynamic one, which would encourage uncovering and openly expressing feelings. (However, this implies a certain rigidity that cannot be worked with and changed, which has not been my experience.)

With Italian-American families, Rotunno and McGoldrick (1982) observe that the therapist often is not trusted, since he or she is an outsider. Even though the family may apparently display considerable verbal expression of feeling, its real and deep secrets are kept tightly locked up within the boundary of an enmeshed extended family. For work to be done therapeutically, this rigid boundary around the extended family needs to be loosened to allow the therapist to enter into the family's world and be trusted with its secrets. Only then could a more optimistic outlook be predicted by these clinicians.

As for Jewish-American families, Herz and Rosen (1982) state that the family structure tends to be more democratic and egalitarian. (One has to question whether this has as much to do with middle-class values as with ethnicity.) These families are found to value complicated and sophisticated techniques in treatment that involve verbally expressing their inner feelings and thoughts, as in psychoanalytic therapy. Behavioral and other short-term directive approaches are seen as superficial and insufficient.

McGill and Pearce (1982) describe white Anglo-Saxon Protestant families as encouraging individualism and self-sufficiency. Thus these families have difficulty in accepting their dependency needs, are emotionally repressed and unable to express their feelings, especially in asking for help. However, once trust is established, they work hard toward achieving their goals in treatment.

There are differences at the beginning of treatment between different ethnic groups; however, I find that if the therapist is sensitive to these differences and is a skilled clinician, they can be worked through in treatment. Clearly, if the therapy is only a brief intervention, there will not be sufficient time to develop a strong therapeutic alliance and work these issues through. However, with short-term as well as long-term therapy, my experience is quite optimistic that these ethnic differences alone need not dictate the choice of treatment, and that a dynamic form of marital or family therapy can be very effective. In the next chapter I discuss the results of an outcome research study comparing behavioral and dynamic family therapy, which I conducted at Bellevue Psychiatric Hospital, that confirms this opinion.

8

Socioeconomic Issues in Family Therapy Choice

SOCIOLOGICAL FINDINGS

Probably the most significant variable in deciding which type of family therapy is most suitable in a particular instance is the socioeconomic level of the family. It supersedes such factors as the severity of mental illness in the identified patient, the individual personality characteristics of family members, and the influence of ethnicity and race. The most profound effect of this socioeconomic variable can be found in the poorest segment of society. This so-called underclass will be termed Class V, using the classification of Hollingshead and Redlich (1958). As a general description, Class I consists of the extremely wealthy; Class II the upper-middle class—professionals and executives; Class III the middle-middle class—owners of small businesses and white-collar workers; Class IV the lower-middle class—blue-collar workers; and Class V the poorest—unemployed or intermittently employed. It is important to recognize that the poor are not a homogeneous group, but comprise both Classes IV and V. Since poverty represents such a profound influence, I will first provide some background material concerning the effects of poverty; then I will describe my research studies on engagement and outcome in family therapy, before making recommendations for effective treatment that takes socioeconomic factors into account.

Such writers as Lewis (1959, 1961, 1966) and Harrington (1962) have described the self-perpetuating "culture of poverty," which contains its own psychology, language, and world view. Because of the stressful and brutalizing life circumstances resulting from poverty and social discrimination, a pattern of disorganization is likely to occur in poor families. This need not always be the case, since many poor families are able to cope and do not remain poor in succeeding generations. However, a danger exists that once the family structure is fragmented it tends to remain so. In addition, decompensation of individual personality can also be one of the unfortunate consequences of poverty. Not only is the poorest segment of society afflicted with more psychiatric disorders than other segments, but those that they have are the most serious, according to the Midtown Studies (Srole et al. 1962, Langner and Michael 1963) and the New Haven Survey (Hollingshead and Redlich 1958). This high level of severe mental illness was found to be due to poverty and not to other factors in Leighton's Stirling County Study (1965). Leighton was able to reverse this process of social disintegration, and thereby reduce the high rate of severe mental illness. In this study of a poor white rural community the members showed the same attitudes as other Class V populations, as found in the New York Midtown Study (Srole et al. 1962) and the study of Negro youth in Harlem by Clark (1964). These attitudes were a pervasive sense of powerlessness, apathy, depression, hostility, cynicism, distrust of each other and outsiders, and a strong intolerance for ambiguity or change. The Stirling group, like other disorganized poor groups, suffered from poor school performance, low educational level, high incidence of broken homes, avoidance of work, lack of future planning, and a higher prevalence of alcoholism and psychiatric disorders as compared to similar but socially organized communities. By providing economic opportunities and facilitating social involvement and group integration, Leighton was able to note a marked increase in family organization, a higher level of educational achievement, and a significant decrease in psychiatric disorders.

How does this disorganization of the family structure come

about? This involves sociocultural, familial, and individual dynamics coming into play. Certainly the history of deliberate fragmentation of black families under Southern slavery, prior to the Civil War, was devastating to the family integrity. Also the lack of economic opportunities in many urban settings added markedly to this family fragmentation. Rainwater (1966) points out that since emancipation after the Civil War in the United States, blacks living in rural areas were able to maintain full nuclear families as well as similarly situated whites, since the male had an important role function.

The Puerto Rican family structure in the United States experiences stress due to conflict between the two cultures. In Puerto Rico, families are organized along traditional, patriarchal lines, with a highly differentiated, hierarchical role structure, and emphasis on extended family ties. On the United States mainland, the breakdown of primary group controls and extended family support in favor of the isolated nuclear family with a more egalitarian, individualistic role structure creates considerable strain. The wife may identify with the American family structure, since it entitles her to more power than she would have otherwise, while the husband will attempt to retain his position as defined in the Puerto Rican culture. On the other hand, both parents might identify with the traditional, more authoritarian role structure, while their children might rebel against the resulting limitations upon their autonomy. This might be reinforced if the children's reference group is another American family. In these instances alienation between the spouses may occur, or between both parents and their children.

The devastating effects on individual personality development that result from social discrimination have been reported by a number of behavioral scientists. When a minority group is held in low esteem and excluded from full social participation, individuals of the minority group often identify with and internalize the majority's negative attitude toward them. Part of the minority person's ego can be said to identify with the aggressor, while another part identifies with the degraded identity imposed by the diminished social role assigned to that minority. The result is self-hatred, lowered self-esteem, self-defeating behavior, and work inhibition, when they turn their aggression upon themselves.

If they turn their aggression outward, others in their immediate environment become targets of their rage. This phenomenon of self-hatred was first investigated by Lewin (1935) amongst Jews who suffered social discrimination. A similar conflict in black identity has been studied and reported on by Clark (1950, 1964), Milner (1953), Johnson (1957), and others. Rodman (1968) reported that most of the residents in a black ghetto identified and judged themselves by middle-class aspirations and values, which is seen as the majority culture, while at the same time adhering to lower-class cultural values and attitudes. The study of Antonovsky and Lerner (1959) found, interestingly, that black children had a higher aspiration level than white children coming from the same income level. However, these aspirations were felt by the black children to be disparate with actual levels that they might expect to achieve, resulting in a higher degree of frustration, helplessness, and disillusionment, and a lowering of self-esteem.

Scanzoni's (1967) study showed that lower-class youth of various races and ethnicity had the same or higher levels of aspiration as middle-class youth, yet their level of expectation of attainment was also lower. The parents of lower-class youngsters were found to inspire their children to achieve, yet were unable to provide guidelines about realistic ways of achieving these goals; moreover, they were themselves not adequate role models of success. Merton (1957) explains one form of juvenile delinquency as partly due to this phenomenon: When middle-class aspirations and goals are internalized, but are believed to be unachievable through legitimate means in society, the resultant condition, which he termed *anomie,* frequently produced deviancy, which he called *innovation.*

Several ways out of this frustrating dilemma are possible. The individual may adapt by assuming a delinquent, exploitative position, seeing the world as a predatory jungle with each person competitively pursuing his or her own needs and using other ruthlessly. In this case, the individual becomes streetwise and keenly sensitive to power relationships. He or she does not expect to gain gratification through legitimate means, and thus to gain it may attempt to manipulate others (hustle, cheat, lie, seduce, or use whatever bag of tricks is available), or else aggressively extract what is wanted through direct force. Another adaptational position is one of defensive withdrawal from an environment that is experienced as overwhelming and depriving. The person becomes resigned to powerlessness, lowers his or her aspiration level, becomes depressed and apathetic, or lives in fantasy. If drugs or alcohol are available, the person may use them to anesthetize him- or herself or to feel better by getting high. Since there is a withdrawal from ego involvement with others, the family structure tends to become looser and more vaguely defined. These findings have been described by Srole and colleagues (1962) and Langner and Michael (1963) in the New York Midtown Studies, by Clark's (1964) study of Negro youth in Harlem, and the study of the poor white rural community of Stirling County by Leighton (1959).

Herzog (1966) and many others have noted that family structure differs more between different socioeconomic levels than between racial and ethnic groups. A middle-class black family is closer to a middle-class white family than to a lower-class black family in terms of its values and structure. The crucial variable that determines family structure amongst the lower classes is the ability of the husband to work and function as a breadwinner. If the husband cannot fulfill this role function, he loses self-esteem, since he loses social prestige. He considers himself a failure. This is especially significant in traditional, patriarchal families, since this role is the foundation that entitles him to power over others (Komarovsky 1940). Lower-socioeconomic-class males may not get from their jobs the kinds of confirmations of their self-esteem as do middle-class males; therefore, to bolster their egos, they tend to rely more upon enjoying their power over their wives and children. Most sociological studies, including our own (Slipp et al. 1974) found that the lower the socioeconomic level, the greater the degree of authoritarianism, with Class V husbands having the greatest authoritarianism. As an attempt to compensate for their social powerlessness and to prevent loss of self-esteem, Class V husbands rely even more on the rights of their position to have power over family members. However, the wife may question the legitimacy of this entitlement, since the husband has not fulfilled his role responsibility as breadwinner. She experiences domination and at times physical abuse without any compensatory economic security. Thus she may find herself a scapegoat, exploited to bolster her husband's poor self-esteem. As a result, the wife may realize that she is better off finding employment for herself, or that she can manage almost as well by rejecting her domineering husband and going on welfare. In the Puerto Rican community, this latter solution was jokingly referred to as "living with Wilfredo," which has a double meaning—referring to a man's name, but also to welfare. The culture of poverty has thus gradually become one in which many families are headed only by the mother. Amidei (1986) reported that the percentage of poor families headed by a female from 1960 to 1980 doubled from 25 to 50 percent. In addition, one third of all female-headed families, and one half of all female-headed minority families, are poor.

If the lower-class adult male is unmarried, he may not commit himself to the responsibilities of marriage, as he may be unable to fulfill his role as breadwinner. Since he cannot find employment, he may protect his self-esteem by avoiding marriage, which would lead to shameful failure and humiliation. If the lower-class woman feels her financial and dependency needs cannot be fulfilled by a husband, she may also avoid commitment to marriage. Rainwater (1966) discusses the role structure of the black slum culture in which both male and female suffer from the effects of this social victimization. The female role model emphasizes self-sufficiency, which defends her against depending on the male. She is more secure when she takes over the leadership of the family and controls or even rejects the male. For the male role model, there is emphasis on expressive, affectional techniques, on the ability to court and ingratiate himself with women. Rainwater noted that there was conjugal role segregation, with husband and wife each pursuing their own separate interests and lives. Neither spouse trusts the other to fulfill his or her economic and personality needs, and neither expects nor feels responsible to fulfill the other's needs. The black ghetto culture, like certain rural and European cultures, demonstrates a considerable distance between the sexes. Often there is segregation according to one's sex that extends from childhood into adolescence and through all of adult life. Same-sexed groups serve as an important support network, validating and enhancing one's self-esteem by providing friendship, a sense of belonging, and a role that one is able to fulfill. For the male it is the street culture, the bar, or fraternal organizations; and for the female it is the church and the matriarchal home.

In the slum culture, the woman's distrust of men's ability to fulfill their responsibilities often hinders her from entering into a permanent heterosexual relationship. As a mother, she can express affection for and gain affection from her children without having to risk disappointment. However, she may become pathologically dependent for companionship upon her children, and unwittingly block their individuation and separation. Since the mother is likely to be the sole source of gratification and security, the child is more prone to submit to this exploitation. The daughter frequently forms an anti-male coalition with her mother, and feels blocked in her ability to separate from her and enter into a permanent male relationship. The Biebers' (1968) study of black Class V unwed mothers showed this to be the case, with unwed mothers themselves being resistant to marriage despite opportunities. Of the unwed mothers, 60 percent came from fatherless homes themselves, whereas 60 percent of the married control group came from intact homes with a father, and the rest of this group had had meaningful relationships with a paternal figure. Without a father, a girl is deprived of a male figure to validate her feminine identity. This was especially important for black women, since until twenty years ago the culture did not validate her except in white Anglo-Saxon terms (Grier and Cobbs 1968). To bolster her own identity, she might look for the imperfections in the male. By undermining the male, and proving that the male is not masculine, she did not have to prove herself to be feminine and could thus avoid an intimate relationship. Another way to validate her insecure feminine identity was to have babies, which often resulted in a three-generational matriarchal family. At times, however, the baby could serve as the price of emancipation by a daughter from her mother's control. The daughter would replace herself with the baby upon whom the mother could shift her dependency, caring for her own grandchild. The daughter could then leave the home and have a life of her own by leaving her baby with her mother.

For the male in the slum culture, social recognition can be achieved by recounting his sexual exploits to his same-sexed peer group. This serves to bolster his weak sense of himself as a competent and masterful person and as a male. Kardiner and Ovesey (1951), Burton and Whiting (1961), and Pettigrew (1964) all have reported on the Class V black male's need to show exaggerated masculine behavior in order to defend against helplessness and an insecure male identity. Within the Puerto Rican group, there exists an institutionalized masculine protest syndrome, termed *machismo,* defining behavior that *proves* one's masculinity to others and to oneself. However, this finding is not more pronounced among blacks or Puerto Ricans than in any other poor subgroup. For example, in England, Spinley (1953) noted that the white slum male has predominantly female identification, shows marked insecurity and feelings of inferiority, and tends to be overly aggressive and narcissistic in order to compensate. This resulted from matriarchal family power structure, which appears to be common in all industrial societies whenever the male cannot fulfill his role as breadwinner, regardless of race or ethnicity.

One of the consequences of these disorganized families lacking a responsible, protective, and effective father as a suitable role model is a variety of disturbances in the children. Research studies have shown that such fatherless disorganized homes have a strong correlation with poor school performance (Deutsch 1962), drug addiction (Chein et al. 1964), homosexuality (Bieber et al. 1962), and delinquency (Glueck and Glueck 1950, Moynihan 1965).

THERAPEUTIC PROBLEMS IN WORKING WITH CLASS V FAMILIES

Many poor families are hostile to and supsicious of the middle-class therapist, since they have different values, expectations of treatment, ability to use language, and cultural patterns. Often the therapist is seen as an extension of the hostile, omnipotent, impersonal outside world or power structure. If the patient or family comes to a clinic, the therapist is usually seen as representing the entire clinic or hospital. Any past frustrations that they may have experienced with doctors and with hospitals tend to be displaced onto the therapist.

The patients in Class V families may also attempt to enter into a hostile–dependent relationship with the therapist, in which they submit to his or her omnipotent authority, but in turn demand an immediate magical cure. Because of this distrust and distance, the family may avoid revealing secrets and hidden conflicts, and may not become intimately involved with or committed to treatment. This attitude may be reinforced, since many Class V families view mental illness as an intrusion by an outside force, whether magical, physical, or mechanical. Thus they may feel that mental illness can be cured by a pill or a special diet, or by undoing a curse through visiting a spiritualist or faith healer. Because of these expectations, if the therapist cannot produce rapid results, the family members may feel deprived and angry. They may jump to the assumption that if they paid, they would get first-class medicine and a quick cure. Instead they feel they have received inferior treatment because they are poor. In an extensive survey of the lowest socioeconomic group, Myers and Roberts (1959) found distrust and antagonism toward doctors, shame regarding mental illness, and critical attitudes toward psychotherapy. However, in studying a blue-collar population, Crocetti and colleagues (1971) did not find this to be the case.

LANGUAGE IN CLASS V FAMILIES

Another major problem in working with Class V families is their inability to verbalize how they experience situations, how they feel or think about what has happened, and their diminished expectation that what they say will be heard by the other and responded to. In the middle class, language is used in an instrumental manner to convey feelings and messages that can be communicated, and to which one expects the other will respond. Thus, language can be employed to discuss problems and resolve conflict, so that intimate relationships and family solidarity can be maintained. Feelings and thoughts can be expressed through a meaningful dialogue to work out compromises and sustain cooperation. Bernstein's (1961, 1962) studies found that lower socioeconomic individuals generally function with a restricted language code, and that their experiences are perceived in a global, diffuse, nonanalytic manner. They may even look down on people who talk things over and analyze what happens. This results in experience not being differentiated and metabolized, so that it does not become meaningful.

Because of the lack of the use of language, experiences are not well remembered, which leads to difficulty not only in reporting but also in learning from them. There is often an emphasis on activity, such as sports or drinking, to dissipate these global feelings or tensions that are remnants of interpersonal experiences. Minuchin (1964) even noted that in lower-class families containing a delinquent, the verbal content of a message was considerably less significant than the command aspect—that is, the communication that defined the power relationships. Thus how does one work with a Class V family, when the primary tool of therapy is language?

WORKING WITH FAMILIES OF VARIOUS SOCIOECONOMIC LEVELS

After I established the Family Therapy Unit at Bellevue Psychiatric Hospital in 1968, it became apparent to me that our staff and students were having considerable difficulty in engaging Class V families. Thus, as part of our ongoing research in developing the family typology, it was decided to conduct a study of factors leading to patients' engagement in or dropping out of family treatment. One of the instruments selected to test these families was the California F Scale that measured authoritarianism (Adorno et al. 1950). Authoritarianism seemed related to our interest in developing our ideas concerning the "symbiotic survival pattern." The F Scale was concerned with ego-defensiveness, other-directedness (Katz et al. 1957), ambivalence, splitting, and projection of sexual and aggressive feelings. It studied extrapunitiveness (scapegoating), stereotypic thinking, and rigid role structures. In addition, the thought and emotional patterns connected with authoritarianism were at the opposite pole from the democratic group structure of most forms of family therapy.

Family therapy encourages a relatively egalitarian role structure, open dialogue, negotiation of differences, and shared decision-making. Authoritarianism is related to a cognitive style that is rigid, considers things and people in black-and-white terms, and is intolerant of ambiguity. Authoritarian individuals are self-righteous, and consider those who disagree with them to be bad and deserving of punishment. This involves the defenses of repression, denial, and splitting, with the projection of unacceptable sexual and aggressive impulses into others who are then scapegoated.

The authoritarian family is characterized by a clearly defined role structure, and a dominant–submissive hierarchy of power with the father (or mother) as the apex of the triangle. Each role is entitled to have power over the next lower role, so that there is no negotiation of differences, only automatic compliance. Communication is vertical down the hierarchy, with none coming from the bottom upward. Failure to submit is seen as questioning the legitimacy of the role structure, and is experienced as a threat to status, self-esteem, and personal identity. This is because one's identity is markedly identified with one's role. The other is thus seen as bad, and may be physically or verbally punished to force compliance, which is similar to Bion's basic assumption of *fight*. Another method to deal with lack of compliance is to withdraw, which is similar to Bion's basic assumption of *flight*. The third alternative is to displace aggression onto a weaker member of the family, or someone or some group outside the family; an example might be the scapegoating of a minority group in society.

An engagement study (Slipp et al. 1974, Kressel and Slipp 1975) of families coming for therapy was initiated. The form of treatment employed was a dynamic form of family therapy, whose goals were to help family members be more open in their communication, to provide insight into how the members currently affected one another, and to give the parents insight into how their present behavior was influenced by their own childhood experiences. Each family was told what to expect from treatment, since they needed to have some framework of how therapy works. The therapist was encouraged to be genuine and empathic, and to establish a therapeutic contract that was consonant with how the family perceived their problems. The therapists were then to interpret how each family member affected the other, so that pieces of behavior did not remain unrelated, but linkages were provided between them to clarify cause-and-effect relationships. In this way it was hoped that the family members would not simply regard themselves as bad or as victimized, but could see that they had control over what happened, and could assume responsibility for their part of the relationship.

We studied fifty-one families, of which thirty-eight, or nearly 75 percent, continued in family treatment. Those families that dropped out of treatment before the completion of three sessions were the lowest socioeconomic classes (Classes I and II had 9 percent, Class III 15 percent, Class IV 22 percent, and Class V 66 percent). The age of the spouses and the stage of the family life cycle was not significant. The degree of authoritarianism increased the lower the socioeconomic level, with the highest degree of it being in Class V husbands. The sicker the identified patient was, the higher the therapy dropout rate (severely disturbed patients 35 percent, and moderately–mildly disturbed 15 percent). Families with a severely disturbed member were especially prone to drop out if they were in Class V (five families out of six). However, in families with a severely disturbed member, where both the parents were low in authoritarianism, we had a 100 percent engagement rate. In terms of motivation for treatment, if both spouses sought family treatment, engagement was nearly perfect. In Class V families, the greatest tendency was for the wife alone to initiate contact. Given the very high rate of authoritarianism in Class V husbands, these husbands clearly felt their position was threatened by their wives seeking family therapy, or they were antagonized by therapy.

We also administered a Family Inventory that measured division of labor, decision-making, communication, and conflict management. We found that when the wife worked outside the home there was a greater division of labor, which also correlated with remaining in treatment (45 percent, as compared to 15 percent with no division of labor). There was a more cooperative pattern of decision-making in those families continuing in therapy; the husbands in these families reported a favorable view of their communication. The more closely the husband felt himself allied with his wife, such as in sharing domestic roles, the more likely the family would remain in treatment. Wives in these families were more likely to disagree with their husbands openly and to express dissatisfaction. This may have been because of the greater freedom and power they had to be openly confrontational than had the wives who terminated. Dropout wives were often married to rigid, authoritarian males; in such marriages, expression of dissatisfaction would only be cause for even greater conflict and defensiveness on the part of the husband. Thus, continuing families had a less rigid role structure, there was a more equal distribution of power between husband and wife, and a greater disposition to negotiate on the part of the husband.

In the next research study (Slipp and Kressel 1978, 1979) we attempted to evaluate the outcome of insight versus a problem-solving form of treatment with lower socioeconomic families (Classes IV and V). The sample consisted of twenty-eight families, 80 percent white and 20 percent black and Hispanic, whose average family income was $8,000 per year. At intake each spouse completed a background data sheet, the Locke and Wallace Short Marital Adjustment Test (1959), the VanderVeen Family Concept Q Sort (1965), and a sixteen-item bipolar Marital Rating Scale we devised. Families were randomly assigned to the insight group and the problem-solving family treatment group. Eight families assigned to the insight treatment group dropped out, and were replaced by other families to equal the problem-solving group. (These dropout families were nearly all Class V, mostly black and Hispanic, with unemployed husbands. All of them had also experienced the death of a parent during their childhood, and they had all been assigned to inexperienced therapists.) At termination of treatment after three months, the same intake measures were readministered to both groups.

At the three-month evaluation, the insight group reported more negative results than the problem-solving group. There was more difficulty in communicating, more conflict, more emotional distance, and more formality reported, especially by the wives. However, at a one-year evaluation, 63 percent of the insight group stated that they were much better, as compared to only 29 percent for the problem-solving group. Only 13 percent of the insight group reported no change resulting from treatment, as compared to 43 percent of the problem-solving group.

That a directive, concrete problem-solving intervention might produce more rapid short-term effects than a permissive insight-oriented therapy is not surprising. Reviews of short-term individual therapy outcome research (Bergin 1971) have indicated more positive effects when specific, concrete therapeutic goals have been targeted. Outcomes for short-term therapy have been less favorable when goals are broader and more diffuse. In terms of the experience of the therapist, it was significant only in the insight-oriented group. This was consistent with the view that insight-oriented family therapy is a complex task, differing in fundamental respects from the trainees' previous life experiences. Under the demands of a concrete, problem-solving intervention, prior experience ceases to be an advantage.

Our successful group receiving insight-oriented family therapy was a blue-collar population. Even though our short-term results were negative, the eventual outcome of insight treatment was positive. This goes along with the findings in individual therapy by Caligor (1969) and Gould (1967) that blue-collar patients can be effectively worked with by modified analytic psychotherapy. This was a group that was not naturally introspective, and for which an outside intervention would thus produce more rapid results. However, it can also be argued that the negative results after three months might even be seen as a positive indicator of the effectiveness of treatment. One can postulate that the initial defenses of repression and denial were penetrated, so that the underlying conflict could surface. Our long-term follow-up thus indicated that with a blue-collar population, the short-term positive effect did not persist, and that the insight treatment group reported better results in the long run. Clearly this small study cannot come up with definite answers, but it does make it clear that blue-collar families can be worked with effectively in a dynamic approach, particularly if the therapist is trained and experienced.

Dynamic or object relations family therapy is least effective with Class V families and is not recommended. For these families, who have become disorganized in their structure and are highly authoritarian, a short-term structural approach in family therapy seems to be most helpful. The structural approach tends to be more effective because it relies more on an action-oriented method that is consonant with their way of operating. These families do not value talking as an effective way of problem solving, and rely on the therapist to take a more controlling and distant stance. Structural family therapy, although applicable for a wider range of problems, is particularly effective with Class V disorganized poor families for whom other approaches may be ineffective.

This recommendation is understandable, since Minuchin and colleagues (1967) developed their approach originally by working with slum families in New York City. Here the discipline of the children by one or both of the parents was often found to be inconsistent. At times the parents would break down and abdicate their authority, whereas at other times they would be rigid and punitive in their discipline. The structural approach thus strengthens parental authority so that discipline is consistent. It may also help organize the family into a more flexible operating group. Through the techniques of joining, mimesis, tracking, and physical spatial rearrangements, the parents are confirmed in their roles, boundaries are reinforced and clarified between subsystems, pathological coalitions are broken up, and better communications and coping ability are facilitated.

Object relations family therapy is particularly suited for and effective with middle-class families. This is especially the case with more sophisticated individuals, who have already had previous individual dynamic psychotherapy. Many of these families are capable of a more intimate and close therapeutic relationship. The fact that the therapist is also middle-class enhances the possibility of developing trust more quickly, since they all share the same values and goals. If the therapist is trained in this approach, and is genuine and empathic toward the family so that a safe holding environment is created, considerable growth and change in the family and in the members' individual functioning can occur.

9

Combining Family Therapy Approaches

PROBLEMS OF AN ECLECTIC APPROACH

Can a therapist start with one approach in family therapy and then shift to another? In the case of strategic and structural family therapy, Fraser (1982) considers that combining these two systemic approaches in clinical practice is all but impossible. Each approach is based on a theoretical foundation and seeks a therapeutic goal that conflicts with the other. I consider that an eclectic approach—in which, like a Chinese menu, you take a little from one column and a little from another—is also impossible. The selection of therapeutic techniques from various forms of family therapy immediately runs into trouble. Each approach fosters the development of a therapeutic framework between the therapist and the family that is considered essential for cure. This therapeutic relationship is markedly different, or can even be contradictory, in each approach. Different family therapies employ techniques that interfere with or disrupt the therapeutic relationship fostered by the other approach. Different therapies also have different goals for the outcome of treatment. However, some technical aspects of the systemic approaches can be modified so as not to disrupt the therapeutic relationship, and can be used in a psychodynamic framework. This is discussed later in the chapter.

THE THERAPEUTIC DISTANCE

The therapeutic distance between the family and the therapist that is fostered and maintained by each of the systemic approaches is considered a pivotal difference by Kanter and Neal (1985). They state, "Strategic therapists are trained to keep themselves detached in order to remain experientially 'outside' of the client system. Structural therapists are taught to work at a 'median' distance from the client system, moving in close or shifting to a more detached stance for brief moments to obtain information or to intervene" (p. 14). I would add that the therapeutic distance between the therapist and the family using the object relations approach is much closer than it is in the structural and strategic approaches, and indeed closer than in any other approach in family therapy. This would include other forms of dynamic family therapy, in which—even though unconscious drives, defenses, dreams, and transferences are dealt with—the therapist's countertransference is not part of the treatment.

Countertransference in dynamic family therapy is seen as a resistance to progress in treatment, and is not worked with openly. This is also true of structural family therapy, in which the therapist also avoids being "sucked into the system," which essentially is a countertransferential reaction. The object relations family therapist tries to establish a concerned and intimate relationship to the family through the use of empathy. In object relations family therapy, the family is allowed to enter into the therapist, and to evoke certain responses from him or her through projective identification. The therapist then attempts to differentiate whether the responses to the family that he or she becomes aware of are due to unresolved neurotic conflicts of a subjective countertransference, or whether these responses are being induced through projective identification from the family, which would be an objective countertransference. After self-analysis, if the therapist feels that the response is due to an objective countertransference, then the transference being projected can be surmised and used by the therapist as a therapeutic tool to enhance treatment. We cover this area in Chapter 11, when we discuss the employment of objective countertransference as a therapeutic technique in object relations family therapy.

THE EFFECTS OF THERAPEUTIC DISTANCE

In strategic family therapy, the therapist maintains a distant therapeutic stance toward the family. Like an abstinent position in individual psychoanalytic treatment, it fosters regression. I would speculate that this distant stance also reinforces the family's regressive group functioning, which Bion (1961) termed a basic assumption of dependency (baD). An omnipotent position is conferred onto the therapist, who is seen as all good and magically powerful. To maintain this idealization of the therapist, his or her "bad" aspects are split off and repressed.

This idealized and omnipotent position of the therapist facilitates the family's submission to and acceptance of the "paradoxical" prescription that is offered to them. The therapist stays within the family's basic assumption level of functioning and does not attempt to establish a work group, as occurs in other forms of family therapy. The bad aspects of the therapist that were split off and repressed result in the therapist being unconsciously experienced as a persecutory bad object. If the therapist were to assume a supportive approach and attempt to establish a more cooperative therapeutic relationship, as occurs in a normal work group, offering a paradoxical prescription would have little impact and in all likelihood would fail. Strategic interventions rely on the basic distrust and oppositionalism already existing in the family, and if the therapist were involved and friendly, he or she would be demeaned and rejected. Acceptance of the paradoxical prescription depends on submission to the consciously idealized therapist, who is unconsciously feared as the bad persecutory object.

The ultimate goal aspired to in strategic family therapy is to change positive feedback cycles, which are viewed as erroneous solutions to problems in the family. Theoretically, the timely use of paradoxical prescriptions accentuates these positive feedback cycles, supposedly going along with the family's homeostasis, and results in the destruction of these positive feedback cycles. I could reformulate this in object relations terms as the therapist going along with the basic assumption level of the family's group functioning (baD), and using the family's dependency on him or her to undermine splitting and projective identification defenses that have resulted in scapegoating of the patient (baF).

Because the family needs to idealize the therapist (O+), it empowers the therapist to be able to reframe the induced role of the identified patient from family scapegoat (O−) to savior (S+). Even though the patient's behavior continues in the same way, it has been relabeled by the therapist from "bad" to "good," since the family is told the patient's role has an altruistic function for the family. Because the therapist is experienced as idealized and omnipotent, the family submits to his or her directives, and aggression and other pathological aspects of the parents are blocked from being dumped by projective identification into the patient.

In strategic family therapy, dealing with process and working through are not even attempted; instead, the paradoxical prescription functions in this therapy as an antidote for the pathological forces existing in the family. The paradoxical prescription is considered by the strategic family therapist as a therapeutic double bind to countermand a pathogenic double bind. Yet here the very same type of pathogenic force that supposedly creates pathology is used to undo it. In addition, the very same type of disturbed object relations in the family that contributes to psychopathology is replicated in the treatment situation. In more seriously ill families, dependence on an idealized good maternal object is maintained, while rage is split off, repressed, and displaced onto the patient or spouse, who is demeaned and scapegoated.

In strategic family therapy, the therapist is split and consciously idealized as the good maternal object (O+), while unconsciously perceived as the controlling, persecutory bad object (O−). This may account for the very brevity of the treatment; the patients submit and then quickly get away from the bad object. In a personal communication, Selvini-Palazzoli informed me that frequently at the termination of strategic therapy, especially when it is successful, the therapist becomes the object of anger. Thus it appears that once the therapist redirects a family's rage away from scapegoating of the patient, that rage is redirected to the therapist, who has all along been unconsciously perceived as the bad persecutory object.

The family continues to use the primitive defenses of splitting and projective identification, and at termination the idealizations within the family are maintained at the expense of scapegoating the therapist or someone else outside the family. One can make the valid point that some families, who are very distrustful, would never become engaged in treatment. Such an intervention is at least beneficial, even though the level of functioning remains primitive and unchanged in the family. Otherwise these families would receive no treatment at all. Strategic family therapy is like karate, in which one uses the destructive force of the attacker for a beneficial purpose.

In structural family therapy, the therapist works to establish a median distance that allows him or her to maintain a position of control, as well as attempt to develop a therapeutic alliance—that is, to form a work group. The techniques of joining and mimesis foster the family's identification with the therapist, who is seen as one of them. By reducing the family's distrust and distance to some extent, structural family therapy can then work with process. The goal of treatment is to break up negative feedback cycles in the family, so that interactional patterns that have become fixed and rigid may become more flexible. Change may then occur as the therapist equalizes the power relations in the family so that there is a better chance for improved interpersonal relations. This would facilitate better conflict resolution, communication, and structural order, which diminishes the need to blame and to scapegoat others and to form pathological coalitions.

The object relations family therapist also deals with these positive and negative feedback cycles in current family interaction, but sees them as arising from an unconscious collusion of defenses between individual family members. In order to facilitate a cooperative therapeutic alliance, the object relations therapist attempts to establish a close and trusting work group relationship. He or she takes a permissive stance that respects the autonomy of the family members, and avoids the take-charge, controlling position of the systemic approaches. The therapist and the family members then cooperate to process and work through systemic, interpersonal, and individual dynamics. By the creation of a safe holding environment, the members' defensiveness is reduced so they can more openly reveal their inner feelings, thoughts, fantasies, and dreams. The goal is to change the defensive structure of the individuals as well as of the family system, which are both interactive. Self-awareness, empathy, intimacy between family members, and more differentiated interpersonal relations are fostered, to facilitate better communication and problem solving.

THE POWER POSITION OF THE THERAPIST

The strategic approach encourages the therapist to take the most directive and controlling position toward the family. The structural approach encourages a similar power position, but to a lesser degree. It also fosters the development of a therapeutic alliance, and does not simply rely on the oppositionalism or submission of the family, as does the strategic approach. Both strategic and structural approaches see the activity and directive interventions of the therapist as breaking up the current pathogenic feedback cycles in the family. The object relations family therapist relies on verbal interpretations and not on activity or control, functioning in a more equal, permissive role. In this approach the therapist both stimulates the family members' curiosity in their self-exploration and collaborates with them in understanding the significance of their behavior, the "why." The family then does not need to automatically repeat behavior that is beyond their awareness, and can themselves make efforts to change.

THE TIME FOCUS OF THE THERAPIST

In both the systemic approaches, the underlying assumption is that if the present family system changes, then individual personality will change as a consequence. All dynamic, Bowenian, and contextual family therapists do not agree with this assumption and feel there is insufficient evidence for it. Instead they emphasize that exploration and awareness of self and of relationships, past and present, are essential for personality change. The object relations family therapist feels that once the family system changes, and problems are no longer projected and acted out interpersonally, then conflicts are reinternalized and experienced egosyntonically. Once a person reowns these intrapsychic conflicts, they can be worked through by that person in family or individual treatment. Change will not only be produced in the family member, but it will also initiate and sustain further change in the family system. On the other hand, both systemic family approaches see change as being imposed by the therapist from the outside and then influencing the inside personality. However, dynamic and object relations family therapists believe change develops more from inside the personality and then affects the outside system.

OTHER DIFFERENCES IN FAMILY THERAPIES

There are other marked differences between these two systemic approaches and behavioral, Bowenian, contextual, and dynamic (which includes object relations) family therapy approaches. Both structural and strategic family therapy focus exclusively on the present interaction of the family, whereas the Bowenian, contextual, and dynamic approaches look into how past conflicts in the family of origin influence the current family interaction. This theoretical difference influences how the presenting conflicts of the family are viewed and treated. For the systemic and behavioral family therapist, the family's presenting conflicts are accepted solely on their manifest level. In particular, the behavioral family therapist sees conflict as arising from maladaptive behavioral patterns that were learned. Thus, to correct the overt conflicts that are presented, the behavioral therapist may attempt to teach the family members communications and/or negotiating skills. Bowenian, contextual, and dynamic family therapists find that the overt conflict usually has its origins in the family of origin. Their goal is to trace the source of the conflicts, and to clarify and help the members rework and resolve difficulties in their past relationships that affect present family interactions. The current relationships are thus decontaminated from past influences, so as to be more appropriate and adaptive.

Neither of the systemic approaches see insight or self-awareness as curative, whereas Bowenian, contextual, and dynamic approaches rely heavily on it. The systemic, Bowenian, contextual, and behavioral approaches do not focus on the individual family members' unconscious processes as significant for treatment. The object relations family therapist, like all dynamic therapists, considers that working with unconscious processes is crucial. Object relations family therapists especially try to resolve collusive processes involving projective identification and splitting, so that conflict is reowned by the family members. In general, all dynamic family therapists look for derivatives, or hidden meanings in behavior and communication that may reflect transferential reactions of one family member to another or toward the therapist. (For a summary of these differences, see Table 9–1.)

GOALS IN MARITAL THERAPY

Paolino and McCrady (1978) discuss in their book the differences among various marital therapies. In many instances these differences would also hold true for family therapy. They compare psychoanalytic, Bowenian, communications, and behavioral marital therapy. One of the most significant areas they bring up is that of process and ultimate goals for treatment, as originally described by Parloff (1976). *Process goals* are defined as those steps and stages that the therapist deems necessary for the patient to go through if treatment is to be successful. The following process goals are high in all four of these forms of marital therapy, and include "(1) the specification of problems; (2) the clarification of each spouse's individual desires and needs in the marital relationship; (3) redefining the nature of the couple's difficulties; (4) encouraging of each partner's recognition of his or her mutual contribution to the marital discord; (5) the recognition and modification of communication patterns, 'rules,' and interactional patterns; (6) increasing reciprocity; and (7) decreasing the use of

Table 9–1

Comparison of Treatment Processes and
Goals of Family Therapies

	Strategic	Structural	Bowenian/ Contextual	Object Relations
Therapist–family distance	Farthest	Median	Closer	Closest
Therapist's power position	Controlling	Controlling/ Alliance	Alliance	Alliance
Use of language therapeutically	High (Semiotics)	Moderate (Activity emphasis)	High	High
Time frame	Present	Present	Past/ Present	Past/ Present
Meaning of presenting conflicts	Manifest	Manifest	Latent	Latent
Insight as curative	Irrelevant	Irrelevant	Important	Important
Unconscious factors	Irrelevant	Irrelevant	Irrelevant	Crucial
Change instituted from:	Outside	Outside	Inside	Inside
Improved intimacy of family	Low	Median	Median	High
Improved interpersonal relations (communication, problem solving)	Low	High	High	High
Reduced blaming and scapegoating	High	High	High	High
Goal	Changing system will change individual's personality.	Changing system will change individual's personality.	Change system, improve relations, foster self-differentiation.	Change system, improve relations, resolve intra-psychic conflict, foster self-differentiation.

coercion and blaming" (p. 542). Other process goals of moderate importance are "(1) increasing cooperative problem-solving (high in all, except moderate in communications); (2) the establishment of a positive working relationship between the couple and the therapist (high in psychoanalytic and moderate in others); (3) the modification of felt individual needs in the marriage (high in psychoanalytic and Bowenian and low in others); and (4) increasing each partner's ability to express his or her feelings clearly and directly, and to 'hear' his or her mate accurately (high in psychoanalytic and Bowenian, moderate to low in communications and behavioral)" (p. 542–543).

The *ultimate* goals go beyond the process and reflect the end state hoped to be achieved. These goals, according to Paolino and McCrady, are high in all four forms of marital therapy and include "(1) increased role flexibility and adaptability; (2) resolution of presenting problems and decreased symptomatology; (3) a more equitable balance of power; (4) open and clear communication; and (5) increased self-esteem" (p. 544).

CURATIVE FACTORS IN PSYCHOTHERAPY

There has been a persistent disagreement in the field of individual psychotherapy and psychoanalysis concerning the relative importance of the therapist's interventions versus the development of a therapeutic atmosphere (Slipp 1982). In individual psychotherapy, behavioral approaches reflect an extreme of the former, while the Rogerian approach is an extreme of the latter. Many classical psychoanalysts, such as Arlow (1975) and Brenner (1979), consider that any behavior of the therapist that is more than an interpretive stance is unnecessary and even detrimental to cure. Even here, what is interpreted by the analyst also varies in significance. Such analysts as Gitelson (1962), Gill (1982), and Langs (1982) consider that most of the patient's verbalizations have a veiled latent reference to the analyst, and that the only mutative (change-producing) interpretations are those that deal with the here-and-now transference to the analyst. However, other analysts such as Rosen (1955), Neiderland (1965), and Schafer (1977) consider that nontransference interpretations, referring to the patient's past or present life outside treatment, are of value as well.

There are also differing views about the importance of drive theory, object relations, oedipal and preoedipal factors, as well as self psychology, that influence how material is perceived and then interpreted. Some analysts disagree on the issue of the primary importance of interpretation. They consider that if the analyst's interpretations are to be optimally accepted and to be effective, a positive therapeutic relationship needs to be established. This has been called a *working alliance* by Greenson (1967), a *therapeutic alliance* by Zetzel (1956), and a *holding environment* by Winnicott (1965) and Modell (1976). Other analysts feel that the role of interpretation is less significant and the therapeutic relationship perhaps of greater importance. Alexander (1954) discusses the "corrective emotional experience," and Kohut (1977) the importance of the therapist's empathic connection with the patient.

Differences of opinion concerning the importance of the therapist's interventions versus the role of a therapeutic relationship exist in the field of family therapy as well. Like the classical psychoanalyst, the strategic family therapist takes an abstinent and distant position, and considers that the therapist's interventions are the most significant mutative factor. The intervention is obviously not a transference interpretation, but a paradoxical prescription to the family. The strategic family therapist does not attempt to establish a positive therapeutic relationship, considering that it might even be counterproductive as many of the families they see are highly resistant. The structural family therapist would come next. Here the therapist's control and interventions are considered paramount; however, some effort is made to facilitate the therapist's effectiveness through the development of a therapeutic alliance. Most other forms of family therapy use a more equal combination of the attempt to develop a positive working relationship and a reliance upon the therapist's interventions.

PSYCHOTHERAPY RESEARCH STUDIES

Experimental studies have been done to determine what is effective in treatment, using Silverman's laboratory procedure of subliminal psychodynamic activation (1971). A two-channel tachistoscope is used to flash subliminally the message of MOMMY

AND I ARE ONE (maternal symbiosis), accompanied by a picture of a man and a woman merged at the shoulders like Siamese twins. In controlled studies of phobic women (Silverman et al. 1974), overweight women (Martin 1975), cigarette smokers (Palmatier 1980), and alcoholics (Schurtman 1979), subliminal maternal symbiotic stimulation increased the effectiveness of the accompanying nonanalytic behavioral or counseling treatment. After their subliminal maternal symbiotic stimulation, research participants in one study (Silverman and Wolitzky 1972) were willing to be more open to express their wishes, feelings, and personal motivations. Linehan (1979) also found that college students in group therapy, exposed to this subliminal stimulation of MOMMY AND I ARE ONE, disclosed more things about themselves than did the control group. Silverman and Wolitzky (1982) compare these laboratory findings with the clinical observations of Fleming (1975) and Nacht (1964), who felt that with certain patients, a positive therapeutic atmosphere provided some degree of symbiotic gratification that improved adaptive functioning. Silverman and Wolitzky point out that studies already carried out have yielded data supporting the notion that symbiotic gratification can further the analytic process, as well as reduce symptoms.

These findings are supported by the psychotherapy research of Sampson and Weiss (1977). These researchers found that when a safe, trusting therapeutic relationship developed, personality change in the patient was most likely to occur. Relationship factors seemed to be of equal or even more importance than the therapist's interventions. The role of interpretation by the therapist was not considered to be as significant, since if a safe environment was developed, occasionally patients would even make their own interpretations. The safety of the treatment situation was believed to allow the patients to lower their defenses and to be more open about their thoughts and feelings.

THERAPEUTIC CHANGE WITHOUT A HOLDING ENVIRONMENT

The individual or family therapist's manipulation of change, even if it is "for the good of the family," does not necessarily instill trust nor develop a safe therapeutic relationship. Can change occur without the development of a trusting relationship? It can, as demonstrated by the effectiveness of strategic family therapy with certain families. Here the family's distrust and oppositionalism is harnessed in the service of change. These resistant families are very limited in their ability to develop a more equal, open, and trusting relationship. Indeed, previous therapists who had attempted to develop such an equal working relationship with them failed.

These families seem to function like a baD and a baF group that uses the defenses of splitting, and needs to idealize or demean others. If the therapist makes an effort to be friendly and accepting, he or she is demeaned. These patients have such low self-esteem that they often feel that if anyone cared about them, that person must not be any good. They have not integrated their ambivalence, and to sustain their self-esteem and/or self-integrity they need to maintain a dependent symbiotic relationship (baD) with an omnipotent, idealized parental figure, who is usually a spouse (although it may be a child in the borderline typology). Rage is split off and projected into the patient (or into the spouse in the borderline typology), who is scapegoated (baF). I would speculate that the family's need also to maintain the therapist as the idealized O+ enables the strategic family therapist to be effective. The therapist goes along with this projective identification, and satisfies the family's need for an idealized omnipotent good object (O+). The therapist's behavior of being distant and controlling also complements the family's functioning at its basic assumption level of dependency (baD). This does not threaten or disrupt the basic assumption group level of functioning that already exists between the spouses, and probably explains what strategic family therapists mean by "going along with the homeostasis."

Functioning as the good omnipotent object, the therapist is empowered to relabel the identified patient; to remove the patient from the role of scapegoat (O−), and into the role of savior (S+). According to my classification, a schizophrenic typology is replaced by a depressive typology; or similarly, working with Bion's concepts, basic assumption fight–flight (a paranoid-schizoid position) is exchanged for basic assumption pairing (a depressive position). Thus the therapist redefines the patient's role in the family as an attempt at curing the parents of their hatred and despair by behaving symptomatically. It does tend to foster perception of the patient as a separately motivated, whole object. The parents' symbiotic relationship is not disturbed; each continues to need the other to function as a good object (O+) and the therapist to function as a good object (O+) for both of them. However, no growth in the family occurs. After terminating treatment, the family members continue to use the primitive defenses of splitting and projective identification, need self-affirmation, cannot confront each other to problem-solve, and still displace their rage elsewhere. It is at this point that the therapist or others may be demeaned as the bad object (O−).

A SAFE HOLDING ENVIRONMENT WITH DISTRUSTFUL FAMILIES

For families that are less highly authoritarian and distrustful, a dynamic approach is applicable. In our own outcome research studies (Slipp and Kressel 1978, 1979), the use of a dynamic approach in therapy with Class IV families was ultimately *more successful* than a behavioral approach in the one-year follow-up. Instead of instruction by the therapist on how to resolve conflict, the dynamic approach offered these families an opportunity for experiential learning to do their own problem solving. A safe holding environment was established in the treatment situation, where the family members gradually were able to open up and to reveal their inner feelings and thoughts.

To develop trust, the therapist must be trustworthy. The therapist in dynamic family treatment tries to establish a genuine, nonmanipulative, nonexploitative relationship, in which each of the family members feels supported and understood. The dynamic family therapist contains their aggression and sets boundaries, so anger can be expressed without blaming, scapegoating, or getting out of control. However, there is no power struggle between the therapist and the family to establish a dominant–submissive relationship as in systemic approaches to the family. Attempting to establish a more egalitarian, shared working alliance serves as a model for the family to identify with and to use outside the sessions themselves. This equalization of power makes their own negotiating of conflict easier. Eliminating the power struggle between the omnipotent controlling person and the underprivileged persecuted one helps to integrate ambivalence. It undermines the need to use splitting and projective identification of idealized and scapegoated roles onto others.

In treatment, the family members experience the relationship with the therapist as providing a safe holding environment. Thus, they are more trusting and more willing to lower their defensiveness, to open up and share their inner secrets and feelings with one another. Hopefully this process will carry over into their everyday life outside of treatment, since therapy has provided them with a corrective experience and taught them to provide a safe holding environment for each other.

INTEGRATING SYSTEMIC AND DYNAMIC FAMILY THERAPY APPROACHES

How can the family therapist employ a systemic perspective with an object relations approach, so that they are not mutually contradictory in their methods or goals? The insights of the systemic perspective concerning circular feedback loops, both positive and negative, are extremely valuable. In many instances, one cannot even start to proceed with family treatment unless the therapist helps the family deal with these reverberating systems of interaction that lock in psychopathology. However, the process of treatment used by the systemic family therapist is contradictory and disruptive to the permissive therapeutic stance of the object relations family therapist. Both strategic and structural family therapists take a position of control and assume that change is due primarily to the therapist's directives.

Whereas the structural family therapist attempts to bring the family up to a work group level, the strategic family therapist does not attempt to develop a therapeutic alliance and apparently remains with the family at a basic assumption group level. For the object relations therapist to assume such a controlling position would go against the development of a trusting therapeutic alliance, which is basic to this approach. The object relations family therapist does not use the power of his or her knowledge concerning systems to exert control, but uses leadership in a more democratic group fashion by sharing with family members this expertise that clarifies their interaction.

How does the object relations family therapist work with the negative feedback that establishes restrictive family rules? The therapist can point out and clarify how the members' shared unconscious fantasy or collusion serves to limit their interaction. For example, the therapist might say, "I've noticed that there appears to be an unspoken rule in this family that the expression of angry feelings will be damaging to family members and lead to rejection or loss. Yet this very rule itself can lead to problems, since it restricts the freedom of what people can feel or say to one another. The rule interferes with the discussion of differences that could lead to their resolution, and seems to contribute instead to the building up of more and more tension." This intervention brings the shared, unconscious, omnipotent destructive fantasy out into the conscious arena for discussion, as well as attempting to integrate the family's primitive defense of splitting—in other words, enabling the individual members to integrate both angry and loving feelings at the same time. The family and the therapist can then join in a collaborative effort to work through this unconscious fantasy, so that each member can resolve conflict without idealizing one person and scapegoating another.

How can one work with positive feedback cycles in object relations family therapy? These positive feedback cycles do not simply arise out of erroneous attempts at problem solving, but the erroneous attempts result as a *consequence* of the defensive operations of the family members. The positive feedback cycle is the first obstacle that must be changed, whereas the defensive structures of the family members is the second and deeper one. To surmount this first obstacle, the object relations family therapist would again point out and clarify the process that develops the vicious cycles of positive feedback. The therapist needs to interpret how the family's problems become escalated by the way each member deals with the other. Each family member has a profound effect upon the others though actions and words. The old saying "Sticks and stones may break my bones, but words will never harm me" is incorrect. Words can inflict deep and permanent wounds in another's psyche. One need not repress conflict out of fear of the destructive consequences, but there is a middle ground where individuals are realistically responsible for their impact on one another.

The therapist can point out how A's reaction and communication in a situation is reacted to by B. B in turn responds defensively, which has an effect on A. A then reacts defensively, and so on, resulting in a vicious cycle of escalating conflict. For example, a wife may be angry at her husband, who she feels is too authoritarian. Her way of expressing her anger is to withhold sex. The husband may resent this, and, to show his wife he will not give in to her manipulation, may have an affair. When the wife finds out about the affair, which the husband may facilitate by leaving around clues, she responds with further anger and withholding. Each spouse reacts to the other behaviorally, as if being punitive will change the other. By the therapist's pointing out to them the vicious cycle of escalating conflict that becomes established as each reacts to the other, the process of blame is diminished. Instead of being acted out defensively through self-destructive behavior, the conflict is brought out into the verbal sphere. Rather than reacting passively and feeling victimized, or engaging in a power struggle, each member can take a more responsible and constructive part in the resolution of the conflict. Through discussion of how each feels in the situation, the other has an opportunity to respond. Both may then modify their own behavior or make certain concessions that reduce, not escalate, the conflict.

10

Evaluating the Family for Treatment

Except for the extremely oppositional family, for whom treatment has failed previously, and for the disorganized poor (Class V) family, for whom a strategic and a structural approach respectively seem more suitable, object relations family therapy is widely applicable. It is suitable for both a blue-collar and a middle-class population, as well as for families ranging from those who are essentially normal or mildly disturbed to those in which a member is suffering from a psychotic illness. In order to develop our treatment plan, we need first to evaluate the members of the family.

THE FIRST SESSION

Let us start by going step by step through the process of evaluating a family, with an identified patient, referred to us for family therapy. After a few general pleasantries, we attempt to establish rapport with each family member. We introduce ourselves and, to foster more total and equal participation, we can ask all of the family members to introduce themselves. After acknowledging the members' anxiety, and giving them an opportunity to express these feelings and to be as comfortable as possible, we begin by finding out why they came for help. Even though we may have been given a synopsis of their presenting problem by the referring source, it is important to hear how they express it in their own words. This will help us understand how they perceive their situation. Is the focus solely on the identified patient, who is seen as the cause of all the family's difficulties? Do the parents blame each other for their youngster's problems? Do they feel that there has been a breakdown in communication, which involves mutual responsibility, and that an impartial third party may be helpful in resolving any misunderstanding? The very way the family presents their complaint will give us some information regarding the degree of projection, of blaming, and of motivation to work together and to share responsibility for change.

We next find out what they have done themselves to remedy this problem. When did it begin, how did it come to their attention, how did it affect other family members, and what did they do to resolve matters? Did they seek help from other therapists, and drop out each time after a few sessions? Did they become punitive toward one of the youngsters, and consider him or her bad? Did they try to sit down and discuss, in an understanding and helpful fashion, what might be bothering the identified patient? How did the patient respond to their efforts? Was the patient defensive, withdrawn, and not responsive to the family's efforts to be helpful? Did he or she resent their questioning as an intrusion? Was the patient able to reveal openly what was bothering him or her? Their answers will give us some indication of how resistant or motivated the family is to working out their problems in a psychotherapeutic setting.

Then we can explore what they hope to gain from this treatment. Is it confirmation that the spouse is to blame for all the problems, or that the child is impossible and should be sent to a military school or mental hospital? Or do they genuinely wish to work together, with the therapist's help, to resolve difficulties that exist between them? Some of these expectations of therapy may be implicit, and one may need to read between the lines. However, one can obtain some inkling of how rigid, defensive, and resistant to open communication the family might be. On the other hand, one can estimate also how flexible and nondefensive they are, and how willing to share responsibility in an open dialogue.

DIAGNOSING THE PATIENT AND THE FAMILY

Next, we need to make a tentative diagnosis of both the individual identified patient as well as of the family. Here a developmental history of both the patient and the family is helpful. A genogram is useful in noting the connection of traumatic incidents during the family's life cycle that may have affected the patient. For example, did the mother's father die shortly after the birth of this child, so that she was in mourning and unresponsive to the developmental needs of her infant? What are the cultural backgrounds and personality characteristics of the grandparents? Was the sex of the child accepted or a problem for either parent? What is the sibling position of the identified patient, and how many years were there between births? The sibling position of the patient is often associated with certain personality characteristics, particularly that of the oldest, middle, and youngest child (Toman 1961). Often the oldest child is the most responsible, while the youngest may be overindulged and infantilized. Traumatic incidents, such as illnesses, deaths, separations, divorces, and so on, are recorded. Thus we get a clear picture of the events shaping the personalities in this family.

A formal diagnosis may be made of the individual patient, based on the symptomatology using DSM III. The family typology is what I use for a family diagnosis. I look for the specific forms of family interaction associated with the four role patterns described in Chapter 5. Is the child assigned the role of the *scapegoat,* as in schizophrenia; the *go-between,* as in hysterical/ borderline conditions; the *savior,* as in depressive states; or the *avenger,* as in the case of the overinvolved delinquent? In the types of family interactions found in schizophrenia and in borderline conditions, there are shared, unconscious basic assumptions— based on fight–flight and dependency. Anger is experienced as destructive to relationships and needs to be split off and projected into a "bad" person so as to preserve the "good" object. In families having a depressive or overinvolved delinquent pattern, there is a shared, unconscious basic assumption of pairing, in that the child through its social performance, either in accordance with or against society, will save the parents from their hatred and despair. One has to keep in mind the following questions: Is the patient preserving the family homeostasis and the parents' self-esteem by being symptomatic? In turn, does the family system of interaction require that the patient remain in this sick role to preserve the family, and its members' personality integrity?

EVALUATING FAMILY CONSTANCY

How do we evaluate *family constancy*? In other words, to what degree is the patient free from having to assume responsibility for the maintenance of the self-esteem and self-cohesion of the parents' personality? One needs to assess the level of the parents' self-differentiation; that is, whether the parents have good self-esteem and a strong autonomous identity, are not excessively narcissistically vulnerable, and do not need constant confirmation by others to maintain integration of their personalities.

One way of assessing the strength of the parents' identity is to understand how they manage conflict. Normally, the parents are not simply self-centered; they are aware of others' needs and motivations and are willing to accommodate to them. In a healthy family the parents can maintain their loving attachment despite conflict, so members feel free to disagree openly and are also able to ask for what they want directly. These are all signs of fairly differentiated and secure individuals. On the other hand, more narcissistically vulnerable individuals may evidence splitting and the need to control and deny the separateness of others. If there is a disagreement, does one of the parents see the other as bad, and then provoke guilt or engage in a personal attack on that spouse to bully or threaten him or her into submission? Are one or both of the parents experienced as narcissistically vulnerable, so that others in the family need to constrict or inhibit themselves in a hidden or unconscious collusion to protect that member's self-esteem or integration? For example, there may even be a conscious family myth that if one expresses anger and gets a parent upset, the parent will become physically or mentally ill, die, or abandon the family. If this is the case, divergent opinions and aggression are not expressed openly, and language may be used for defensive purposes to cover up potential conflict.

Other ways of masking divergent feelings and thoughts are to disqualify them. If a child expresses hurt and anger about an occurrence, a parent might say, "Oh, you are too sensitive and thin-skinned; that shouldn't bother you." In submitting to this disqualification, the child comes to feel that he or she is not entitled to have these separate and unacceptable feelings. In other families the parents are involved in continuous conflict, with each inflicting severe narcissistic wounds on the other through personal attacks, particularly on the other's weak spots. Then the children may be caught in efforts to mediate and patch up the conflict between their parents. We also need to know what the conflict stems from. Does it come from their efforts at mutual control and exploitation of each other, from the lack of genuine intimacy and communication, or from dissatisfaction with their socioeconomic status? Does the wife feel unimportant, since her husband earns little, particularly when her sister has married such a rich husband?

STRUCTURAL DIAGNOSIS

Minuchin's (1974) structural family diagnosis is useful in delineating the boundaries between individuals, subsystems, and the family as a whole. Is the power hierarchy in the subsystems appropriate? For example, are the the parents' working together as a team having authority over the sibling subsystem? Is there a transgenerational coalition between one parent and a child against the other parent? Is the parental subsystem too tight, so as to exclude the children from nurturance? Is one child excluded from the sibling subsystem? Are the individual members too distant or too symbiotically merged (enmeshed)? Is the boundary around the entire family too rigid and encompassing, so that outside support networks are lacking? When the family becomes socially cut off and resembles a closed system, it establishes what Wynne and colleagues (1958) termed a *rubber fence*. This makes it more difficult for children to break away and separate. In other families, the family boundary may be too open. Towne and colleagues (1962), for example, found that married female schizophrenic patients might remain so attached to their families of origin that the parental coalition and authority structure of the women's marital families was undermined by their own parents.

With a family boundary that is too open, such as this, grandparents or other family members may become too intrusive and create conflict between the spouses.

NONVERBAL CLUES

Another way of observing individual and family functioning is to observe the members directly as they speak and engage in nonverbal behavior. Often the first person coming into the office, or the one who speaks first, is the most dominant family member. This person may take the most comfortable chair, and either sits directly opposite the therapist, or at the extreme side of the family, like a bookend. Spatial seating arrangements also offer clues to alliances, triangles, and subgroup formations. Who sits physically closer, or further away, from whom also reflects emotional closeness or distance. If a child is scapegoated, that child will usually sit peripherally to the family, often with head lowered or eyes averted. If a child functions as a go-between, he or she will usually sit between the parents and may even function as a conduit for communication between them.

In addition, the family members' grooming and dress may reveal additional evidence concerning self-esteem and personality functioning. A person having low self-esteem usually dresses poorly or sloppily. On the other hand, the same type of person may attempt to overcompensate by considerable attention to superficial appearances or dress. A child who is infantilized by a family is usually dressed too young for his or her age. The reverse is also true; if the child is parentified, he or she dresses in a manner too old for his or her age, and behaves or even speaks that way.

Scheflen (1963, 1964) found in his family therapy research that certain nonverbal (kinesic) signals occurred in families that served to regulate intimacy as well as the direction and speed of interaction. These included quasi-courtship behavior (grooming), parallel postures, leg blocking, and gaze holding or aversion. Scheflen noted that, to indicate disapproval, certain *monitoring* signals such as nose-wiping and brushing-off hand movements were used when there was deviation from the family's rules for behavior. If videotape equipment is available, the therapist can review the session afterward for nonverbal clues. Some analytic family therapists, such as Alger and Hogan (1969) and Berger (1978), use videotape playback with the family as a therapeutic procedure to explore the discrepancies between nonverbal and verbal communication.

VERBAL CLUES

Careful listening to verbal interaction also provides one with valuable information. Do the family members listen to one another and respect what is said? Do they look at each other attentively, and respond appropriately? These are good signs that they are able to use language for conflict resolution, and that they respect each other's individuality. On the other hand, there may be what Wynne and Singer (1977) term *communication deviance*. In such cases communication becomes obfuscated and stripped of its meaning by the lack of a shared focus of attention. What is said has a vagueness about it, and there are sudden shifts of topics that throw one off. Is there intrusive behavior, with one family member showing lack of respect for the others' individual boundaries by speaking for them or telling them how they feel or think? For example, a mother may tell her child, "You are sleepy and should go to bed." She may say this just because the child is fully awake and actively climbing the walls, which invalidates the child's real feelings.

Are the family members so acutely tuned in to each other that they almost do not have to speak, but seem to read each other's mind? Do members use the pronoun *we* to deny individual differences? Do they always use the pronoun *you* to generalize, to distance themselves from responsibility, project blame, or deny their own individuality? Here, the therapist may suggest the use of *I* language instead of *you* language to help the process of differentiation.

PRECIPITATING STRESSES

At this point I investigate the precipitating stress that seemed to bring out the patient's symptomatology. Usually stresses occur at transitional points in the family life cycle. At the beginning of the parents' marriage a marital contract is formulated, which can be openly verbalized, may be nonspoken but conscious, or may even be entirely unconscious. Sager (1976) describes this "marital contract" as what each partner is willing to give, and what each expects in return. For example, I recently worked with a couple whose marital contract was that each would save the other from despair and make the other happy. Each would function as a savior (S+) for the other. To fulfill such a marital contract each couple then develops an interactional script or some family rules regarding how to fulfill its covenants. The contract of making each other fulfilled and happy is doomed to failure, since one individual is not able to fulfill another totally.

Thus some contracts are unreasonable, or they may be incapable of being continued because of intervening circumstances. The interactional script may become disrupted by the birth of children, the stresses of work, health, or loss of family members. Paradoxically, the marital contract may even be broken by the return to health of a sick family member or the personality growth of one of the marital partners. For example, a newly liberated woman may revolt against being the traditional home-oriented wife who selflessly supports her husband, insures him against loneliness, and takes a submissive role. She may now assert her own needs, go back to college, and pursue her own independent career, thus disrupting the original marital contract that had been made.

POSITIVE ASPECTS

I also evaluate the positive aspects of the family. These include the loving and caring feelings amongst the family members. I explore whether or not there is firm family cohesion and support that also allows the members to have independent identities. One can investigate to what degree members acknowledge and validate each other's achievements and are genuinely involved in each other's lives, and the extent of warmth, comfort, and nurturance they provide each other.

BEGINNING TREATMENT WITH A MODERN CAIN AND ABEL

The following case illustrates how these evaluative procedures may be specifically applied at the beginning of therapy.

A young, upwardly mobile, middle-class family, consisting of the husband Joe, the wife Jenny, and two adolescent sons—Cain, 15, and Abel, 13—were referred because of the older son's repeated episodes of running away from home and being a disciplinary problem. After introducing myself and establishing rapport, I asked the family members to introduce themselves. This set the framework of the treatment, establishing the fact that each family member was important and would have an equal chance to talk and be listened to carefully. I then asked how I could be of help to the family. The father began by stating the problem was their son Cain's inability to accept discipline. "Cain is so rebellious that my wife and I cannot control him, and this is placing great stress on the entire family. Cain will not clean up his room, he is messy about the house, refuses to obey curfew, fights with his brother, and sasses his mother."

Here the father focused the blame on the older son, Cain, for all the family difficulties. Cain seemed to be assigned the role of family scapegoat.

The mother then spoke up and said that their younger son, Abel, was respectful and responsible. He was no trouble at all, but she had great difficulty with Cain who did not respect her and constantly challenged her authority. When the boys were asked how they saw the problem, the younger son, Abel, said, "Cain is trying to break up our home by causing all this trouble." When I inquired of Abel what he meant, the father interrupted and answered for him. Joe stated, "I have to choose between my wife and my son, and I need to back up my wife. Then Cain feels that I don't care about him when I don't support his side, and he gets angry, sulks, or runs away." When the older son, Cain, was asked how he experienced the problem, he said, "Mom prefers my younger brother to me. Even though Abel and I both have messy rooms, she only comes down on me, not on my brother."

Thus I noted that Cain did have the ability to be open about his thoughts and feelings, to disagree, and even to defend himself with a concrete example. He had not simply accepted the role assignment of scapegoat, but he had sufficient sense of himself to fight back. What crossed my mind at the moment was the question of why the father needed to put himself into such a position as having to choose between his wife and his son. Why did he need simply to support his wife, instead of attempting to negotiate and calm the situation between them? Was the wife narcissistically vulnerable? Was Cain acting out anger for his father? Moreover, the father did not acknowledge Cain's statement that the mother showed preferential treatment toward Abel. There seemed to be the use of the defenses of splitting and projective identification with one son being viewed as all good and the other as all bad. The family did not seem to acknowledge that other family members besides the identified patient had any responsibility for his behavior problem. Their approach to handling Cain was to see him as bad and to punish him by further restrictions. This in turn was a further insult to the self-esteem of Cain, which made him even more rebellious and increased his acting-out behavior. A vicious cycle (involving positive feedback loops) had been established that escalated the conflict.

This was the family's first attempt at seeking professional help. They had mentioned the behavior problem they had with Cain to their family physician, who had referred them to me. I questioned the family as a group about what they hoped to gain from treatment. The father, who was the family spokesman, wanted me to fix up their son Cain to be more obedient. The mother said that if Cain were more obedient and more like Abel, she would like him just as much. Cain was labeled a difficult child. Abel had nothing to say, and Cain repeated his perception of the problem that his mother's preference of Abel had contributed to his disobedience. He reiterated that he was not that much worse than Abel, and that even if he were as obedient as his brother, his mother would still prefer Abel. I remarked that the problem was perceived differently in the family, and that this was a good starting point for discussion.

Neither parent seemed to acknowledge Cain's perception of the problem or his feelings of rejection by the mother. In fact, Cain's comments were met with disconfirmation by the mother. On superficial inspection, then, this family appeared to be highly defended and judgmental, holding rigid views and lacking in real dialogue. The parents seemed unsympathetic to Cain's views, and to deny any of their own responsibilities even when confronted by Cain. Even though Cain's comments were not confirmed, he did have the strength to speak up for himself and to fight role induction as the family scapegoat.

Diagnostically, the identified patient seemed to be suffering a moderate adjustment reaction manifested by a behavioral problem. How would the family fit into the typology? Most obviously, Cain had been induced into the role of *scapegoat;* and possibly the other, more subtle role inducement was Cain as the father's *avenger.* It was unclear what Abel's role was, but it appeared to be that of *go-between.*

I obtained a history of the family, which included developmental information on both sons. The father came from a family in which his siblings were super-achievers, and he had had difficulty in competing with them. He felt that in his family of origin, his father preferred his sister, and his mother preferred his brother. When he was a young man, Joe had remained a loner; he did not have much confidence in his ability to attract women, fearing that all women would, like his mother, prefer other males and reject him.

I commented that Joe must be able to understand how angry Cain feels, since he also experienced his mother as preferring his brother. (This was an effort to probe into whether Joe might connect that his own anger at his mother was being put, via projective identification, into Cain, who was expressing it toward his own mother, Joe's wife.) Joe did not pick up on this comment. He said he had been attracted to Jenny because she was outgoing and attractive. Jenny said, laughing, "I almost had to seduce him, he was so shy with women." After the marriage, Joe was possessive and remained jealous of other men.

In Jenny's family of origin, she had been her father's favorite up until the birth of her younger brother, whom the father then favored. She admitted to then feeling rejected by her father. However, as she developed into a beautiful woman, she felt she could compensate for the rejection by being attractive to men.

The births and early development of both Cain and Abel were uneventful and normal.

Joe's insecurity is more evident, but Jenny is also insecure even though she is able to present a better facade. Both of them are narcissistically vulnerable and have deep concerns about their lovableness and self-worth. They each seem to need to maintain an idealized relationship with the spouse as an O+, to avoid the possibility of marital conflict going out of control and destroying the marriage. This would then be experienced again by each as a parental rejection, and be the repetition of a severe narcissistic wound. The result was an unconscious collusion between both spouses to deny their aggression and displace it onto Cain, who would function as a scapegoat. Cain would be the bad one (O−), and Joe would defend Jenny as the good one (O+), which is an expression of the defense of splitting. In terms of shared, unconscious basic assumptions, it would be baF and baD. The family was consciously aware of the possibility of a dissolution of the marriage, but this was blamed on Cain.

In the seating arrangements in the office, Cain sat apart from the family. However, he was not downcast or defeated, but looked to the therapist for support, sitting closer to me. Abel sat between his parents, which is usually the position of the go-between who attempts to hold a marriage together. On being questioned about where he went on the nights that he ran away, Cain admitted going over to his paternal grandmother's house. His grandmother was someone he could talk to, because she was empathic and understanding. Since he experienced his grandmother as nurturant and not rejecting, there were no disciplinary problems with her.

This support from his grandmother would account for Cain's strong sense of himself and capacity to resist assuming the role of family scapegoat, despite the parents' disqualifications of his thoughts and feelings. It also explained why he looked to the therapist for support. Cain had seen me in terms of a grandmother transference, as someone who would also be fair and understanding.

The development of a structural diagnosis of this family indicated that the parental coalition and the power hierarchy were apparently intact. There was a transgenerational coalition between the mother and Abel. Some of her behavior toward Abel seemed somewhat seductive. The sibling subsystem had been disrupted, and Cain was left alone. The boundary around the entire family, however, seemed open. There were fairly good relations with relatives and grandparents.

Based on the description of the beginning of the marriage, when Joe's insecurity had caused him to be distrustful and possessive, one could be alerted to a great potential for marital conflict. However, this was denied during the initial evaluation. I would not expect such a highly defended family to reveal their secrets during the early phases of treatment until there was sufficient trust established. There was evidence of one kind of intrusive behavior by the father, who interrupted and spoke for Abel. One got the impression here that Abel was parroting the words of his father about Cain breaking up the marriage, so that the father may simply have spoken up since they were his sentiments anyway.

To an inquiry about the precipitating stress, none was offered by the family except for the fact that Cain's behavior had become gradually worse over the past year. The marital contract would probably read like this: "I, Joe, promise to make you, Jenny, feel more adequate about yourself as a woman; and I, Jenny, promise to make you, Joe, feel more adequate about yourself as a man." Jenny's picking Joe as a suitable mate was flattering to him, since she was so attractive. It compensated for his feeling of not being preferred and special to his mother. Joe's support for Jenny in preference to their son reinforced her feeling of worth over a male, especially since her father had preferred her brother. The interactional script probably was that each would not say anything critical or rejecting of the other, but would be mutually supportive to sustain an idealized relationship. However, there appeared to be an underlying conflict. The cohesion and stability of the marriage seemed shaky, but this was blamed on Cain's angry behavior.

The first session ended with my making some general nonthreatening comments that did not side either with the parents or with Cain in this dispute. I said that individuals in a family always deeply affect one another, and that we would work together to try to help alleviate the discomfort experienced by all of them, each in his or her own way. I then asked the parents and Cain if I could interview the paternal grandmother, since she seemed to be an important individual in this situation. They agreed to this procedure, and I arranged to interview her.

The paternal grandmother was found to be sincerely concerned about her grandchild, Cain. She was happy that he had turned to her, and that she was emotionally available to him. She confirmed his statement that she had no disciplinary problems with the boy; he was obedient and respectful with her. She also confirmed my suspicions that there did exist considerable underlying conflict in her son's marriage. Joe had been insecure about his wife's fidelity during the early phases of the marriage, and had suspected that she had had an affair. Whether this was the case or not, Jenny provoked Joe's jealousy by being flirtatious with other men in his presence. Jenny, because of her rejection by her father, felt unlovable, and needed constant validation of her desirability and attractiveness from her husband and from other men as well. The flirting in front of her husband probably was also an expression of her rage at her father for preferring her brother and rejecting her, rage which was displaced onto her husband. In response to Jenny's flirtatiousness, Joe had become a workaholic, withdrawing into his job and frequently going off on business trips, leaving Jenny alone a good deal of the time. Jenny thus turned to Abel, in a seductive fashion, and became overly involved with him. She displaced her rage at her husband for being away, which she experienced as abandonment (as with her father), by being punitive in disciplining Cain. She was unable to confront Joe directly, since she needed his confirmation in the role of a good father figure (O+) to sustain her low self-esteem. The grandmother informed me that Jenny had started drinking alone; she worried that Jenny could become an alcoholic and said that Joe was aware of her drinking, and had spoken to her privately about divorcing Jenny.

However, he had decided against this because Abel seemed so attached to his mother. A divorce might be too devastating to Abel.

Here I speculated that for Joe, Abel represented his own idealized self (S+) by being what he would have liked to have been, his mother's favorite. Joe projected his own feelings of devastation into Abel, in contemplating a divorce, and felt too guilty to be the one to disrupt this idealized relationship. Cain, on the other hand, in not being his mother's favorite, represented what Joe had actually been. Cain represented that part of himself that Joe disliked, his rejected, angry, lonely bad self (S−). Thus Joe, instead of feeling depressed and unworthy himself, externalized this intrapsychic conflict and was critical of Cain. Cain was therefore seen as the angry, destructive, bad son; and Joe, by not interfering with Jenny's punitive behavior toward Cain, had joined her in an unconscious collusion to scapegoat their elder son.

Joe was unable to deal directly with his own anger at Jenny's flirtatiousness and possible infidelity because of his own narcissistic vulnerability. He feared that if he expressed his anger, it would destroy Jenny's love for him, and she would reject him. Unconsciously, this represented again being rejected by his mother and feeling worthless. Joe needed to defend against this at all costs, since his self-esteem needed to be constantly confirmed by Jenny, who represented transferentially the good mother (O+). Thus Joe unconsciously induced Cain, through projective identification, into expressing his own angry self (S−) at Jenny. Then Joe could avoid responsibility for his anger even though it had been expressed, and could blame Cain for being such a difficult and destructive person who threatened the marriage. Joe could thus have his cake and eat it too. He could vicariously have his aggression expressed at Jenny for preferring other men by having Cain serve as his avenger, yet also come to her support against their son Cain, and so make her feel special.

Joe could thereby express through Cain his own angry feelings at his wife, and at his mother for being the rejecting bad object; and he could punish Cain directly and through Jenny for being his bad self (taking the side of his own superego). By siding with Jenny against Cain, Joe remained in the role of her validating good father, thereby safeguarding her self-esteem. In exchange Jenny remained the idealized good mother for Joe, thereby protecting his own self-esteem.

Even though Joe turned this intrapsychic conflict into an interpersonal one, this did not address the basic problems with Jenny nor with his earlier difficulty in feeling rejected by his mother. Jenny's seductive overinvolvement with Abel, and his functioning in the role of *go-between,* were not helpful to Abel's needs for growth nor did they address her problems with Joe. Both the parents and the two sons were caught up in a web of defensiveness that prevented their working out their problems. The marriage was being kept together but at great cost to all the family members.

In this difficult case, our goals would be to get Cain out of the roles of avenger and scapegoat as well as Abel out of his role as go-between. By the therapist providing a safe holding environment and eventually interpreting the parents' need to use splitting and projective identification, the family system that requires the boys to hold the marriage together may be changed. Then the couple could admit to their marital conflict, and give up the denial of their problems and acting them out through their children. They could then communicate directly and attempt to work out and resolve the problems in the marriage. The competition between the sons should diminish as they become disentangled from their parents' problems, and they could hopefully establish a supportive sibling subsystem.

Overlapping and following the work on these interpersonal issues, both spouses will also have an opportunity to work through individually the source of their low self-esteem, stemming from the rejection by the parent of the opposite sex in their families of origin. In the next chapter, we trace more closely this process of treatment in family therapy.

IV

Object Relations Techniques in Family Therapy

11

Interventions During Phases of Object Relations Family Therapy

THERAPEUTIC CHANGE

There are various levels of change that one may hope to accomplish in any form of psychotherapy. There is the level of symptom removal, the level of improvement in interpersonal relations, and the level of deeper structural changes in the individual personality. In individual therapy, these can be observed respectively in behavioral therapy, interpersonal approaches, and psychoanalytic psychotherapy. Each modality is suited for a specific purpose, and may not be most appropriate for certain other types of problems. At times, combinations of these approaches in individual therapy are most effective, as with a patient who, while in dynamic therapy, has behavioral therapy as well to deal with a specific phobia. Another combination might be with someone in individual dynamic therapy, who has explored intrapsychic conflicts and now is ready to try to change the way he or she relates to others. Here, combining individual with group therapy, in order to explore new ways to deal with interpersonal issues, is often most effective.

When it comes to family therapy, drawing from the best of each of the three approaches is most effective in bringing about change. By first working on the systemic level in the beginning phase of treatment, the therapist may break up the defensive interaction that blocks any further progress. In the middle phase of treatment one can address the interpersonal issues, so that conflict is reowned; and finally, in the last phase, individual issues are dealt with that are now intrapsychic. This order of the phases of treatment is the reverse of their historical evolution, as described in Chapter 1 on the three revolutions in psychotherapy.

THE SYSTEMIC LEVEL IN THE BEGINNING PHASE OF TREATMENT

In the example of Joe and Jenny's family, a strategic therapist might shake up the system drastically by prescribing a "paradoxical" intervention to diminish the symptomatology. The strategic therapist might instruct Abel to get closer to his mother, perhaps even to climb on her lap and hug her, thereby accentuating one aspect of the symptomatology. As for Cain, the therapist might suggest that he isn't really angry enough, and that maybe he should become even more angry, more often.

The paradoxical prescription might also reframe each of these moves so that Abel is perceived as showing how much he loves his mother, and Cain's rebellious acting up as helping to bring the family together. A positive change in the boys' behaviors may very well result because the paradoxical prescription breaks up the process of projective identification that induces these behaviors. It reveals the seductive interaction between Abel and his mother, which is embarrassing for a teenager, by presenting him as being infantilized by her, a "mama's boy." This is indeed what is happening, as generational boundaries are being breached and Abel is unable to resolve his Oedipus complex in order to separate and individuate. The paradoxical prescription with Cain takes him out of the scapegoated role, but ignores the manipulative and controlling aspect of the family's relations. The prescription interferes with Cain's being his father's avenger, but it provides no underlying understanding. The father needs to provoke Cain into acting out his—the father's—own unacceptable angry feelings toward his wife and mother. Then he can blame and punish Cain for being bad without assuming responsibility for his own anger and guilt. If Cain should be presented as being good, the father could not ally himself with his internalized superego objects, nor use a manic defense and take out his aggression on Cain. Also, the prescription undermines the shared unconscious fantasy that aggression would be destructive to the cohesion of the family. The intervention states the opposite, that aggression is good and helps maintain the family's cohesion. This provides an altruistic motive for Cain. It also facilitates the integration of ambivalence, so that aggression need not be split off and projected into Cain.

On a higher level of theoretical abstraction, this intervention may exaggerate the symptomatology of the boys to the point that the stabilizing forces in the family may become activated to restore homeostasis. However, even though these paradoxical interventions may work, neither the family nor even the therapist understands why it is effective. They are at a dead end, and it is a mystery to all concerned. In addition, there may have been so much resentment generated toward the therapist's intrusive, manipulative role, that even though the symptom was cured, the family would not continue in treatment. Unresolved interpersonal conflict would remain, and, at an individual level, intrapsychic issues would continue to bleed the parents of their self-esteem. All this may then be dumped into the therapist temporarily, until the family finds another object to scapegoat—perhaps this time Abel.

Object relations family therapy attempts to deepen the self-awareness of each of the family members by analyzing their unconscious internalized object relations and verbally interpreting the genesis of their behavior. It does not remain at an action-oriented level as in systems therapy, but links current behavior to past interpersonal occurrences in the marriage, as well as past individual relations from each parent's family of origin.

How is object relations family therapy then different from systemic family therapy, when it also makes a systemic intervention? First of all, like all dynamic therapies, object relations family therapy recognizes that there is an unconscious, in which drives, fantasies, and thoughts exist out of conscious awareness. It recognizes that individuals use a variety of defenses to avoid anxiety and danger so as to protect their self-esteem and integrity.

It acknowledges that repressed past relations are replayed in the present, with those currently around us—in other words, that transferences are developed that shape how one perceives and reacts to others based on one's past experiences.

The defenses and transferences form circular feedback systems to sustain repressed past experiences in the unconscious. Object relations family therapy sees the circular system that evolves between people in the family as an outgrowth of these elements, particularly the defensive interaction between people. It does not see the system as inexplicably coming into existence through spontaneous generation, nor disappearing at the stroke of one single intervention. The system evolves out of the parents' individual circular feedback systems, composed of defenses and expressed in transferences. With sicker parents, there is also an attempt to mold each other's personality response through projective identification.

Instead of using the knowledge about the system to control and manipulate it like the systemic therapist does, even if it is for the family members' benefit, the object relations family therapist uses verbal interpretation to share this knowledge with them. The circular system of interaction that reverberates between the family members can be directly pointed out, and the system can be linked to their efforts to resolve a problem as well as to their defensive need to protect their self-esteem. The same goals of diminishing blame and emphasizing positive aspects that are important in strategic interventions can be employed without a controlling approach.

Interpreting the reverberating system of interaction is usually not done until there is sufficient trust developed, so that the members will listen carefully and not simply feel criticized. The therapist does not judge or blame, but objectively points out the way individuals bounce off one another (positive feedback), or how they protectively restrict their interaction because of a family myth (negative feedback). To facilitate the development of trust, the therapist must provide a safe holding environment. The therapist needs to be genuinely concerned about what each of the family members feel and think, and be empathic for each of their experiences in the situation. It is important that the therapist not take sides, but be a participant-observer who is empathic, calm, and objective, and who can contain anxiety and conflict. The family members need to know that the therapist has no ulterior motive to control or manipulate them for his or her own gratification, not even for their own good. Even a benevolent despot infringes on one's autonomy.

With the establishment of a trusting relationship, a therapeutic alliance is formed between the therapist and the reasonable, observing ego of each of the family members. Not only does the therapist point out the interaction that reverberates back and forth between family members, but in order to eliminate blaming, a reason or meaning is inferred for this circular system. This makes the delineation of the system more understandable to the family, and (1) defines how it began, (2) what was hoped to be gained or avoided by it, and (3) describes its effects on the family members.

In the example of Joe and Jenny and their two sons, the therapist might point out the interaction involving splitting, even if only superficially by saying, "Your labeling Cain as bad and punishing him was the way you felt would correct the situation. You hoped that Cain would then become good. Yet you, Cain, were already feeling misunderstood and alone, and the punishment unfortunately resulted in your feeling alienated all the more. Instead of diminishing the conflict as you, Joe and Jenny, hoped, it only added more fuel to the fire, since it only made Cain feel less important, and more alone. This in turn contributed to an increase in Cain's rebelliousness, which was his way of coping with the situation. In turn you both redoubled your efforts to get Cain into line to be good through more punishment, which unfortunately only created a spiraling level of escalating conflict. Clearly, you as parents and son were not able to connect with each other even though you tried what you felt was best." This clarification of the systemic circular interaction, though remaining at a behavioral level, does sensitize the family members to the effects they have on one another. It does not address the deeper interpersonal and intrapsychic levels, and the parents' need to dump anger into Cain through projective identification.

THE INTERPERSONAL LEVEL IN THE MIDDLE PHASE OF TREATMENT

One technique useful in working with a family to understand interpersonal issues is to be acutely sensitive to one's own counter transference reactions, both to the family as a whole as well as to each of the individual members. The therapist has certain feelings, thoughts, or behavior, which are not characteristic of his or her usual manner, or which breach the frame of treatment. These may serve as a signal to a possible countertransference reaction that is outside the therapist's conscious awareness. The therapist needs to evaluate them carefully to find out whether they are due to a subjective countertransference, stemming from unresolved issues in one's own past. If they appear to be objective countertransference responses, they were induced through the very same process as that of role induction in the family — that is, through projective identification. If this is the case, the therapist needs to contain these feelings, understand where they are coming from, and then weave them into an interpretation of the projective identification that is presented to the family.

The objective countertransference experienced by the therapist represents an externalization of either the good or the bad self or object image of one or more of the family members. For example, the therapist may represent an internalized parental figure, and be experienced transferentially as one of the family members' parents. On the other hand, the member may identify with this internalized parental figure in his or her superego, and do to the therapist what the parent was perceived as having done to him or her. (This may be actually what the parent *did* to the child or how the parent was subjectively *responded to* by the child, or both.) If the objective countertransference can be *contained*, and not ignored or acted out by the therapist, then the therapist can think through what the transference is that the member is using in the here-and-now interaction. This is termed *metabolizing* the countertransference. Thus the therapist can experience how that person felt he or she was treated by the parents as a child. If the objective countertransference is interpreted in an empathic manner, and tied to a genetic reconstruction that links the present interaction with a past relationship, the net result usually is an increase in the depth of empathic understanding and a furthering of the therapeutic alliance.

The most important task of the interpersonal level, in the middle phase of treatment, is the *interpretation* of *projective identification* processes in the family. Through interpretation, dissociated aspects of the personality may be reowned by the individual who uses projective identification. Instead of being projected and acted out interpersonally, these issues reenter the intrapsychic sphere, where they can be worked through and integrated.

But how does one interpret the projective identification process of dumping one's pathology into another without being critical? For example, one cannot say you are using your son to express your anger at your spouse, so you don't have to take responsibility. That person would just feel attacked and become defensive. Here are three techniques in interpreting projective identification that I find useful:

1. *Reframing* the aim of projective identification away from a pathological or negative process, and attributing a positive purpose to it.

2. *Linking* the projective identification to a past genetic reconstruction clearly indicates that the therapist is trying to provide understanding or meaning, and not simply blaming the person. It provides him or her with insight into the fact that past relationships are repeated in the present, which can be further explored collaboratively with the therapist.

3. *Clarifying* the reason for the patient's past conflict about owning the problem is helpful, since it may have originated in the desire to protect others, to preserve self-esteem, or to respond to family rules. This indicates the therapist's empathic understanding of the need of the patient to disown and project problems, and serves to diminish guilt and aid self-acceptance. The therapist thereby diminishes the defensiveness of the projecting person. The person does not feel blamed or diminished, and can continue to explore the problems further with the therapist.

In the Cain and Abel family, the therapist needs to interpret Joe's projective identification of his negative self into his son Cain. In order for Joe not to become defensive, the interpretation needs to be reframed in a positive fashion and stripped of its pathological significance. The interpretation is tied to a past genetic reconstruction, and then the reason for its existence is provided. The substance of the interpretation is that Cain is expressing unacceptable, dissociated aggressive feelings for his father. This is necessary because Joe experiences his wife Jenny in a mother transference. When this interpretation is made empathically in front of the family, all the family members can then understand and care about Joe's attempt at dealing with and mastering a difficult relationship with his own mother. The current relationships become defused from their intensity, and shame and guilt are diminished. Joe can then reown his projective identifications in a therapeutic setting that provides a safe holding environment, and work openly on his intrapsychic conflicts.

The therapist thus might say, "I guess you, Joe, even as a child, had great difficulty in expressing your anger at your mother because you were afraid that you might be rejected further. Thus you felt you had to sit on that angry part of yourself, and you needed *help* from Cain in finding a way even now to let that part of yourself be expressed and to feel more whole. Since you and Cain both shared the same experience of feeling rejected, and of your mother's preferring the other son, you each sensitively knew how the other felt. Since Cain's expression of anger at Jenny did not destroy the family, which was one of your fears, this opened the pathway for you, Joe, to be more open in the expression of your own feelings and thoughts. Thus Cain was helpful to you, in opening the path for you to communicate better with your wife and to be a more complete person."

Through such an interpretation Joe reowned his projective identification of his split-off angry self (S−), which was no longer labeled as bad. Cain was now relabeled from the bad self (avenger) to the good self (savior), which enhanced his self-esteem. Joe became aware that he did not need Cain anymore to act out his angry self. It was safe; his wife (transferentially his mother) would not reject him, and the family and his world would not crumble. In the safety of the treatment setting, he was able to test out the omnipotent, destructive fantasies he unconsciously harbored, and did not have to avoid his wife by being a workaholic. Joe then continued to explore his problem of expressing his anger at his wife and mother. In turn this helped Jenny open up to be more communicative about her own loneliness and her anger at Joe for being away from home so much, like an abandoning father who did not value her. She had coped with her despair by turning to Abel and to alcohol. In resolving this she released Abel from his go-between role.

When family members reown their projective identification and are thereby able to experience their conflict or developmental arrest within themselves, they can then work through these intrapsychic issues either in the family setting or in individual therapy.

SUMMARY OF BEGINNING, MIDDLE, AND LAST PHASES OF TREATMENT

During the beginning phase of treatment, the techniques are:

1. Developing a safe holding environment through empathy, evenhandness, and containment; an environment that facilitates trust, lowers defensiveness, and allows aggression to be worked with constructively.
2. Interpreting the circular positive or negative systemic interaction in a sequential nonblaming manner by
    a. defining its origin
    b. defining what was hoped to be gained
    c. describing its effects

During the middle phase of treatment, the techniques are:

1. Interpreting projective identification by
    a. reframing its purpose to give it a positive aim
    b. linking it with a genetic reconstruction
    c. clarifying why an aspect of the self needed to be disowned and projected
This diminishes defensiveness, enhances the therapeutic alliance, and facilitates continued work with the reowned projective identification.
2. Using the objective countertransference as a tool to understand the transferences, and to provide material for interpretation of projective identification.

During the last phase of treatment, the techniques are:

1. Working through individual conflicts and developmental arrests in the intrapsychic sphere. This is a gradual process that may continue in individual therapy after the family treatment terminates.
2. Termination of treatment (see Chapter 14).

Each of these therapeutic techniques is described in the case illustration that follows. A brief summary of how a Bowenian, structural, and strategic family therapist might handle this case is compared to how an object relations family therapist might do so.

HARRY AND ROSE:
COMPARING BOWENIAN, STRUCTURAL, STRATEGIC, AND OBJECT RELATIONS INTERVENTIONS

Harry and Rose came for marital therapy because of Rose's threat of divorce after twenty years of marriage and two children. Rose expressed her rage and exasperation: "I can't take it anymore. It's just too much! I've gotten so little out of this marriage. He's such a bastard; I hate him!" Harry was impassive, with a beatific smile on his face. He seemed to get sadistic satisfaction out of irritating his wife. Harry remained calm and assumed a reasonable demeanor, while Rose became increasingly incensed and appeared to be the impossible one who was out of emotional control.

Harry, who had been an only child, was 6 years old when his father was killed in an auto accident. Shortly thereafter, his mother had a "nervous breakdown" (probably a psychotic depression) and was hospitalized. Harry was sent to a relative's home because his mother was "sick." Information about these two traumatic events was withheld to protect him, "for his own good," and thus he did not have an opportunity to understand these losses or to mourn his father. After being reunited with his mother, he did not express his anger at her leaving him, for fear that if he did so she would become sick again, and he would be abandoned a second time.

Harry defensively anesthetized himself, cutting off and repressing his angry feelings. He developed a withholding and obsessive personality.

Rose had been the eldest daughter in her family of origin, and had responsibility for her younger brother while her parents worked long hours in a mom-and-pop grocery store. The parental subsystem in this family seemed close, with each parent being mutually supportive of the other, but excluding the children from nurturance. Rose did not receive the attention and caring from her parents that she wanted but instead had to be a parent to her younger brother. She wore hand-me-down clothes from her cousins, and felt too unworthy to demand much for herself. She felt that asking for anything was selfish and that she should be content to have clothes and food, and to have a roof over her head. Thus this marriage of Harry and Rose was between a man who could not give and a woman who did not feel entitled to receive.

When Rose married Harry, she hoped for a financially secure future. Harry was an accountant, and they both expected that he would become a partner in the firm he worked for. Because of Harry's personality limitations, this never materialized. They barely managed financially, especially after the birth of their second child.

In the course of treatment, it became apparent that Harry had projected his angry self (S−) into Rose, who would then express his angry feelings for him. Rose had unwittingly become Harry's avenger. Rose, however, no longer wanted to play by these rules of the game; her masochistic titre had been surpassed. Rose said, "It's not fair; he knows how to push my buttons, but I can't even find his buttons to push." She had lost hope. She had unconsciously wanted to change Harry from a withholding and depriving parental figure (O−) into a nurturant, good one (O+). She had doggedly persisted, since she needed this transformation to enhance her poor self-esteem. Then she had realized, as she stated to Harry, "You are like Typhoid Mary. You're a carrier; you infect others with your anger." This was an apt, though accusatory, description of Harry's defense of projective identification.

Rose represented for Harry his weak and dependent mother who had abandoned him (O−), and toward whom he was unconsciously enraged. He could not express his rage directly, and needed to have Rose express these angry feelings for him. How did Harry accomplish this task? First of all, Harry denied his feelings. He was like a stone wall, unresponsive, even when directly confronted by Rose. When Rose demanded an emotional connection, Harry responded with intellectualization, trivializing her feelings. Harry also procrastinated, so that others had to wait for him. In this way he put his frustration into other people. When he promised he would do something, he would forget or delay. He always had a reasonable excuse, which drove Rose to distraction. Thus Harry was always in control, enraging others by frustrating their needs and expectations.

This same frustrating behavior was directed toward the therapist. When asked a question, Harry would often not answer. He might change the topic, digress into irrelevant details, go back to a previous conversation, or act stupid. Harry would say, "I heard what you said, but I don't understand it. Maybe I'm not smart enough." He would disqualify himself, and thus feel not responsible. He also would ask for advice about what to do and then dismiss what was suggested as ineffectual. He had tried it already, and it didn't work anyway. The implication was that you were not very smart either. Thus, Harry would not gratify others' needs for his emotional responsiveness; he would avoid dialogue, and not satisfy their expectations. He had identified with the aggressor, and did to others what he experienced had been done to him as a child. This time, the other person would be the helpless, frustrated, and angry one. They would have to wait for him, and he would be unresponsive to their needs. It was his way of mastering the helplessness, loss of self-esteem, and trauma of his father's death and his mother's emotional abandonment.

How would a family therapist trained in Bowen's approach work with Rose, who is frustrated over Harry's cutting off his feelings and distancing himself

from her both emotionally and physically? The Bowenian therapist might tell Rose not to run after a distancer.
In this way, Harry's use of projective identification
would be disrupted, and he could not frustrate Rose and
live out his anger at his mother through her. A structural family therapist might join Harry, sit next to him,
mimic his speech patterns, and support him in openly
confronting Rose. A strategic family therapist might
give Harry a paradoxical intervention, such as telling
him to continue to be withholding toward Rose; that he
was thereby being sensitive and helpful to her, because
she was used to being deprived ever since childhood;
that she expected such treatment, and would be extremely uncomfortable if he were to be giving and
nurturant. (Psychoanalytically, this goes along with
Rose's resistance to and fear of change.) This reframing
of Harry's behavior into good terms would break up the
projective identification of his angry feelings by en-
listing Harry's oppositionalism. Harry's need was not to
gratify but to frustrate Rose. Thus, in order to frustrate
his wife after this paradoxical intervention, he would
need to become gratifying.

The Bowenian approach explores issues such as differentiation, distance, closeness, and triangulation through several generations. The structural and strategic approaches, even though they
may break up the pathological interaction, do not explore the past
but restrict themselves to the present. This does not lead to
introspection about the causes of why people establish such a
system in the first place, but remains limited to their actions and
behavior. Dynamic approaches differ in that they consider that
people's insight into their past relationships influence their present
behavior. Transferences are interpreted, genetic reconstructions
are made, and unconscious fears and drives as well as defensive
structure are worked with throughout the course of treatment. For
permanent change in the system, as well as in the sphere of
interpersonal relations, dynamic therapy considers that structural
changes and personality growth in the members of the family are
necessary.

In object relations family therapy, a safe holding environment needs to be developed in order to lower defensiveness and to

increase the level of trust. Here, the most important factors are the therapist's genuine concern for all the members of the family, refusal to take sides or to be judgmental, and willingness to consider each member's perspective and feelings. The family members also need to develop confidence in the strength of the therapist to contain the expression of aggression. The therapist acts like a referee to prevent low blows and the occurrence of a free-for-all. This is particularly important for families in which there is the fear that aggression will get out of control and will be destructive to the cohesion of the family.

At one point in treatment, Harry came close to openly expressing his aggression by making a cryptic remark that thinly masked his hostility toward me and the treatment. He made a joke about the lack of effectiveness of the treatment process. I saw this as a derivative of the transference, in that I represented his ineffectual mother from whom he could not expect help, and instead whom he had to help. I acknowledged Harry's efforts to be open and honest about his distrust and anger toward me, and his concerns about how effective I might be in helping the family. (I felt it was too early at this point to make a transference interpretation.) I further stated that I realized how difficult it was for him to express his anger, and I acknowledged his effort to do so.

In this way I attempted to establish a corrective emotional experience. I could show him that I was able to accept and contain his anger without retaliation (like Rose) or falling apart (like his mother). I would not abandon him emotionally or physically. This had been exactly his fear concerning his weak and depressed mother; she would become sick and abandon him again if he expressed rage. Thus he did not need to deny responsibility for his anger now but was entitled, and indeed encouraged, to express it openly and honestly, *himself*. This undermined his false self and the need to use projective identification as a defense.

The systemic level of interaction was dealt with by describing how Rose and Harry's conflict became escalated by the very way they dealt with each other. The more Rose demanded, the more Harry withheld; and the more Harry held back, the more Rose demanded. This created a vicious cycle—a circular process in which each one of them reacted to the other, a process that ran away with itself. An objective description was made of their interaction, which prevented the focus of blame from falling on either one of them: "Both of you are victims of this process; it is a no-win situation. It may be that this is how each of you have felt since childhood, as if you've been a victim of others." This sensitizing of them to the fact of their bouncing off each other defensively alerted them to the systemic process, to its transferential significance, and contributed to their working on controlling it.

One way of resolving Harry's use of projective identification was through the use of the objective countertransference he evoked in me. I experienced a sense of frustration and annoyance with him which I contained. When I felt that Harry was sufficiently engaged in treatment, I revealed my own countertransference feelings. I did this in a way that was calm and not accusatory. I reframed my countertransference feelings in a positive way and tied them in with a genetic interpretation that described the source as well as the purpose they served. In this way, I tried to diminish Harry's defensiveness, guilt, and loss of self-esteem.

I said, "I sincerely have been trying to help, but at times I've experienced myself feeling helpless and frustrated in my efforts. Then as I was mulling over these feelings in my head, I realized that you must have felt this same way when your father died. Perhaps you wanted me to feel the same way, so that I could empathically understand how helpless and frustrated you felt then. Your mother became sick, and there was no one there to help you mourn the loss of your father. You were alone and unable to express your feelings openly. This continued even when your mother returned, for fear that she would become sick again and leave. This must have left you feeling trapped, impotent, and angry."

The conflict was thus placed back into Harry. He could now own it and did not need to project it into others and act it out through them. He then began working through his fearfulness about being openly expressive and taking responsibility for his anger. He acknowledged that he had feared that if he expressed his anger at his mother, she was so narcissistically vulnerable that she would only become sick and leave again. Thus he could not get his own needs addressed, and felt he had to function as a protector of his mother. This same conflict, this fear of being open and honest in expressing his feelings, was reflected in his distant and angry relationship with his wife.

In the past he had dealt with his helplessness and anger by projecting this aspect of himself into another, thereby rendering the other person helpless and enraged. This solution gave him some sense of mastery over his own helplessness and rage by externalizing these feelings and controlling the other person. But he did not really address the underlying issues of his rage, insecurity, and lack of self-esteem, which continued to be acted out in the interpersonal sphere. The obsessive defenses Harry erected were constricting his freedom of expression and his vitality, and were punitive and self-defeating. Insight into the genesis of his obsessive behavior enabled him to recognize the source of it, ventilate his rage, and stop taking it out on his wife. In turn, Rose had grown sufficiently in her self-esteem to feel entitled to receive better treatment. The marriage would not have lasted much longer had Harry not changed and become more considerate of Rose's feelings and needs. Harry and Rose continued on in individual therapy with separate therapists, to work through the conflicts that each of them had become aware of in marital therapy.

12

A Continuous Case of Object Relations Couple's Therapy

It would be useful to demonstrate the stages of object relations family therapy in a continuous case report of marital therapy. The same process of treatment is followed, starting with the systemic level, then proceeding to the interactional and finally to the individual level. In this clinical case the wife served as both the avenger (the bad self) and the scapegoat (the bad internalized mother) for the husband. For the wife, the husband represented her exploitative and rejecting parents, whom she internalized (the bad objects) and for whom she performed with the hope of changing them and gaining some security and a sense of importance. Each spouse functioned as the split-off negative parent for the other, and served to complete the other's personality needs.

They had been locked into a complementary unconscious collusive system of object relations, which was recently shaken because of the wife's having undergone individual therapy. Before therapy, the wife had unconsciously continued in the marital relationship the type of relationship she had had with her mother. But now she no longer needed to find security in feeling needed by performing for the other, and this disrupted their unconscious collusive system of relationship. Neither spouse felt loved, and each expected to be controlled by the other.

ANNIE AND TOM: AN AVENGER ROLE AND MUTUAL SCAPEGOATING

Sessions were generally fifty minutes long, and the couple was seen by me weekly or every other week. These descriptions of the sessions were taken from my process notes, which have been summarized and disguised to protect confidentiality.

Tom and Annie entered couple's therapy because of constant arguments that escalated into shouting matches. Each blamed the other for their mutual unhappiness. There was no resolution to their conflicts. Both felt resentful and victimized, as well as helpless and hopeless about their marriage. This was the second marriage for both of them, and Annie had two children from her previous marriage.

Annie's parents had divorced when she was in her teens. She had been reared by her narcissistically needy mother, to whom Annie had functioned as a good mother (O+). This role made her feel more important than her younger sister, with whom she competed. She was her mother's confidante, and heard continuous complaints about her father. Annie felt needed and like the favorite child, but the price she paid for this position with mother was having to split off and repress her own needy self. If she did not, she would have risked her mother's rejection. The mother herself was never able to confront her ex-husband directly. Annie took on the role of challenging her father, as her mother's avenger (S−). The mother would then condemn Annie for not being polite to the father. This would result in Annie feeling like an orphan, abandoned by both parents.

Tom had been raised on a farm in the southern United States, where his parents had suffered hard times. They desperately needed his labor on the farm in order to survive economically. His younger brother, however, had been spared having to help out with the heavy labor because he was frail. Thus, Tom had to carry the burden for his brother as well. Helping out on the farm deprived Tom of having friends and playing with his peers. Tom idealized his relationship with his parents, and split off and denied any anger toward them or competitive feelings toward his brother. He did have contempt for "those soft city kids who were given everything." This was a derivative displacement of his anger at his brother onto other children.

Tom did not feel entitled to experience or express any angry feelings toward his parents or brother. The repression of his anger was fostered by the family myth that his mother had a "nervous condition," was vulnerable, and was unable to handle anger. His father emphasized that no one was to upset the mother by being disobedient or selfish. The family rule was, "If you have nothing good to say, don't say anything." Aggression needed to be suppressed. Tom was therefore unable to integrate his ambivalent feelings and to function as a separate and whole person.

In previous individual therapy with another therapist, Tom had been able to admit to himself that he felt cheated out of a childhood because of his work on the farm. His childhood had been grim and humorless, and he had felt like a slave. He had confronted his mother, who responded by being hurt and withdrawing emotionally. Tom then dropped out of individual treatment and did not proceed to try to deal with his ambivalence toward his parents. He retained a false compliant self, and remained a slave to himself.

BEGINNING PHASE: THE SYSTEMIC LEVEL

During the first month of marital therapy, the couple arrived ten minutes late for their third session. I remarked in a nonaccusatory manner about the lateness, and suggested we talk about it. Each blamed the other and felt victimized. This demonstrated the kind of escalating conflict they were engaged in. Annie reported that she had observed Tom starting to make a large breakfast for himself, even though they were pressed for time. She then also took her time in getting ready. Tom said that when he had seen Annie not rushing, he concluded that he could eat his breakfast. Neither owned up to his or her share of responsibility for the lateness. I commented that each took cues and was reactive to the other; that each put responsibility for the lateness onto the other. The result was that Annie blamed Tom, who in turn blamed Annie, to create a vicious cycle of mutual recrimination. Here the systemic level of interaction was pointed out, in order to clarify the lack of separate autonomy and the defensiveness that prevented resolution of their conflict. This intervention set the stage for the investigation of how and why they did not function autonomously, and how each gave responsibility for the self over to the other, resulting in their both remaining reactive and feeling controlled.

In the first month of marital therapy, they talked about pressure from Tom's parents to celebrate Christmas on the farm. Annie did not want to go because Tom's mother was cold to her and excluded her from conversations, as if she did not exist. Annie felt angry at Tom for not speaking up to his mother and protecting her. She had told Tom about her feelings, but he made no move to deal with their relationship. When Tom told his mother of their decision not to visit, he said it was Annie who had not wanted to come. He took no responsibility for his own feelings. Again he implied that he was only reacting to Annie's not wanting to go. Annie was depicted as the bad one, and Tom remained the good one. As they had done in the earlier session, Tom portrayed himself as a victim of Annie, and Annie experienced herself as a victim of both Tom and his mother.

MIDDLE PHASE: THE INTERPERSONAL LEVEL

The following sessions demonstrate the work on the couple's interpersonal interaction, and how an interpretation of their projective identification was made. After the interpretation, each spouse began to reown his or her own conflicts that they had put into each other through projective identification. They then continued to work them through on an intrapsychic, individual level in the last phase of treatment.

SESSION FIVE: INTERPRETING TOM'S PROJECTIVE IDENTIFICATION ONTO ANNIE AS HIS AVENGER

Tom: Annie, you don't communicate with my parents, and I don't want to be the channel between you and them. I don't like being caught in the middle. [Tom has projected his S− onto Annie, who serves as his avenger and whom he can blame for his poor relationship with his parents. His intrapsychic conflict is thereby externalized and acted out through Annie.]

Annie: You defend them and don't show concern for me that they hurt me. It's you that hurt me, not your parents! I was disappointed that they weren't like surrogate parents for me. Instead, they excluded me. Your mother seemed jealous that you didn't marry her. I don't expect anything from them now and maintain my distance. [Annie can tolerate rejection by Tom's mother, but she feels betrayed by the fact that he blames her and is not protective even though she unconsciously serves as his avenger.]

Tom: I realize I have been insensitive to your feelings when they were hurt by my mother, and I'll try to empathize.

Annie: You say that you will try to understand and be good; did you get that out of a textbook? You always seem to put yourself in the position of being the good guy, with your parents and with me as well. [Annie describes Tom's intellectualized comment as being compliant and as coming from his false self so that he can deny responsibility.]

Therapist: I can understand your annoyance at Tom, Annie, but it has always been important for Tom to be the good guy. You, Tom, in fact said you *had* to be the good guy, since you weren't permitted the full expression of your feelings. There were three reasons that you have mentioned: (1) There was a family rule in your home that if you didn't have something good to say, you weren't supposed to say anything; (2) you were told that your mother had a nervous condition, so you weren't supposed to upset her; and (3) you did not feel entitled to be angry or rebellious, since the family needed you to work hard on the farm just to survive economically. Thus you felt blocked by shame and guilt from expressing your feelings, especially your "negative" ones. Since you, Tom, couldn't express these "negative" feelings yourself without feeling bad, selfish, and hurtful to your mother and family, you needed Annie's help to express them for you. But, since you condemn yourself for these feelings, you also needed to condemn Annie, who expressed these blocked-out, unacceptable feelings of yours toward your parents. I know that probably both of you are wondering why you, Annie, accepted this painful role of expressing Tom's anger. This is something we will also need to explore. [This interpretation listed in an understanding way the reasons why Tom needed to use projective identification—that is, the family rule, the family myth, and his unconscious guilt if he shirked his responsibility for the emotional survival of his mother and the economic survival of the family as a group. Tom's projective identification into Annie was dealt with as follows: (1) It was *reframed* into something positive, wherein Annie was assisting Tom in completing himself by expressing his anger for him; (2) it was *linked* to a genetic reconstruction; and (3) the need for the use of splitting and projective identification was *clarified*. This took away from the need to blame, and set up a framework of self-understanding and self-acceptance by both Tom and Annie. In addition, Annie's collusion with this process was mentioned, which also mitigated against blaming, and which would be further opened up to enable Annie to grow and change as well.]

Tom: I would like to go to my parents to express my "negative" feelings toward them myself now. [It was unclear whether this was real change due to the interpretation, or just superficial compliance and his wanting to be the good guy with the therapist also.]

Annie: I want him to express his own anger. I did the same thing for my mother, and I'm tired of it. Tom is doing the exact same thing as my mother did to me as a child. [Annie does not see herself entering into the collusion, as had been pointed out, but feels victimized by both her mother and Tom as if she had no choice in her role induction.]

Tom: But I would like Annie to have honest communication with my parents. [Tom projects his own conflict into Annie again.]

Annie: It's not me. You need to have honest communication for yourself with them. It is between you and them, not between me and them. [Annie corrects Tom's externalization, and wants out of her induced roles of avenger and scapegoat for Tom.]

Tom: But I need you to help me. [Tom feels unable to confront his parents and openly calls for Annie to rescue or support him. He resists her wanting out of her role as avenger.]

Annie: Why do you need me? You need to look into yourself. Remember how you couldn't get angry at your parents during our vacation there last time? I've already gone through my own stuff and looked into myself in individual therapy. I know how painful and difficult it is. I felt that if I said anything against my mother, she would die. I saw her as so vulnerable and weak. I had thought my father was in the wrong, and I fought him for her. I felt he had all the power. But my mother only punished me for not being nice to him. It didn't help me come closer to my mother, even when I had worked it out in individual therapy; but I became more my own person. You can do likewise. [Annie refuses to be reinduced into her role of avenger since it had not worked with her mother or Tom. She supports his working through his conflict with his parents intrapsychically, and expresses confidence in him.]

Tom: My relationship with my parents is at rock bottom. [He pleads for her help, feels inadequate to reverse the relationship with his parents.]

Annie: But don't blame me for that. [She recognizes that if she takes on the role of avenger, she will also be blamed for problems in the relationships between Tom and his parents, becoming the scapegoat as well.]

Therapist: You, Annie, are tired of expressing Tom's anger and then getting blamed, and would like Tom to own his problems and work them out toward his parents. Yet you, Tom, always felt you could only be half a person. You felt you needed to be nice to be accepted by your parents. If you expressed your anger, it would result in more distance, which you didn't want and still don't want. [Annie's wanting out of the avenger–scapegoat roles is acknowledged, and Tom's intrapsychic structural conflict between id and superego is pointed out and clarified.]

Tom: I feel I can change for the better. I do see that I have problems with my parents myself. I want to be more honest with them, but at the same time I also want to be closer. I'd like to talk with them more on an emotional basis, tell them of my scars from childhood, but not to make them feel bad. [Tom further elaborates on the guilt he feels about his anger hurting his parents and alienating them from him. His conflict continues about expressing his genuine self and also being accepted.]

Annie: Why do you have to keep protecting them, Tom? You know your mother is made of steel. You don't really feel free in confronting your mother, but she isn't that fragile. You also know that your parents aren't going to accept that responsibility for your childhood, and to avoid your feeling guilty you want to see me as the bad one. They'll blame me for putting you up to it. [She tries to dispel Tom's family myth that anger will hurt the mother, but also acknowledges that Tom's family is not receptive to his honesty and need to blame her.]

Therapist: Annie, your experience then is that both sides, both Tom and his parents, have a vested interest in dumping their negative feelings into you, to scapegoat you so as not to feel guilty and to heal their relationship. [Their resistance to allow Annie out of the avenger–scapegoat roles is brought out, and the secondary gain achieved by Tom and his family in blaming Annie is clarified.]

Annie: Tom, you don't need me to heal your relationship with them, it's up to you to heal your relationship with them. Why can't you write to them yourself and work on your difficulties with them instead of putting me down? [Annie answers Tom's need for her to heal his relationship with his parents, and suggests he can do it and offers a way, writing, in which the confrontation would not be so direct.]

Therapist: Annie, you feel that you don't need to be the scapegoat to heal Tom's relationship with his parents; you feel confident he can do it himself without your help. [Annie's statements are reiterated in order to support her and reassure Tom of his ability to own and deal with his ambivalence and fears.]

Tom: I will go visit them, and I'll start with the three items Sam (the therapist) described, and talk with them on an honest basis about my life. Since you won't be there, how would you want me to refer to you? [Again, Tom seems to want to involve Annie in his relationship with his parents.]

Annie: The three of you (Tom and his parents) have been using me, especially your mother, and you have been the most manipulative. You are close to them so long as I've been the bad guy. [Annie recognizes Tom's wanting and needing to pull her back into the avenger–scapegoat roles to preserve his idealized relationship with his parents.]

Tom: When I come back are you going to quiz me about what I said? You complain about them to me, and that bothers me. [Tom seems to be experiencing Annie as a controlling bad maternal figure who does not trust him.]

Annie: You will be out there to work on your relationship with them. I want you only to understand my feelings; the rest is up to you; I want a relationship with you only and not with them. I realize that your family does not want honesty and closeness; they want distance. [Annie emphasizes Tom's autonomy in dealing with his parents, the importance of her relationship to Tom, and of his family's resistance to change.]

Tom: Do you think that the end result and reality of the relationship with your own parents, where they couldn't change, might influence your hopelessness about the possibility of change with my parents? [Tom confronts Annie's pessimism, and possibly her envy that his outcome might be different from that of her family.]

Annie: If you don't change, Tom, and they don't change, I'll still be needed to be the bad guy. I shouldn't have allowed myself to be used, by reacting and expressing my anger. I should have contained myself, been more passive and cool. I don't know why, but I know I allowed myself to be used. [Annie is curious and takes responsibility for permitting herself to be used by Tom. It presents an opportunity for not just feeling victimized but for owning her part of the collusive interaction. Annie can now or later introspect and explore her unconscious participation. Her current relationship probably serves as a negative feedback cycle to confirm her expectation that she will be exploited by others as she was by her mother. By again being used as an avenger, and then scapegoated for another's narcissistic needs — as she has been by Tom — she reinforces her defenses and she therefore need not come out of her cocoon of distrust and self-sufficiency.]

Tom: Is it OK, Annie, for me to communicate more honestly with them? [Tom is again assuming a compliant false self and relating to Annie and to his therapist as controlling parents.]

Annie: You don't need my permission. [She refuses to be induced into the role of a controlling bad parent.]

Tom: Can I visit them without you? [He questions how controlling she will be.]

Annie: I would like for us to discuss the weekends when you want to go there so it will be a cooperative decision.

Tom: If I go without you, you don't want me to talk about our fights. [Tom seems to try to provoke Annie into anger, and to experience her as a controlling parental figure.]

Annie: Why would you tell your parents more negative feelings about me? You'll only fuel them more into seeing me in the bad role. I don't care what you say about our relationship, but if things get more negative, I'll never go out there again. If you portray yourself as the poor innocent victim, mistreated by me, I'll never go out there. [Annie questions Tom's motivations, recognizes his resistance to change, and sets an ultimatum if he continues to present her as the bad one.]

Tom: But I'm concerned that you don't want to go out there yourself now, and if things get worse, you'll be the judge. You might set up things so that there will be no further relationship by interpreting them negatively. [Tom distrusts Annie's motives, as if she has a vested interest in his relationship with his parents not getting closer, as it did not with her parents.]

Annie: What you want is to be closer to them, for them to think you are terrific. I'm worried you'll get support from them by using me. You did that with your ex-wife. You told them that she was the one that prevented you from getting close to them. You weren't honest, since if you wanted to be close to them you would have gotten close to them yourself even if your wife didn't. [She confronts Tom with his putting his own conflict about closeness into her. Tom still needs validation from his parents and wants closeness, yet to be honest with them means violating the family rules and myths about what behavior is acceptable to them and suffering rejection. Annie thus distrusts Tom's desire to change, because of his conflict between autonomy and acceptance.]

Tom: When I tell them about myself, I will take responsibility that it wasn't my ex-wife, and I will tell them the three reasons for my difficulty in expressing my feelings. I was ashamed of what I was doing with my life at that time, when I was previously married. I was living a bohemian life-style and didn't want them to know about it. [Tom takes responsibility for his previous need for distance from his family because of shame over his behavior.]

Annie: I'd go to your parents if you take responsibility for yourself and don't use me. In the last few sessions you have started to listen, but are not there yet. [Annie recognizes Tom's ambivalence about change.]

Therapist: It will be hard for you, Tom, to deal with your mother. It is a conflict; you want to be honest with your parents, yet it may interfere with your wish to be close to them. [Tom's intrapsychic conflict is recapitulated.]

Tom: Annie, I think it would be helpful for me to see the connection between your relationship with your parents and the relationship to my parents. [He questions Annie's motivation and pessimism.]

Annie: I know I had unrealistic expectations of what would happen with your parents, since I was so deeply disappointed in my own parents. I wouldn't have been so upset if I didn't already feel like an orphan. My expectations of your parents were too high, so their distancing themselves from me was so much more hurtful. Every time we have been with your parents, especially your mother, they do hurtful things, and then you add salt to the wound by yelling at me. [Annie expresses her disappointed expectations about being parented and protected.]

Tom: You seem to see yourself as a naive victim of them. [Tom wants Annie to accept some responsibility also.]

Annie: I withdraw when I'm hurt. I say to myself, I don't need you, I don't need other people. I put up a wall. Eventually, with people I need, the wall comes down. But with your parents, I don't need them, so why take my guard down? I don't give a damn about them. I care about you and me, and your not using something to become angry at me. You are so angry at your mother from the past, and you project it onto me. That upsets me. Unless I feel comfortable that I won't be scapegoated again, I don't want to go out there. When you confront your mother, she will say that what you tell her isn't true; that she checked it out with your brother, and it is not true. That's what happened before. [Annie is aware of her narcissistic defenses of self-sufficiency, and her anger at and distrust of Tom's parents. She recognizes Tom's mother transference and displacement of his anger from his mother onto her as the O −.]

Tom: When I told my mother previously that I felt I had worked too hard on the farm, that life during my childhood was grim, and that emotional expressions were blocked, she reacted by feeling hurt. Then she wouldn't talk to me for a month. She checked it out with my brother, who said that he didn't have that experience at all. [Tom relates what happened when he previously confronted his mother, who invalidated his statements by getting her other son's support. Indeed Tom's brother did not have the same burden of labor on the farm, since he was frail.]

Therapist: You experienced that she disqualified your statements, became defensive, got support from your brother; and I assume you both anticipate that this will happen again. [Reality is tested in order to counter Tom's denial and wishful thinking, and his blaming Annie for the thwarting of his wishes for closeness with his parents.]

Tom: I'll tell her not to check it out with my brother. It's how I felt, it was between you and me. He had a different experience. If she can't accept what I say, then it's her problem. It seems as if there has been a curse on our family not to be able to express feelings. I still hope my confronting her will result in better communication. [Tom still wishes for validation and acceptance, and acknowledges the family rule and family myth which he calls a curse on his family preventing expression of emotions.]

Annie: But it is important for your own growth, even if it doesn't improve your relationship with them. [She expresses support for Tom.]

Tom: I said it was important to me, but I hope it will improve my relationship with them and with you.

Annie: But if you see your mother more clearly for who she is, with her limitations, it may affect your relationship with me. Then it wouldn't bother me what your parent said or did, if you were different. [Annie encourages integration of Tom's splitting, and seeing his mother as both good and bad. If he can accept his mother's imperfections, he need not be totally disappointed. By integrating his ambivalence, Tom would not need to idealize his mother and scapegoat Annie.]

Tom: But it doesn't resolve anything in the relationship between you and them. [He still externalizes part of his conflict with his parents onto Annie.]

Annie: But Tom, you are not in the middle. A husband and wife listen to each other, especially about things that upset either of them. If I say something upsets me, you respond by saying go do something about it. I feel that you don't care. [Annie expresses her need for Tom's containing and supporting her in coping with her problems, instead of distancing himself.]

Tom: But when you are upset or hurt, it comes out with a lot of anger. You blame me, and I feel accused. Then you sulk, and I don't know what to say. [Tom interprets how Annie defeats herself, so that she does not get her need for support met.]

Therapist: What Tom seems to imply is that the way you, Annie, express your hurt is by being critical and withdrawing, and it does not enable him to give you the support you want and need. It is probably especially difficult for Tom, since the way his mother reacted when she was hurt, by criticism and withdrawal, is the very same way you react when you are hurt. [Annie's reactions to hurt are like Tom's mother's, which reinforces Tom's transference onto her. This transference interpretation also deals with the systemic interaction between Tom and Annie that forms a circular feedback cycle to reinforce each one's pathology.]

Annie: I have tried not to attack and withdraw. I am working on that and am continuing to try to change that behavior; I know it is self-defeating. [She acknowledges the accuracy of the interpretation.]

SESSION SIX: EXPLORING ANNIE'S ACCEPTING THE AVENGER ROLE

Therapist: In the last session you, Annie, were wondering why you allowed yourself to be used to express Tom's anger for him, just as you had for your mother. I was wondering if you had some further thoughts about this, particularly since in both instances you wound up also getting punished for doing so. [Annie's questioning of her own motivation, as brought up in the last session, is explored and opened up.]

Annie: I feel more comfortable giving than receiving. I don't feel I deserve to ask for things or to be taken care of. If I'm needed, the other person will be there for me, and I feel more in control. With my mother, I was angry that she used me when I realized it later, but as a child I felt needed by her, and special to her by expressing anger for her. I didn't get any positive strokes from her for expressing her anger at my father, and it made me feel worse. I couldn't get angry at my mother; I didn't even feel anger at her then. My mother also did not openly express her anger; she is passive-aggressive. Once I recall I did express anger at her directly, and she started to cry. Another time, when I was in individual therapy, I confronted my mother, and she cried again. I felt I was nasty, but the therapist thought I was walking on eggshells. I felt I was cruel, bad, hurting my mother.

Several years ago, my mother started using my children against me; she'd tell them bad things about me. I wrote her a letter that she had done the same thing to me as a child that she was now doing with my children. I wrote that if she was angry at me for something, to talk to me directly and not to involve my children. I showed the letter to Tom, and he said it was too harsh. My aunt, who "makes nice" all the time, also said tear it up and write your mother a loving letter. My uncle said that's right on, it's terrific, go ahead and send it. But I listened to my aunt and Tom. However, I instinctively felt I needed to express my anger at my mother before I could feel loving toward her. Then I would be able to forgive her. She wasn't all bad; there were times when she was loving and good. What was bad was the unconscious part of her that was destroying me. [Annie did not trust others to be responsive to her needs, and she needed to have control by behaving in a conforming way, and developed a false self. Her self-esteem and security were increased by allowing herself to be used by her mother; otherwise she felt too unimportant and insecure to expect others to care for her, just by being herself. She also felt she was damaging her mother if she demanded things or was angry at her, and thus she also made reparations by performing.]

Therapist: So you entered into a collusion with your mother to express her anger as a way of engaging her, of feeling needed and special; otherwise, what did you feel would happen? [Her fears of abandonment, if she did not perform in the role of her mother's avenger toward her father, are explored.]

Annie: I felt my mother would only be there for me and be loving if I took care of her. [Annie took on a good mother role (O+) and was parentified to gain love and security from her mother.]

Therapist: So if you didn't take care of your mother, you felt she wouldn't take care of you. [Her statement is repeated so she can hear her own words: Annie gave up her autonomy and her own developmental needs in order to feel secure with her mother.]

Tom: Not only would she not be there for Annie, but she would become actively deceitful and manipulative of others against her. I remember at your divorce, she allied herself with your ex-husband and not you. [Tom is supportive of Annie.]

Annie: I had gotten to the point where I didn't want to take care of her and my ex-husband. I wanted to take care of myself and my children. I was letting go of both of them. My mother would say that I was not being a good mother to my kids, since I was going to college. I shouldn't go out; I should stay home with the kids. As soon as I started having a life of my own, then I wasn't a good mother. [Annie was told she was bad if she separated and was autonomous from her children, but really from her own mother, who was a dependent, clinging childlike person.]

Therapist: If you separated and were autonomous, you were labeled as bad and rejected by your mother. It was a difficult dilemma for you, I suspect. [Conflict over close relationship with mother versus autonomy is brought out.]

Annie: All the workshops on women's liberation that I went to in the 1970s gave me support that it was OK to think about myself, and that it was bad to be selfless. When I grew up women weren't supposed to be selfish or conceited. It was OK for men. But I even went beyond social convention. People would tell me I was *overly* modest. If anyone complimented me, I'd have to undermine that. I'd blush or stammer if someone said anything positive to me. [Her mother's injunctions about being a selfless good object for others was even more than society-dictated. She had to be a selfless O+ for her mother, but received support for independence from her women's group.]

Tom: That one about your not accepting compliments from others, that you mentioned, made me angry, since you also discounted my positive overtures to you. You interpreted my positive behavior negatively, you didn't believe it or discounted it. It has always bothered me, and now I understand it a bit better. [Tom took Annie's behavior personally, but now understands it as a more general issue of her inability to feel important. She had considered it being conceited, and was therefore unable to accept compliments from anyone.]

Therapist: It bothered Tom, but now he can see that you, Annie, had a general problem of being unable to accept compliments from anyone, since you felt it would have been bad and conceited.

Annie: Even though I am getting better, I know I can't ask for what I want. If Tom gives what I ask for, and does it grudgingly and not with love, I feel hurt. Then I realize that if I really need something, even though it is not given lovingly, that is *his* problem. It was a relief, whereas before I'd feel hurt and rejected. My relationship with my father could have been better if I could have accepted him and his limitations and taken what he was able to give me. [Annie was unable to ask for things, fearing rejection, but when she did not receive them she felt hurt and worthless as with her father.]

Therapist: It sounds like you experienced your relationship with your father in black and white terms, of being either accepted or rejected, and now feel some regret that you didn't receive what you could have, had you accepted your father with his limitations. [Therapist reinforces Annie's efforts to integrate her splitting of her ambivalence toward her father and Tom, and to view them as separate whole objects—in effect, achieving a depressive position.]

Annie: My mother helped me view things like that. She made my father seem like a bad guy. I remember I was so excited when he would come home, and then it would deteriorate into a fight between him and me. He would be critical of me, and I'd get angry and thought he was terrible. It was less about how he treated me, and more about how mean I felt he was toward my mother that caused the arguments. The last few times I saw him, I wanted to talk about the past, but he refused. The past is the past, he'd say. Let's not dwell on it. Then he'd lecture me about what he wanted to talk about. There were no feelings; he just reported events or complained about people screwing him at work. [Her mother reinforced splitting of ambivalence toward her father, and her being the mother's avenger alienated the father.]

Therapist: He didn't connect with you. How did you feel about not being able to resolve issues with your father? [Therapist explores her ambivalence and conflict over her lack of closeness to her father, and feeling unimportant to him. This gives her an opportunity to mourn the loss.]

Annie: His current wife says to him that he should stop lecturing at me. I felt he didn't love me, and I feel sad about that. He never hugged me. He was so controlling, if you didn't agree with him he'd want to kill you, he'd get so angry. I felt rejected. When he was a child, his parents traveled a lot; he felt helpless and rootless, living out of suitcases. He hasn't given me a birthday present since I was twelve. It's hard for him to give of himself. Now I realize that this is him, he didn't get and was incapable of giving emotionally. Now he can give materially at times, though before he didn't even give materially. After the divorce he did not give anything in child support, when we were raised by my mother. I don't even get a birthday card from him now. I used to feel hurt and angry. He isn't even involved with his grandchildren. I realize that's him. When my father heard from someone that I had an automobile accident once, he called to ask about the car and not about me. Then he started talking about himself. I just laughed to myself, that's him, he can't be intimate. I was able to separate myself from him, but I've always felt sad and missed having a father. [Annie is able to see her father more objectively as a separate, whole object, is less vulnerable narcissistically, and mourns her loss.]

Tom: That's interesting, since I remember you were upset that I would be like him and only be worried about the car. [Tom questions her resolution and giving up of the bad father.]

Annie: I'm struggling to get rid of that critical father within me who says that whatever I do it's not good enough. [Annie acknowledges that she is still trying to let go of the bad internal father object.]

Therapist: Annie, you seem to have been more able to see your father's limitations and integrate that, but with your mother and Tom, you still have difficulty functioning as a separate person. You felt that your father was not there and accepted that fact as reality; but with your mother and Tom, you still feel compelled to perform for them and express their anger for them or they will not be there for you. [Annie seems to have been more able to separate and integrate her ambivalence toward her father, but not moved into a depressive position with her mother and Tom. The maternal transference toward Tom is emphasized, and the fear of rejection if she is autonomous.]

Annie: Tom really helped me to see my father's limitations. But when Tom withdraws, I still get hurt and also withdraw.

Therapist: Annie, you seem to feel the only options open to you are to act out your mother's or Tom's anger, or to be totally separate and to withdraw. [Annie seems to remain in the paranoid-schizoid position with her mother and Tom, losing boundaries, and needing to fuse and act out the others' impulses.]

Annie: I really never knew who I was, and I'm still struggling to find out who I am as a separate person from other people.
Up until 30 years of age, I thought I was just a mother. [Annie
acknowledges her boundary and identity problems.]

Tom: But now you are seeing yourself in so many other
roles. [He is supportive of Annie.]

Therapist: Was it because you felt you had to be a mother
to your mother? That being a mother was the only role that was
acceptable? [Annie was unable to differentiate from her mother,
needing to be an O+ for her mother to be accepted.]

Annie: Yes, that was the thing I got the most strokes for,
especially when I became an actual mother also. I felt unworthy
otherwise, and when I take care of myself, I feel guilty. I realize
it's OK to mother myself, to put myself first, not that I won't also
mother other people. I got the most reinforcement from my
mother in that role, and received anger from her when I pulled
away from that role. If I pulled away from being a mother and was
not totally there for my children, my mother told me I was a bad
mother. I wasn't as good a mother then, only if I remained totally
a mother who took care of others, including her. After I gave up
that role of being a mother to my mother, my sister took it on. My
sister sensed that I was my mother's favorite. I was seven years
older than her and more like another parent, especially after my
father left. It was my mother and I and then her. I guess my
mother felt guilty having to work, and may have put her feelings
into me of not being a good mother. I was also like a husband to
her, and she shared intimate secrets with me. [Annie becomes
aware of her mother having dumped her guilt into her about being
a bad mother, and of having felt special by joining her in a
parental role over her sister. She is working through the internalized values and gratifications received from her mother for
performing the O+ role.]

Therapist: Did you feel that your sister was jealous of that
intimacy with your mother, and your being the favorite? [The
sibling rivalry with her sister is explored.]

Annie: Yes, my sister was jealous but wouldn't admit that to herself. She was always angry at me for being the favorite. Also my mother would tell my sister bad things about me, and influenced her against me. Tom, I feel guilty I monopolized the session. [Tom may also transferentially represent the sister, toward whom she felt guilt for having monopolized their mother; now she felt she had monopolized the therapist.]

Tom: But I got a lot from it myself. [He is supportive.]

Therapist: Perhaps you are apologetic to Tom now for feeling you monopolized me, just like you felt guilty toward your sister for monopolizing your mother? Yet in this instance Tom felt it was helpful to him, your getting something for yourself. Thus Tom does not seem to be like your sister, or even your mother, since he felt he got something as well as you when you gave to yourself in the session. [Tom is differentiated from transferences onto him of her sister and mother.]

SESSION SEVEN: TOM OWNS HIS CONFLICT WITH HIS PARENTS

At this point in the treatment, Tom wrote a letter to his parents indicating that he had avoided taking responsibility for his own anger at them about having felt enslaved during his childhood. He courageously admitted that he had blamed Annie for the alienation that existed between him and them, and had used Annie to express his negative feelings toward them.

Tom: I haven't gotten any response from my parents about the letter, even though I've had several conversations with them the past several weeks. My father did thank me for the letter, but didn't say anything else. I want a response, and if they don't give it, I plan to call them up. My father was in the hospital with heart trouble; they think he possibly had a heart attack. [Tom probably feels some anxiety that his expressing anger had hurt his father, in accordance with the family myth.]

Annie: When Tom asked his mother how she was feeling about his father, she said "I'm OK."

Tom: She did say that she had supportive friends; that she expected him to die before she did; and she cried. My brother did send a letter addressed to me in which he said, "I talked with Dad. Why don't you come for a visit? Dad may not make it through this." He thought that a brief visit every other year was not too much. He said, "Come to celebrate and not to mourn, and come with Annie, or come alone if necessary." He underlined Annie. I then wrote my brother a letter, also addressing it to his wife. I told him that I share his anxiety about Father's health. I appreciated his wanting us to come, but had felt pressured and resented that. We have done all the visiting. How about you coming out here? I also asked him why he didn't address his letter to Annie also. I had mentioned to Mom over the phone that Annie didn't want to come out. I had asked Annie and Mom to speak to each other directly, and for my brother himself to address letters to Annie and speak to her directly also. I told him I missed them all, and would welcome a session with a family therapist there to help resolve issues between us. [Tom reports communication with his brother, in which he encourages inclusion of Annie.]

Annie: His brother had been the problem child when they were growing up. We heard about how he almost killed his mother by expressing his feelings. He's the most expressive, but now I'm the bad expressive one. [She comments that the scapegoat role, which is assigned to the one expressing the family's feelings, has switched from Tom's brother to her.]

Tom: He was always the artistic one, and was a hippy before.

Annie: But now he's pushy like your mother. He implies that this is what you should be doing or else you are a bad person. [Annie implies that Tom and his brother have also switched roles regarding who is the compliant good one and who the rebellious bad one.]

Tom: But he did say come for celebrations and not only for mourning. [Tom does not feel scapegoated but welcomed.]

Annie: I'm the bad one now, and before me your brother was the bad one for being distant. There always needs to be a scapegoat so that your mother does not have to express her own angry feelings. [Annie recognizes the family's need to scapegoat either her or Tom's brother.]

Tom: I feel good I've expressed my feelings directly, and am asking for a response. Now it's up to them.

Annie: I had been presented as the problem, and still feel it's defined that way. Your brother only wrote to you and not to me. Would you write him and not his wife also, and then tell him about his wife? You don't defend me until I made a fuss about it. You keep encouraging me to take the initiative. If you resolve your problems with your family, things will be automatically fine between them and me. If you express your feelings honestly, I won't have to do that for you. I won't take the initiative to write to your mother. It's not that important to me; it's important for you. [Annie recognizes that she has caught the hot potato, the scapegoat role, so that Tom can remain idealized. She hands it back to Tom as his own.]

Therapist: Tom, there still seems to be a conflict in dealing with your parents. You've been able to express your anger, but you also risk not getting their acceptance and love, which you want. [The conflict is redefined as Tom's, while the progress he has made in risking a confrontation with his family is recognized.]

Annie: I just get Tom's anger, and they get his love. [She recognizes Tom's splitting of his ambivalence.]

Tom: I want to get rid of the family curse of emotional tightness, of also being unable to give. I have a lot of fear even of expressing love; I'll be vulnerable to being controlled, yet I want an honest relationship with my parents.

Annie: A lot of time and attention is still being focused on his parents, and not on his own family with me. It seems little positive energy is being put into me; I don't hear you say "I love you." I want to hear about what you like about me. I want to feel cared for. [She exposes her needy self to Tom, and her wish for protection and caring.]

Tom: I have fears of being controlled and vulnerable if I'm open, even though I do want to be honest to myself and with others. [He expresses his fear of and wish for closeness.]

Annie: When you are open, I feel secure, and am less critical and need to control you less myself. I am different than your mother; I'm not controlling of your feelings. I never feel critical unless you start to pull away. [She tries to differentiate herself from the mother transference, and expresses her own fear of abandonment.]

Tom: I guess it's all my fault. [He withdraws, feeling she is projecting blame.]

Annie: Sometimes I feel I need a boyfriend, not a sexual partner, just to say nice things to me and make me feel good as a woman, like you used to do. [She reveals her need for narcissistic supplies, to feel special to Tom.]

Tom: I don't feel I can satisfy your needs sometimes. I feel like a failure financially, and I can't make you happy. I feel you have the high ground. You define what makes you happy, and I'm supposed to do it. [He experiences Annie's need for protection and affection as a demand to which he has to submit, like with his mother.]

Annie: But our relationship is so much like the one you had with your first wife and your mother. Your main concern was not to have any conflict, instead of just being loving and affectionate. When I'm loving toward you, you also push me away. [She describes Tom as avoiding a dominance–submission battle with her as with his mother.]

Tom: But you abuse me. The other day you cursed at me. [He fears being hurt if close.]

Annie: But you abuse me also. I said that after you provoked me by leaving when I asked you to stay. [She had felt abandoned and had responded with anger.]

Tom: I have accepted that I need individual therapy. [This was said in an angry tone of voice.]

Therapist: It sounds like you are just complying with Annie out of anger. [The therapist explores if Tom is again demonstrating a false self, compliant but sarcastic.]

Tom: She defines how I have to change, and she feels justified in being angry at me and saying whatever she wants to say. [He notes Annie's not taking responsibility for her comments.]

Annie: But you can't accept responsibility for your problems from your past that are unresolved. No, I'm not just defending myself because you say it's my fault. If you want individual therapy, you have to do it for yourself and honestly believe you want help, and not do it to give in or spite me. [She interprets his motives.]

Tom: But my anger only comes out with you and not with others. [He projects blame onto Annie.]

Annie: But those are superficial relationships you have with others. What kind of loving relationships have you had? You should want to change for yourself. You're being Mr. Nice Guy for everyone. It's like my father, who used to buy drinks for everyone. He wanted everyone to think of him as the good Joe. But others didn't know how he really was with his family. [She interprets her transferential perception of Tom being like her father and assuming a false self, Mr. Nice Guy, to feed his own ego.]

Therapist: Clearly Tom has his own problems stemming from his childhood, but Annie, you yourself notice that you overreact with anger when Tom's behavior reminds you of your father's. [Tom's problems are acknowledged, but Annie's father transference onto Tom is noted as well.]

Annie: Both Tom and my father could only express anger and not loving feelings to me. [She verifies this interpretation.]

Therapist: I know that's a sensitive area for you that's still raw. [Empathic response is made and encouragement given for further exploration.]

Annie: I used to cry a lot; I needed more and felt unloved by my father. With Tom, I feel he loves me. But both of them direct a lot of anger at me.

Therapist: That must have affected the way you felt about yourself. [Exploration is made of the genesis of her lowered self-esteem, self-blame, and anger at her father.]

Annie: My mother set me up to express her angry feelings, and then my father would dump his anger on me. He even said to me that I ruined their marriage. That made me feel terrible about myself. Now I realize neither he nor my mother could take responsibility for themselves. That's what gets me angry. [She is now not self-blaming, but aware of the limitations of both her parents.]

Therapist: You're tired of getting others' anger dumped on you.

Annie: I have my own anger about things, without theirs being added.

SESSION EIGHT: TOM OPENLY EXPRESSES ANGRY AND COMPETITIVE FEELINGS

Tom: There hasn't been any response to my letter, and I'm upset. I plan to call my parents for a response; it's hard for me to stand the silence.

Annie: Did you ask for a response in your letter? With your family if you don't specifically ask for a response, and especially if it's an uncomfortable issue, they don't reply. Maybe they thought you were just sharing your feelings. [She mentions avoidance being used by Tom's family.]

Tom: I did get a nasty note from my brother recently, saying cut the bull and get your ass out here, your parents are ill. He implies that my father is about to die. (Turning to Annie) I want to handle this myself, is that OK? [He shows anger at Annie, anticipates she will interrupt.]

Annie: Fine. I keep telling you it's your issue. I'm happy you are handling it.

Tom: I'd like to visit my folks in late March, and invite all of them out here for next Christmas. They've only been here a few times before. I would have liked to invite them to come, but they did not show any initiative either. The initiative could come from either end. I'll call for a response, and if they refuse to give it I'll express my dismay. If they do respond, I'll listen. I'm also going to call my brother to tell him he's being manipulative. [Tom shows initiative and self-assertion.]

Annie: Weren't you hurt by your brother's letter? I'd be. [She is supportive.]

Tom: He was discrediting what I was trying to say. He's now the protector of the status quo in the family. [He feels displaced by his brother.]

Therapist: Are you implying that he's the family spokesman, and is expressing your parents' feelings? [Suggestion made that his parents express their emotions and communicate now through his brother.]

Annie: I'll bet your mother set him up to write the letter.

Tom: I wouldn't be surprised if my mother did, but I will not say it is so unless I have real evidence. [This is said with annoyance.]

Therapist: Tom, you seem annoyed at my suggestion. [His anger is picked up, and he is encouraged to express it toward the therapist.]

Tom: I'm hesitant to say he's the spokesman, though I'm sure my mother did talk to him. I did challenge him in my letter that he was the pawn for Mother. [He does share the same assumption regarding his brother.]

Therapist: Yet, Tom, you appeared angry at me for suggesting the same possibility. How do you account for that? [His transference to the therapist is explored.]

Tom: I'm upset at my brother and both you and Annie for speculating who is expressing feelings for whom. I don't express feelings for the family, although I did sum up the feelings for the family at my grandfather's funeral. [He expresses his anger openly, and relates to a time when he was a family spokesman.]

Annie: Maybe you're annoyed that your brother is the spokesman now, and you feel you should be it. [She reveals the competition between Tom and his brother, and his displacement of his anger onto Annie and the therapist over that.]

Tom: Maybe I am jealous. For a long time he was the bad guy, and I was the spokesman. Now we have reversed roles and he is the spokesman, and I'm the bad guy. [Honest acknowledgement is made of his hurt feelings over loss of special status to his brother.]

Annie: When you were younger, your brother was more expressive of his feelings. He expressed the unacceptable emotions for the family.

Tom: How could one person express another's feelings?

[He suddenly reverses his field and challenges Annie and the therapist, using denial.]

Annie: Wow, your mother doesn't express her negative feelings, and your brother seems to do it now. It's like what my own mother did with me against my father, when she couldn't express her feelings to him directly herself.

Therapist: Are you angry at me for suggesting that your brother is now the spokesman and the good one, close to your mother, since you have reversed roles, and that now they feel you are the bad one? Perhaps in a parallel fashion you feel the same way here, that Annie and I have teamed up against you, like your mother and brother, leaving you as the outsider. [Interpretation made of his sibling (and probably oedipal) rivalry. He is angry at me due to his brother transference on me and his mother transference on Annie; and of his experiencing himself as left out as he was with his mother and brother (and probably father). His brother is special, and he is bad.]

Tom: We seem to be competing here, I agree, for who has an accurate perception of what is going on. I was upset at my brother's note and his lack of concern for my feelings. He implies I should run home immediately as if my parents were going to fall over dead any minute. I'm in touch with them by phone and know what's happening. [He avoids the transference interpretation and also avoids expressing anger at the therapist directly.]

Therapist: I guess you feel competitive with me just as with your brother, who feels he has the truth and is closer to your mother. Is that why you are angry at me? [The brother transference interpretation is repeated to Tom, to explore his anger at being displaced by his brother in the favored position. There is probably sibling rivalry and oedipal conflict as well.]

Tom: You harp on that too much. At times people express their own feelings; it's an individual thing. One person's unique feelings cannot be expressed by another. [He expresses denial, and resists dealing with the transference interpretation. Since this may be too threatening, it is decided not to pursue it any further.]

Annie: But in my case my mother was angry at my father. She didn't go to him and say directly "I'm angry at you." She told me "your father is terrible," and I confronted him.

Tom: I call that her looking for sympathy. I was also looking for sympathy, and unwilling to express my anger, and inadvertently made you a scapegoat with my family. But that's not asking you to express my feelings for me. [He denies projecting his anger into Annie.]

Therapist: I guess what you are saying is that Annie shares some responsibility in taking on the role of expressing your anger. [Tom points out that people are differentiated and not fused. Therapist acknowledges that people may have their own motivations for accepting the role of avenger and acting it out.]

Tom: Yes, the other person is not will-less and mindless, is not a clone. Something is operating in the other person when he or she decides to express another's feelings. Something in you responded to the vibrations from your mother, Annie. You had some responsibility of your own for expressing her feelings also. [He wants to avoid feeling blamed, to share responsibility, and to point out that people are differentiated rather than fused.]

Therapist: In the last session Annie agreed with you, Tom. She did say she took on the role of expressing her mother's anger, since it gave her a special position with her mother over her sister, and she felt needed and closer. I guess, Tom, you are alluding to the same issue, that one person is not a victim of the other.

Annie: Yes, it was my way of getting closer to my mother, but it only occurred when she needed me. So I took the role that she offered. Now that I have left that role, my sister took it on and plays it to the hilt. [She acknowledges the gratifications she received by accepting the role of avenger, even though mother was coercive. Now her sister has won the sibling rivalry by adopting the same role vacated by Annie.]

Therapist: How about your family, Tom. Were there rewards for assuming the role of family spokesman? [The triangulation and splitting in Tom's family is explored.]

Tom: I got personal gratification for giving the family eulogy at my grandfather's funeral. I felt good about that, but people didn't give me strokes. When I said something negative about my grandfather later, however, I did get the opposite response, all negative. It was like there was a taboo against saying anything negative. I still have difficulty and am unable to speak, but I can write well. That's why when I had something negative to say to my family, I didn't call them but wrote them a letter. [He explains his verbal block as due to the family rule about not *saying* anything negative, explaining also his fear of verbally expressing criticism directly at the therapist.]

Annie: It's not that you can't express yourself; you do very well in writing. It's when you are confronted directly by your mother or your brother or me that you inhibit yourself from speaking and draw back. [She supports his ability to express his negative feelings in writing, though he is blocked verbally.]

In an individual session with Tom, he did express his feeling that Annie and I [the therapist] were close and that he felt left out, an outsider. He felt competitive, just as he did with his mother and brother. He was able to acknowledge that he experienced feelings of rejection and anger, but feared expressing and admitting his anger toward me. He feared that it would alienate him further, just as he feared that his expressing his anger would alienate his narcissistically vulnerable mother. He was also fearful of acknowledging and expressing his jealousy of his brother, who had gotten out of doing many of the farm chores, because he was smaller and frail. Tom had followed the family rule about not *verbally* expressing anger or other negative feelings.

SESSION NINE: CONFLICT OVER CLOSENESS AND BEING CONTROLLED

Tom: We've accomplished the best planning for the holidays that we've ever had since the beginning of the marriage. It takes into account everybody's interests. I got a letter from both my father and my mother. My father was gracious, philosophical, and understanding. He was not defensive, but he was protective of my mother. [Tom and Annie seem to be working together cooperatively now, and Tom is happy with the response from his father.]

Annie: But he did agree with everything his wife wrote, he said in his letter. He wrote that she has been a wonderful and sensitive wife to him. [She points out limitations in the father's response.]

Tom: Yes, he said that, but he said it about her as a wife. He did not say she was a wonderful parent or mother. He experienced her differently than I did. [He clarifies the difference, and still feels validated by his father's response.]

Annie: It sounded again to me as if he was saying don't get her upset, she's so wonderful and sensitive. [Annie interprets the father's letter as repeating the family myth of the mother's vulnerability.]

Tom: When I was a child he used to take us aside and say that Mother was sensitive and not to upset her. It felt like a club held over our heads; the club was guilt. But the letter was different, the way I perceived it. My mother's letter, however, was defensive. She said she had felt loved as a child and was secure, and that it was I who was distant. She also said she tried to accept Annie as my wife, and at first their relationship was good but then it totally changed. [Tom acknowledges his feeling controlled by guilt about his mother's vulnerability, the family myth, as well as her continuing to put responsibility for their alienation onto him.]

Annie: She took no responsibility for her own behavior, whereas his father, who was never cold or manipulative like her, asked if there was anything he had done to alienate Tom. He said to please let him know because he wants to work it out, so we can have a close relationship. His mother said she thought the pain from the past was over, and she just doesn't want to discuss it anymore. [She clarifies the different positions of Tom's parents, the father receptive to resolving conflict and the mother defensive.]

Tom: My father suggested that I come out alone to clear up things. It was a different parental response, but my mother stayed the same. I don't know how to respond further; I've expressed my feelings openly to them and left it up to them. [Tom is working through his feelings regarding his parents.]

Therapist: It is a change, as you say, since in the past you had to swallow your negative feelings or you would feel guilty that you had not followed your father's instructions about not upsetting your mother. [Now his father is willing to open up negative issues and attempt to resolve them, instead of suppressing them to preserve his wife's self-esteem and survival in the symbiotic survival pattern.]

Annie: Even when you wrote those negative things in your letter, they were not hard or nasty, yet your mother responded in a cold, defensive way. You said "I love you" to them, but also that there were painful experiences from your childhood that you need to talk to them about. She responded by calling your brother, who then sent you a nasty letter, and then she wrote her own letter that was defensive. I don't think you'll ever get more from her; the close relationship that you had wanted with her will have to remain superficial. [She supports Tom's handling of the matter and his accepting his mother's limitations.]

Tom: I now don't expect a close relationship with her, but expect it not to be disruptive to our marriage. I had a dream last night I wanted to talk about. I was a new recruit in the Army, or exposed to a fraternity hazing that was humiliating. I had to hold my hands and feet a certain way, and a drill sergeant was shouting at me. It was dehumanizing and was breaking down my self-respect. I had to say, "Yes, sir, thank you, sir," in the midst of being brutalized. I think it reminds me of my lack of freedom at home, of having to behave in a self-limiting way that was expected of me, in terms of what I could say or do. To add insult to injury,

I also had to be polite, and accept the restrictions on my freedom without saying anything negative about it, which was doubly humiliating.

Therapist: So, you felt controlled and restricted in your speech and behavior in your family, Tom. You felt you had to obey, and, in addition, to put up a smiling front, which was further hurtful to yourself. [Tom's statements are repeated so he can hear himself again, and can continue to work through the conflict and the need to split off anger. On hindsight, the therapist felt Tom and Annie should have been encouraged to associate more to the dream. Most of Tom's associations were to the past, which avoided the expression of his affect in his current relationships. The therapist then questioned (to himself) whether he was also being overly protective of Annie, like Tom's father, because of a countertransference reaction.]

Tom: I had to bury parts of myself in order to do what was prescribed in my family. In my work, I don't give people orders or try to control them. I have more confidence in people's good will and ability to do things, though I am against an extreme level of individualism in society. I exert my leadership in a low-keyed democratic way. When I come up against someone very verbal or aggressive, I can't respond in kind, however. I would have gotten farther in my career if I could have been more assertive. [He recognizes his inhibitions, which block his growth in his current career. In hindsight, the therapist thinks Tom probably felt the same control and constriction in the expression of affect with him as well, which should have been inquired about. Allowing Tom in therapy to deal just with past relationships goes along with his distancing himself from his current relationships.]

Annie: But you lump together being assertive and being aggressive. You keep in what is bothering you even now, and it later comes out in passive-aggressive ways. [Annie, feeling more secure, brings his past conflicts into his current relationships and encourages their expression. She also differentiates assertion from aggression — saying, in effect, that it does not have to be hurtful.]

Tom: But sometimes it isn't necessary to say everything that bothers me each time it occurs. Sometimes I see you as pretty aggressive. [He talks about here-and-now issues and is critical of Annie.]

Annie: But when I say something you don't agree with, you could say that what I said bothers you or that you disagree. Instead you don't respond and you become cold and distant. You restrict and control yourself. Is it aggressive for you to say that something bothers you? [Annie points out that Tom feels constricted and controlled not by others but by his own fear of assertiveness.]

Tom: I wish we could get away from the mutual blaming. It's baloney—when you become hysterical and overexcited, you perceive things about me all in a negative light. Then you have to push, and pick, and nail me down like that drill sergeant in the dream, about how I should behave. And there is always another step I need to take. You always say that I should do all the changing, and you are not responsible for your stuff.

Annie: What do you mean?

Tom: You dominate discussions like this, as to who is right and wrong. You get mad and stomp off when we have a fight. It's me who comes back and wants to talk it over. [Tom sees Annie as the controlling drill sergeant, who rejects if he does not obey.]

Annie: But you want to talk things over only long after the problem has persisted for several weeks or months. I have taken responsibility for the way I treated you. I thought you were like my father. I feared that you would leave and abandon me like he did. But part of you is unpleasant. You present yourself as lily white, and I've been that part of you that is disgusting to you. If you were more honest about your own feelings, you wouldn't sulk before you eventually get around to talking. [Annie points out his share of the responsibility, and his using her to express unacceptable split off aspects of himself.]

Tom: But you'd throw things at me or want to throw me out the door at times. [He points out her responsibility in the conflict.]

Annie: That is only after you sit there calmly and say to me, "What's wrong with you, why are you so upset and hysterical?" That's what gets me furious. Then later, I used to pout and feel unloved when Tom got angry at me.

Therapist: It sounds like you, Annie, were inadvertently behaving like Tom's mother, becoming defensive and withdrawing when you felt hurt and angry. You experienced Tom as an abandoning father. [Annie's father transference onto Tom, and how her response stimulated Tom's negative mother transference onto her, are pointed out.]

Annie: Initially, I used to yell and get it all out, but that terrified Tom. Then he would pout and feel rejected. He couldn't stand my yelling, and would leave if I did that. He reacted to me the way his mother reacted to him, withdrawal if confronted with anger. [Annie also points out Tom's identification with the aggressor, his mother, doing to her, Annie, what his mother did to him. She, out of fear of abandonment by a father figure, inhibited her aggression, became defensive, and withdrew. This in turn reminded Tom of his abandoning mother.]

Tom: But you would say that you don't need any man, that I was just like your father, and I should get out of your life. [He points out Annie's father transference onto him, a manic defense against dependency.]

Annie: And you'd say, "I don't know if I love you, you're so controlling and hysterical." You knew that by calling me names and by withdrawing, or calmly saying, "I don't know what you are so hysterical about," that it would upset me. You were saying, "I'm lily white and you're all the problem," which is just what your mother did to you. [She spells out his identification with his mother and the use of splitting and projective identification.]

Therapist: It sounds like the problems each of you had—Annie with your father abandoning you, and Tom with your mother controlling you—entered into your current difficulties relating to one another and caused the escalation of your conflicts. [This points out that their transferential reactions interact in a circular manner to create a vicious cycle of escalating conflict.]

Annie: I have tried to work on myself in individual therapy to change, and have not tried to change Tom.

Tom: A deep mutual respect is lacking between us, and I always feel in a subordinate position.

Annie: But I feel you control the relationship.

Therapist: Then each of you feels the other controls the relationship. [Both feel dominated and victimized by the other due to their transferential relationships.]

Annie: I accept that you, Tom, are more proficient than I am in certain areas, but you don't think anyone can do anything better than you. [She presents an issue.]

Tom: I don't understand that; give me an example. [He takes a nondefensive and problem-solving approach.]

Annie: I'm a good cook, but if you go into the kitchen to cook, and I say anything, you right away say, "Don't tell me what to do."

Therapist: Both of you felt you were manipulated and controlled in your childhood, and you each still experience yourself in the same way, as subject to the other. [Transferential feelings are being experienced in their current relationship.]

Tom: You're damned tootin'! And I'll not let anyone do it again. Why don't we experiment in letting go of control. We made a bet that if we got more than twelve Christmas cards in the next two days, I'd win; and if we got less, you'd win. We bet money, but why don't we change that in terms of who initiates activities the following day. [He proposes a game to loosen control and generate some trust by structuring activities, which some family therapists actually prescribe.]

Annie: I don't see why that has to be done, especially winning a competition. [She is concerned about the competitive nature of the game.]

Tom: We have been at loggerheads on the control issue. Instead, why don't I take Saturday, and I'll initiate our activities, and you take Sunday, when you can initiate all the activities. Instead of a competition, we'll just alternate. How's that? I'm proposing that we do something where we can get out of this power struggle. [He accommodates to Annie's concerns about competition and changes the format.]

Annie: Do you think that this one exercise will change everything? I don't know.

Therapist: Perhaps the exercise will not work, and you may be disappointed, Annie, but Tom is trying to propose some way of developing mutual trust and respect between you and thus diminish the need for control. [He is supportive of Tom's intent, and both of their desires for a more trusting cooperative relationship.]

Annie: But he started out by proposing it as a contest, and I became suspicious.

Tom: It's not a contest; it's only a silly game. We could simply flip a coin on taking turns. It's not winning over the other and dominating them. I enjoy it when we are able to make light of things and just have fun. [Playfulness coming back into the relationship.]

Annie: OK, but it shouldn't be a competition. We can alternate, and it will be just fun.

SESSION TEN: TRUST AND OPENNESS ALLOWS CONFLICTS TO BE RESOLVED

Annie: Things are much better between us. The game didn't turn out as we hoped, but we are working out our problems together. There is much less tension. But I still worry that you, Tom, keep things to yourself and build up anger. [She acknowledges change is occurring for the better, but fears a recurrence of conflict if Tom buries his feelings.]

Tom: I don't just keep things to myself, although I know it's a troubling issue for Annie. I simply forget the issue if it is something she feels strongly about and I don't. If she likes it, I'll do it. [He denies he is complying and storing up resentment.]

Annie: An issue did come up, and we resolved it. I couldn't go to a group session at our church that was held about stress. I wasn't feeling well, so Tom went alone. My friend Sally later called me up and told me what happened there. The participants broke up into small groups. She saw Tom expressing his stress in the form of a mime. He was holding his head and saying "Oh, Oh!" A woman in his group was holding her back where she felt stress, and complained. I thought Tom had instructed her to be like me, like a psychodrama, but I later found out from Tom, when I asked him, that the woman was just doing her own thing. I had assumed he resented my complaining about my back, and I put two and two together and was upset when I asked him about what happened. He was surprised I would be upset, and became angry. [Annie is still distrustful of Tom's openness and empathy toward her.]

Tom: You make assumptions. You put two and two together and get six. I hadn't said much about the evening, since I thought it was a waste of time. I also resented Sally calling you up to report what happened. When I put my hands on the sides of my head, I moved it from side to side as if I were torn by conflict. I get tired of your suspiciousness. [He expresses his anger directly and verbally to Annie.]

Annie: It has to do with your resenting my being sick with a bad back at times. [She gives reasons for her suspiciousness.]

Tom: You exaggerate the matter. I'm not resentful. If I challenge what you say, you become defensive and make me the issue. You always feel in the right, as if it is always my fault. What is your responsibility? [Tom resents always being seen as the abandoning bad object.]

Annie: Shouldn't I have talked to Sally? I didn't call her. She called me to talk.

Tom: You should have checked it out with me before jumping to negative conclusions about me.

Annie: But in the past I would have withdrawn and said nothing. I did come to you to check it out, and you became upset. No matter what I do, I feel I can't win. You want me to go around with a grin pasted on my face at all times. [Annie draws attention to her change in behavior, but still has difficulty containing Tom's anger and dealing with it.]

Tom: But nothing terrible happened when I got angry; I apologized when I got angry. I took responsibility for my anger. I wish you could have held your feelings in abeyance for a few minutes, until you checked out the information that you got from Sally. [He comments on her impulsivity and lack of trust, and points out that anger need not be labeled as bad.]

Annie: You should know that people can control behavior but not feelings. I did check it out with you, and I told you I believed you.

Tom: It upset me that you made a negative assumption about me. You didn't trust me, and I trust you.

Annie: But I don't feel I know you well enough to trust you. You keep a lot of yourself hidden, and you make fun of me about being sick. So I wonder what you say to others. [She explains her difficulty in trusting Tom now as due to his past behavior.]

Therapist: Both of you are quite sensitive. You, Annie, feel hurt if Tom makes fun of your not feeling well, and you, Tom, are hurt that Annie doesn't trust you.

Tom: I know that who I am triggers off who your ex-husband and father were.

Annie: Just like I trigger off issues between you and your mother. I am now 90 percent more trustful. When I first met you I was trustful, and then you did things that were hurtful. You'd withdraw each time we had a fight and would threaten to leave. Most people have differences, but don't threaten rejection. [She explains how Tom's behavior activated her transferential fears of abandonment by her father.]

Tom: But if two people continue to have such differences without resolution, I felt there would be too much pain for me to be able to stay. [He is working through conflict from his perspective.]

Annie: I always felt you had one foot out the door.

Tom: I always felt you had a dagger at my back.

Therapist: You each had great insecurities. [He encourages them to avoid blame and to share responsibility for conflicts.]

Annie: For Tom, not having pain or conflict is more important than the relationship.

Tom: But if our relationship had continued without love and trust, it would have been impossible for us both. [He tries to resolve conflict.]

Annie: Now we are working on it and are committed to each other. [She agrees and is hopeful about their relationship.]

Tom: I agree. But if we get into a period of continuous unresolved conflict, I wouldn't stay. I think too much of myself to just be masochistic.

Therapist: That's a sensitive area for Annie, the threat of a man's leaving her like her father. [He interprets father transference.]

Annie: That's why he says it. [She feels he inflicts wounds on her Achilles' heel, where she is narcissistically vulnerable.]

Tom: You should believe I love you, and you know I want to work on our relationship. You also threatened to leave when we fought. It mucks up painful stuff from the past that I feel has already been resolved. [Annie also inflicts wounds and threatens rejection, Tom states.]

Annie: I asked you not to bring up leaving, and you promised not to say it. Maybe you don't want me to trust you, when you know the effect it has on me. [She questions his resistance to change and unwillingness to give up his internal bad maternal object (O−).]

Tom: But I want you to have whatever feelings you have.

Therapist: It seems that both of you are fearful of expressing your anger, fearful that the other will move away or reject you. We know that you, Tom, felt compelled to be the good boy, not to say anything if it wasn't nice or else your mother would withdraw and side with your brother. And you, Annie, you know that your mother was fearful about expressing her anger at her ex-husband. He might reject her, and you had to express her anger for her. Then when your mother later became angry at you, she sided with your ex-husband and turned against you. Thus expressing anger for each of you was associated with rejection, and was a source of pain and unhappiness. [He describes fear of anger as destroying the relationship to the good object.]

Annie: When I moved here my mother was angry at me for

leaving; and when I married Tom, she rejected me. It was very hurtful, but I got support from my other relatives and friends. I expressed my feelings of betrayal by her to others. When I wanted to write her a letter, you, Tom, and my aunt told me not to do so and were against it, so I didn't.

Tom: I was wrong, you should have expressed your anger at your mother. Even your aunt, through the years since then, has seen how cruel your mother has been. Sending a letter to her with your honest feelings might have unburdened you. [He admits his mistake and is supportive.]

Annie: If I write her now, I'll get no reaction from her. [She still fears rejection.]

Tom: But I see you burdened by your angry feelings toward her. It helped me when I wrote to my mother. I felt clean and good, even though it didn't get the response I had hoped for and wanted. There is no reason to keep those feelings from your mother. You have nothing to lose. You still seem to feel guilty and burdened by your having moved here. You felt you had to leave your mother and abandon her for your own sanity. [He shows support and understanding.]

Annie: I used to feel my mother needed me, and I left and abandoned her. [She expresses guilt over separating from her narcissistically needy mother, whom she hurt by leaving.]

Therapist: You felt you were supposed to rescue her and take care of her, as if you were the mother and she the child. [He acknowledges her expectations of herself and the role reversal.]

Annie: Yes, I did, and then I gave the role over to my sister. When I first left and came here, I felt guilty, since I had taken her grandchildren away. When I left my ex-husband, I gave up the role of taking care of him and also of my mother. I only wanted to be a mother to my kids and take care of them. My sister was jealous of me and my closeness to my mother and took on that role. [She discusses her sibling rivalry and her ability to separate by the sister's assuming the O+ role for mother.]

Therapist: That situation with your mother and sister sounds so very painful, and I guess you felt betrayed by them. [He attempts to work through her distrust after having been exploited and rejected.]

Annie: And my father too. Maybe I deserved it, maybe I was a bad person. I got negativity and rejection from my father also until I was 30, and then got it from my mother. I was never good enough. Whatever I did, they wanted more. My father wanted me to perform more, and my mother wanted more of being taken care of. I feel that way with Tom, that I should be a tall strong farm-girl, who doesn't show her feelings. He doesn't like that I'm small and emotional. He makes fun of my little chicken-bone wrists. Tom, I feel you are always putting me down. [She expresses her feelings about being bad and inadequate, which stem from her relationship with her parents, and now from Tom.]

Tom: About your smallness, I thought it was only a joke. I was teasing and it was my way of expressing my caring.

Annie: Maybe that is your way of showing your affection, but I wish you would be more direct.

Tom then hugged her and did express his admiration for Annie. After five more sessions the couple discontinued treatment, since they were getting along very well. I heard from Annie six months later that their relationship was supportive and loving.

13

The Narcissistic/Borderline Couple

ATTRACTION FOR EACH OTHER

One of the most frequently encountered types of dysfunctional couples is that composed of a narcissistic person married to a borderline person. The narcissist, who is obsessional, finds the borderline person's expressiveness exciting. The borderline person experiences the narcissist as calming and containing of emotionality. After a honeymoon period, these narcissistic/borderline relationships are prone to develop friction. Such couples later come to therapy because of severe marital or family conflict. Each feels a victim of the other, helpless and reacting to the other's abuse. Each feels justified in demanding that the other change first, places responsibility onto the other, and makes no real effort to change. The result can be a stalemate.

Lachkar (1985), using self psychology concepts, noted that these couples had a shared unconscious fantasy. The narcissist and the borderline each need mirroring by the other as a selfobject (O+), but feel they can never attain the object. But each experiences disruption of the relationship to the other as a selfobject in a distinctly different manner. The borderline is dominated by the overt fear of abandonment, and feels worthless and depleted. Because of the lack of impulse control, the borderline tends to be clinging and demanding. The narcissist, fearing being invaded and taken over by the borderline's demands, withdraws. A to-and-fro dance ensues. The borderline person experiences this withdrawal as an abandonment and may respond in two ways: (1) to criticize or to make suicide threats, which only tends to further the withdrawal of the narcissist, or (2) to become compliant. If the latter option is chosen, the borderline may submerge personal needs and "be good," to gratify the narcissist's grandiose needs to be appreciated as special. The narcissist then returns, but ultimately is ungratifying toward the borderline, who again feels abandoned and becomes demanding. Thus a vicious cycle is established, with both seeking selfobjects $(O+)$ to confirm their personalities. Each feels victimized by not getting what he or she needs and tries to manipulate, control, or punish the other.

REPETITION OF PARENTAL RELATIONS WITH THE SPOUSE

The relationship in the marriage is similar to that in the family of origin. To diminish parental conflict, the narcissist had been used as a go-between $(O+)$, which enhanced his or her infantile grandiosity and feelings of entitlement. At other times, the individual was scapegoated $(O-)$, feeling abandoned and demeaned. There is no integration of these polar opposite or split roles, being alternatively either all good or all bad. The narcissist experiences others similarly in terms of these alternating relationships, with others either feeding the grandiosity $(O+)$ or being perceived as an abandoning object $(O-)$. In turn, narcissists may idealize or demean others, treating them just as they themselves had been treated in their family of origin: The other is either special or nothing. In the Solomon child syndrome, the child's grandiosity is enhanced by performing as a savior $(S+)$ for one parent. But since the child is seen as an ally of that parent, the other spouse displaces anger and scapegoats $(O-)$ the child. This same process occurs with the opposite parent. The child's absorbing the parent's anger preserves the marriage. The child serves as a peacemaker by complying to one parent and absorbing the anger of the other parent, being *alternately* valued or rejected.

With the borderline, during the rapprochement subphase of separation–individuation the mother first clings to the child and then rejects the child for separating (Masterson and Rinsley 1975). This process is repeated later, especially during adolescence and young adulthood. The child is stimulated seductively, used as a go-between (O +), then *permanently* discarded (O −). Thus borderlines do not learn tension control, nor do they need to repress their rage to retain the object, since there is little hope of their being valued again. Because of a feeling of being thrown on the trash heap by the object, a borderline may discard him- or herself by making a suicide attempt (Stone 1988). The borderline can be compared to the psychotic depressive, who destroys and merges with the bad object; whereas the narcissist is like the neurotic depressive, who retains the bad object through compliance.

COMPLEMENTARY PROJECTIVE IDENTIFICATIONS FILLING DEFICITS

There is a shared unconscious collusion between the couple, involving dependency and anger at an abandoning bad parental introject. Since the narcissist idealizes the bad object, and the borderline is openly enraged at the bad rejecting object (Gunderson and Singer 1975), it is easier for the borderline to express rage for both of them. Through projective identification, the narcissist puts anger into the borderline, who serves as an avenger to act out the split-off bad self of the narcissist. In addition the narcissistic individual denies dependency and appears to be self-sufficient. Through projective identification, the clinging and overtly dependent borderline can also express the split-off dependency needs of the narcissist.

The narcissist's obsessive organization is experienced by the borderline as compensating for his or her own deficit in tension control. The borderline hopes his or her impulsivity will be contained by the narcissist, who will function like a powerful good parent (O +) to provide care, protection, and comfort. The borderline may test to see how much anger will be tolerated before he or she is rejected. The narcissist absorbs anger, having been rewarded in childhood for being the parents' peacemaker. Having had to perform this role and complying to the parents' dependent demands is experienced by the narcissist as exploitative and draining. To sustain some autonomy and to express rage indirectly, the narcissist withdraws to create distance. The borderline, who has been used to gratify the narcissist's needs, then feels used and abandoned. This is a repetition of their experiences in their families of origin. The borderline experiences the narcissist as the abandoning bad parental object, and the narcissist sees the borderline as the demanding, dependent, and exploitative bad parent. Each distrusts the other, and does not expect gratification from the rejecting bad object $(O-)$. Each does not have to face the dread of giving up the bad internalized persecutory object and thereby suffering an identity crisis, pain, loss, and mourning. At times these marriages seem to function for long periods of time in a complementary way, with the borderline expressing the dependency and anger for the narcissist, and the narcissist containing the borderline's impulsivity. Rarely each spouse may reown the split off part of the self and individuate. Most often, however, there is a considerable ongoing sadomasochistic interaction, and these marriages remain stuck together. I think the glue is the inability of both the spouses to tolerate intimacy and sharing, and the fear of autonomy, which for them represents abandonment by the bad object. By holding onto this undifferentiated relationship, they minimize the risk of loss of self-esteem which might be entailed in trusting another as a separate person. They each perpetuate their being used and rejected by the other, which is the relationship they expect.

THE NEXT GENERATION

The borderline and narcissistic couple often pass their pathology onto the next generation. Masterson and Rinsley (1975) find that, in cases of children who turn out to be borderline, the mothers cling to their infants during early phases of development, and withdraw their emotional availability when the child makes efforts to separate and individuate during the rapprochement subphase. It is the mother's insecurity and need for control that makes her experience the child's efforts at individuation as a major threat. Thus the child is rewarded for remaining fixated at an undifferentiated level, and punished by abandonment for separation and individuation. Masterson and Rinsley consider that the borderline child has a borderline mother, who is available only if the child remains clinging. My finding with the female borderline is that she is able to separate to some extent from the mother, but attaches to the father, who then functions as a surrogate mother. However, the fathers were narcissistic, and instead of being nurturant also interfered with separation by exploiting the child for their own needs. If the child separates from the father, the child is emotionally abandoned, which recapitulates the earlier trauma with the mother.

The work of Edward Shapiro and colleagues (1975) also found a family constellation with complementary projective identifications between the parents of the borderline patient. There is an unconscious fantasy found in these families that the borderline's efforts at autonomy, along with his or her dependent needs for nurturance and support, have an aggressive and bad intent. The parents see themselves as unidimensional, either "strong and autonomous" or as "lovingly dependent." The dissociated aspect of these traits in each parent is put, through projective identification, into the borderline, who is then punished. If the child is autonomous, this is seen as hostile and rejecting; if dependent, this is seen as ravenously dependent. Thus the conflict that usually occurs openly between the narcissist/borderline couple gets placed into the child. This finding would explain why some investigators, such as Singer (1977), did not find the parents of borderline patients to be overtly disturbed. Here the child's expressing the conflict between the parents could preserve their relationship and their individual functioning.

INDIVIDUAL TREATMENT OF NARCISSISTIC AND BORDERLINE PERSONALITY DISORDERS

In individual therapy with the narcissistic patient, Kohut (1977) recommends that the therapist function as a good selfobject and provide mirroring (admiring responses). By so doing, and also by satisfying the idealizing needs of the patient, the therapist can help the weakened and defective self of the patient to grow into a more authentic and differentiated self. The patient no longer needs to retain an archaic grandiose self, nor to fuse with an omnipotent, idealized selfobject. Modell (1976) similarly recommends that during the first phase of treatment with the narcissistic patient, when the patient maintains a grandiose self as a defense against dependency, a safe holding environment needs to be established. Acceptance without interpretations during this initial "cocoon" phase is needed, with the therapist empathically functioning as a transitional object. This permits sufficient ego consolidation so that the patient can separate sufficiently to express anger. In this second phase, the therapist can interpret the patient's defensive grandiosity and fantasy of self-sufficiency. In the third phase of treatment, a transference neurosis develops which can be interpreted along with other defenses.

Kernberg (1975) suggests that, in individual psychoanalytic psychotherapy of the borderline patient, there needs to be a systematic elaboration of the negative transference in the here and now, without an attempt to achieve complete genetic reconstruction. As these patients develop a negative transference, interpretation of their defenses needs to occur, particularly primitive defenses which contribute to ego weakness and the blurring of boundaries. The therapist has to set firm limits so that acting out of the transference can be blocked; and to effect as much structuring of the patient's outside life as necessary, while protecting the therapist's own neutrality. Distortions of present reality and perceptions of the interaction with the therapist need to be systematically clarified. The positive transference, which is less primitively determined, need not be interpreted in order to foster a therapeutic alliance. Kernberg makes an exception for some borderline patients, who have a high degree of honesty and integrity, and who can undergo unmodified psychoanalytic psychotherapy from the beginning. With others, it is only after working through the primitive level of internalized object relations as manifested in the transference that these patients can accept the shortcomings of their parents, separate from them internally, mourn the loss, and accept their aloneness.

TREATING THE NARCISSISTIC/BORDERLINE COUPLE TOGETHER

Marital or family therapy can serve in a similar way to the beginning phases of individual therapy, and in fact has certain distinct advantages (Slipp 1980). First, the intensity of the primitive transference is diluted, which is particularly useful with the borderline patient. Because of the dilution of the transference, there tends to be less distortion by both spouses. Second, the primitive transferences which involve splitting, denial, idealization, or demeaning of the other already exist with the spouse. These factors enable the therapist to be seen more as an objective observer. The therapist can then join in an alliance with the couple to look at their present interaction in a parallel fashion. The therapist is also more able to contain and acknowledge each of the spouse's feelings and experiences. This acknowledgment not only diminishes tension, but enables each partner to hear the other, and diminishes their egocentric perspectives. Concentrating on their interaction lessens the possibility that each would feel criticized, which is more likely to occur in individual treatment. One danger is the need on the part of both to have the therapist judge one as being the "good" victim and the other as the "bad" persecutor. This is particularly important with these couples, since the narcissist may be seen as the strong, reasonable, good one and the borderline as the weak, angry, demanding, and bad one. By being impartial and empathic to both parties the therapist can point out how aspects of one are put into the other through projective identification—for example, that the borderline is expressing anger or dependency needs for the narcissist. Thus there is a greater chance for integration and reowning of these split-off parts of the personality. Once the partners reown their projective identifications, they tend to experience their problems intrapsychically, and develop more profitably in individual therapy.

The following guidelines for treatment are offered:

1. Set a firm therapeutic framework, with boundaries to prevent acting out.
2. Establish a secure holding environment, by taking an empathic and unbiased position toward both spouses.

3. Be keenly aware of your countertransference reactions, in order to avoid siding with one spouse or reinforcing pathology.

4. Focus on the present interpersonal relationships, especially on circular systemic processes, in the beginning phases.

5. Do not simply gratify the patients' demands to make up for past deprivations, but foster a therapeutic alliance so that the couple can join in exploring and becoming aware of how each of them affects the other.

6. Interpret splitting, so the couple does not perceive others, including the therapist, simply from an egocentric position of whether or not the other gratifies their demands or needs—that is, as either all good or all bad. Help them become aware of others' independent motivations and needs. This enables them to accept interpretations later and enhances their ego growth and differentiation.

7. Interpret projective identification, so that they can reown aspects of themselves that are split off and projected. This facilitates the integration of their ambivalence, and the ability to continue to work on their problems intrapsychically.

8. Interpret their transferences toward each other and the therapist. Help them work through idealization and denial of past conflicts with their parents, so these are not acted out with their spouses in the present. Enable them to become aware of their rage, and to work through past deprivations.

9. Help them give up bad internalized objects, and resolve their fears of the abandonment and lack of survival that might occur if they become autonomous.

10. Help them to separate from past roles and identities, to mourn and work through the deficits they experienced during childhood, and to work out new and healthier ways of relating in the present.

SOL AND DORA: COMPLEMENTARY PROJECTIVE IDENTIFICATIONS

Sol and Dora, a middle-aged couple, came for marital therapy because of a history of long-term conflict. They blamed one another for their problems and felt controlled and victimized by each other. Recently their conflict became escalated, and Sol had moved out because he felt Dora was making too many demands on him emotionally and financially. This was the second marriage for each of them. They had met at a social gathering ten years earlier, and married shortly thereafter. After a year of marriage, conflicts began to emerge. Dora's first husband had been wealthy, and had taken pride in her attractive appearance. She continued to spend large sums of money on clothing, jewelry, cars, and beauty salons. This provoked Sol's anger. He felt used and inadequate, which resulted in his becoming distant. Dora then felt deprived and unhappy, and, in order to compensate, bought more items. She became critical of his emotional unavailability and his controlling behavior. Sol was angry and exasperated with her constant criticism, felt used and invaded by her, and contemplated divorce.

Sol presented himself as an overly responsible person, who wound up always torn between conflicting pressures. He was obsessed over Dora's demands and those of his children. He would set up appointments that were too close to one another, so that he would feel pressured to leave one to be on time for the next. Before he finished one project, he would start another, so that he was constantly pulled in opposite directions. This repetitious pattern was brought out in therapy for investigation, since it caused him to feel pressured and dominated by opposing forces. He acknowledged that all his life he had lived with a high level of tension and anger, and felt constantly invaded by others' demands. He experienced himself as a victim, even though Dora saw him as a domineering bully.

Sol recalled that growing up with his parents was like living in a civil war. His father was athletic and encouraged Sol's playing football, often coming to watch him in games. However, his mother objected to his playing football, and would often come to the playing field, collar him, and take him home to finish his chores and to practice piano. If he played the piano, his father thought him a sissy. He always felt torn between conflicting loyalties. He had been a Solomon child, torn between his parents' conflicting demands and developed a narcissistic personality. In adulthood, Sol unconsciously created dilemmas by setting up situations that would create conflicts of time and energy. Now he was caught between Dora and his children, his job and his therapy, and too many work commitments. He was angry because he felt pressured, out of control, and that he could never succeed. He dealt with these feelings by distancing himself.

Dora complained that Sol treated her as if she were an idiot, and made unilateral decisions for them. She was especially sensitive to this because her father had also demeaned her mother and treated her as an incompetent. Her mother had had low self-esteem, having been treated this way by her mother as well, and thus not feeling entitled to be treated with respect. Sol complained that he took control because Dora could not make decisions. He felt forced to take over and then was criticized by Dora. This seemed to be a variant of his Solomon child syndrome, with one person playing both roles: He performs for Dora and then is criticized.

As a child, Dora had idealized her father. He seemed like a romantic figure to her, who preferred her to her mother. Her father was critical of her mother, and Dora also felt her mother was incompetent. The father seemed to dump his feelings of inadequacy into his wife, who accepted being mistreated by him. The mother could not do anything right for him, even though she constantly strove to please him. He would compare his wife to Dora, and say she ought to be like her daughter. Thus Dora was treated more like her father's wife, and she was discouraged from identifying with her mother. Dora identified with her father and sometimes joined him in demeaning her mother. At other times Dora played the role of mediator in her parents' disputes. Thus Dora was parentified (O+), and also assumed the role of go-between or surrogate spouse to her father.

When Dora was a young child, her mother could not make such simple decisions as what to prepare for dinner, which frustrated her father. However, when Dora reached adolescence, she became ill and her father was not attentive to her. He had started working long hours and was away from home a good deal of the time.

Her mother proved to be the nurturant and reliable parent. Then it was learned that her father was having a long-standing affair. Dora felt betrayed and abandoned by him, and guilty that she had joined him in being abusive to her mother. He then died in an automobile accident. Dora felt that his death was a final betrayal and abandonment by him.

After the father's death, her mother blossomed into a competent woman who obtained employment and demonstrated leadership skills. Dora could not understand this sudden metamorphosis, from being unable to make the simplest decisions to now supervising a number of employees. I suggested that perhaps, by acting indecisively, her mother had unconsciously expressed her anger by frustrating her husband for demeaning her. What better way was there to do that than by using the very incompetence she was accused of by him as a weapon against him. If he put his incompetence into her, she could put her anger into him. Dora came to recognize that she was behaving like her mother toward Sol. Her own indecisiveness was also an unconscious way of frustrating Sol, who she felt controlled her and made her feel inadequate. She felt that if she functioned inadequately for Sol, then he would pay the price by being frustrated. Was she also unconsciously provoking Sol into being like her father, out of her guilt and her identification with her mother? Dora was a high-functioning person with borderline features.

The following sessions deal with some of these issues, since the couple was ready at this point to accept interpretations.

SESSION FIFTEEN: INTERPRETING DORA'S TRANSFERENCES

Dora: I really feel hopeless. We can't have a disagreement without a power struggle. I don't have the privilege with Sol to express anger or have human frailties. He feels he can't win, and needs to steamroller over me to feel adequate. He needs to be in control, but I need respect as a person.

Therapist: As you were talking about Sol, I recalled your saying in the last session how your father behaved similarly. Your father dumped his feelings of inadequacy into your mother, and also didn't seem to tolerate your mother's anger.

Dora: Sol has a stake in keeping me feeling childlike, inadequate, dependent on him, so he can feel better about himself. When he asks a question, and I express an opinion and it's not the answer he wants he'll badger me. Then I become so upset that I begin to feel inadequate like my mother. I feel trapped and unable to make a decision of my own. I know I also play a part in it as well as Sol. It's a familiar scenario; maybe we need it.

Therapist: Dora, what part do you play? [He discourages externalization and encourages introspection.]

Dora: I want someone to take care of me in some areas, and yet I need to be dependent. I don't give up the expectation that this time the relationship will be different. I hope he won't get angry. I keep biting, and hope there won't be a problem this time.

Therapist: How would you like things to be different? [He asks for clarification.]

Dora: I want us to be partners and equal. To allow the other not to have to be perfect all the time. I remember how it was when we first met. Sol was a friend. Now I don't trust him to be helpful, especially when I feel frail or inadequate. If I were sick, he would take care of me physically, but emotionally he would not be comforting. He beats me up emotionally.

Therapist: I recall from the last session how you felt your father also could not be depended upon when you became sick. [Her father transference onto Sol is interpreted.]

Dora: My father couldn't deal with sickness emotionally; he'd withdraw, and my mother did come through consistently.

Therapist: How about you, Sol, what are your reactions to what Dora has just said? [He encourages Sol's self-expression.]

Sol: Dora has a stake in destroying me and us; to destroy me physically and financially. I feel castrated by her, I feel like a nothing. She constantly criticizes me. She's discontented all the time. For example, this morning I asked her if she had her keys, since I won't be home till late tonight, and she gave it to me with both barrels.

Dora: He asked if I had the keys two seconds before I left. I said that I would have appreciated the courtesy of his telling me in advance that he wasn't coming home till late. I thought he would just say I'm sorry, but he couldn't accept that request as legitimate. He interpreted that as my controlling him. I didn't scream at him. I'm simply not allowed to be a person who may not agree with him. I can't express a need without his feeling I'm castrating him.

Sol: That's an example of her anger and rage that are there all the time. If I would have told her earlier, she would have said "not now." I waited till later, and then I was criticized. She should have her keys anyway with her. I don't have to say anything. Am I supposed to be her keeper?

Dora: I had other plans, and suddenly you changed your plans. I'm scared stiff to make any plans of my own, I have to fit myself always into your plans. When I express my needs he tells me I'm castrating him. Can't I get angry without being called castrating?

Sol: I feel frustrated too. I wanted to sit down and discuss expenses and set up a budget. I asked her what she is spending and she refused to cooperate.

Dora: He asked me a question concerning what we needed. I said that I haven't decided yet. He then said I just want to leave everything open-ended.

Sol: But you don't make decisions and get things correct.

Dora: You see he tells me I'm inadequate or stupid.

Therapist: You are experiencing Sol calling you inadequate like your father did to your mother, and I guess you want me to help stop Sol from doing that. [She wants therapist to rescue her, help her to function as an effective mother and set limits with the father.]

Dora: Yes, he doesn't want me to have any independent thought. He chops me apart for the slightest thing. I recently bought two baskets for twelve dollars to please myself, and he accused me of buying them to provoke him. I can't even make a separate decision, even when it's simple.

Sol: But you only make small decisions and not big ones.

Dora: When I don't give him an answer he wants, he badgers me.

Therapist: It sounds like your indecisiveness may be your way unconsciously of expressing your anger at Sol, just as it seems to have been used by your mother. If you were called incompetent, how appropriate to behave indecisively to frustrate the one calling you that. The punishment fits the crime. [He points out her vengeance, which is like a symbolic suicide to punish the other through indirect aggression.]

Dora: I do try to express my anger directly, but he won't allow it. I probably do provoke him into anger, but it's easier not to make decisions than to battle for the decisions I want to make. It's too powerful and terrible a fight if I do it directly. I can't tell him I can't make a decision. Then he'll attack me. He knows my weak spot, my fear of being like my mother. If I fight back we are at war. The choices I have are to be compliant, to battle with him, or to become indecisive and take the rage out on myself.

Sol: You play both roles, however. You tell me you will handle our moving, for example. Then you give me the phone to make the arrangements when the movers call. Then I make the arrangements and you criticize me. I feel set up.

Dora: You told me you wanted to move on Friday, and I asked the movers. They said they weren't able to come till Saturday. I handed him the phone instead of talking back and forth. I told him they can't move us on Friday. Now I hear I'm an incompetent child, who can't do my job. I have to be a good little girl, and do it exactly his way, or else he'll punish me with withdrawal. He treats me like one of his kids and not like an adult. Why do I have to be a clone of you or be badgered?

Therapist: Sol, I was wondering if you experience Dora's requests as orders or commands. We are out of time now. Let's explore that in our next session.

SESSION SIXTEEN: INTERPRETING SOL'S TRANSFERENCES

Therapist: In our last session Dora's experience was that when she made a request of you, Sol, you experienced it as a command, and I was wondering about it from your perspective, Sol. Is it that part of you that feels you have to be a good boy and comply to others' wishes, as if you had no choice, while another part of you is angry and rebellious? [He is exploring Sol's conflict between his compliant false self and his desire for autonomy.]

Sol: I do feel that way. For example, this morning Dora said to me those pants and jacket are horrible together, and I felt I had to change it, but at the same time I resented it.

Dora: But you told me to tell you if things don't look good on you.

Sol: I feel horrible when she tells me my clothes are horrible looking. I'll feel bad all day and feel like a nothing. [Sol's self-esteem is dependent on mirroring.]

Dora: I wasn't saying he's a nothing, just that his clothes did not match or look good together.

Sol: I give in to you for the sake of peace. I've done that all my life. I try to cajole people when they are upset to keep the peace. [Sol assumes the role of savior—a false self—to diminish conflict with others, probably originally to cure his parents' conflicted relationship.]

Therapist: Did you do that with your parents, Sol?

Sol: Yes. I always tried to keep the peace by giving in, but I got more and more angry inside. I didn't want my mother screaming at me. She was worse than my father.

Therapist: You had to be the good boy and give in to your mother's demands or she would scream. [He implies that the false self was also assumed to avoid rejection by his mother.]

Sol: She was very controlling. I had no freedom. I don't know what freedom is. I feel harried and pressured all the time. Even coming here, it conflicts with other things on my schedule.

Therapist: You feel you are being a good boy for me also and giving in like with your mother. [Transference is interpreted.]

Sol: Sure. I feel guilty I'm not at the office if I'm here. I feel compelled to come here. My nerves are on edge all the time.

Therapist: Then you must also feel some anger at me also, since giving in generates a lot of anger. It seems that when someone makes a request, you feel you have to comply to avoid conflict, as you did with your mother; but it is as if you were not a separate person, able to make choices of your own. What were you afraid would happen if you did not comply? [He acknowledges and contains Sol's anger and proceeds then to explore Sol's fear of abandonment if he were to be autonomous.]

Sol: I was afraid they would break up, and I felt responsible to keep them together. I couldn't imagine what my life would have been like being alone with my mother. Even at age 7, I received an award at summer camp for being a peacemaker. I've never had a life of my own. My father wasn't as continuously demanding as my mother, but he wasn't around as much. I'd hear my mother repeatedly saying that she didn't want me to grow up to be like my father. He was never around to take care of things. [He discusses his problem in identifying with his father, because of dysidentification messages from his mother and because of his father's absence.]

Therapist: You felt you had to take care of things?

Sol: I accepted the burden. I learned it was my role to take care of things for others.

Therapist: What about you and your life? [Underlying anger is explored.]

Sol: There is no me, just a mechanical device that does things. [He reveals his lack of a genuine self.]

Therapist: But the part of you that wants to be a separate person is what makes you angry. It seems that only part of you needs to comply to avoid conflict or loss. It sounds like the conflict is about accepting this burden for security reasons or giving up the burden and risking rejection.

Sol: I'm always in a dilemma, torn apart, and nobody cares about me. Maybe I can't be understood. [He blames himself for others' narcissistic exploitation of him.]

Therapist: You feel that people just use you for their own ends, including me. [Transference interpreted.]

Sol: I know I allow others to use me. I know no other way. I've given up, and don't understand another way. I just irritate others. [He has insight that the conflict is internal, but fears change, and blames himself.]

Therapist: Then you are aware that the conflict is inside you. You give in to others' requests, then resent it, and wind up irritating others. Yet in the first place you started being compliant for fear of losing your father, and preserving your parents' marriage.

Sol: But I make it so that everybody does eventually leave me. I bring about what I'm afraid of. I'm fearful that if I do anything positive with Dora, I'll get rebuffed by her and be criticized.

Therapist: You expect Dora to be like your critical mother. It's interesting that, in the last session, we noted that Dora experienced *you* like her critical and demeaning father.

Dora: My father also saw himself as the peacemaker or mediator. My father always sought to prove himself to his father, to be a good boy, and never succeeded. Sol always reminded me of someone. Now it's clearer, it's my father. One thing I noticed is that since his father died Sol changed in his way of relating to me. He became punitive, not supportive or understanding, and disdainful, unable to have fun. He took over his father's personality. When I met Sol, he couldn't stand his father. He was unable to please his father in business or elsewhere. Neither parent said they loved Sol. Now he wants me to be a clone of him just like his father did to him. [She suggests he internalized the lost bad father object.]

Sol: Some if it is right. I was looking for an identity; I felt like a nobody.

Therapist: You say you took on your father's identity when he died, but you didn't like him. How's that?

Sol: He also had some positive attributes. People seemed to like him and he had friends. But I didn't really know him, and his friendships were superficial. For example, I thought my sisters liked him, and were closer to him. But I talked with them recently, and their telephoning him every week was just duty. It was without real affection, and they didn't like him either. Maybe I want to be disliked or hated like my father, at least part of me does. [He mentions identification with his father.]

Therapist: So you think you want others to hate that part of you that is like your father.

Sol: Maybe I need to punish myself.

Therapist: You had said that when you left your father's business because you were so frustrated and angry, your father's business failed. You implied that your father then fell apart, lost his zest for life, and turned into a dried-up old man. Do you feel guilty that when you were not a compliant good boy your father fell apart? You had assumed the compliant role initially to preserve your parents and their marriage. Do you think you need to punish yourself for giving up that role, for separating and leaving your father? [He explores Sol's guilt, and identification with his destroyed and destroying father.]

Sol: I do seem to have a pattern of starting something, then getting shot down and feeling destroyed myself.

Dora: Sol sets up situations so that they can't be successful; he seems to be self-defeating. Then he may blame others for the failure, like me, or he calls himself a failure. We were trying to set up a party for his kids under the most trying of circumstances. Unless he sets up the situation to be almost impossible of attainment, it's valueless. Then when it doesn't materialize, he'll be angry at himself. He'll say, "See, I can't even get a party worked out." If I point out the difficulties of everything falling into place realistically, he'll attack me as fighting him. I become the enemy then.

Therapist: I was just thinking about the dream Sol reported in the session before last. As I recall, you were in a wilderness in Africa surrounded by hostile cannibals. A helicopter lands, and you do not have time to go to your tent to get your possessions, so you leave precipitously. Then you discover as you are flying away that you left your medicines in the tent, and will become sick and die anyway. You couldn't win, no matter what the decision was that you made in this dream. I wonder if you experienced your father as the hostile cannibals. If you stayed in your father's business, you felt you would be eaten up and killed as a person. But you experienced your flying off and being separate as killing your father. He could no longer live off of you, and when you left the business it failed and he deteriorated. Is that sick part of yourself, your guilty self, what causes you to be self-defeating? Are you unconsciously punishing yourself for feeling you hurt your father by not being the good boy and staying, and that I also can't help you since you don't take my medicine? [He interprets the unconscious fantasy of either being murdered and consumed by his father, or murdering his father, which created conflicts over separation and individuation. Did he consume his destroyed and destroying father after his father's death as Dora implies he did?]

Dora: He does have a scenario of trying to be a good boy whom nobody appreciates. That was how he was with his father, and it was the reason he left his father's business. He was never understood or praised. So he then turns around and becomes the bad boy. He can't stay with one or the other, be compliant or rebellious, but vascillates back and forth between them. I've had to live with these two sides of him as if he has two personalities, and I don't know when he will suddenly turn from one to the other.

SESSION SEVENTEEN: INTERPRETING THE COLLUSIVE PROJECTIVE IDENTIFICATIONS

Dora: The other day I asked Sol for a scissor, and he became angry at me, instead of just saying that he didn't have a scissor and letting it go at that.

Sol: She was always looking for a scissor, so I bought her one for her sewing last week. Then yesterday, she again asked me for a scissor instead of using the one I bought her. I feel burdened by her, she always is needy and wants something from me. I have to be her caretaker all the time, like with my mother.

Therapist: That reminds you of feeling burdened by your mother's demands, and having to be a peacemaker and give in to her when you were a child. [He is working through Sol's mother transference to Dora.]

Sol: Yes, it is exactly the same type of burden, and I resent it now as well.

Dora: But he also resents it if he can't be the caretaker. He is always looking to see what I am doing, as if he is the only one who can do it. He finds something for himself to do so he can be the caretaker, and gets agitated until he fills that role.

Sol: She doesn't put herself out for anything, and then I have to do it. If I don't do it, it doesn't get done. She is behaving like her mother, who acted as if she couldn't do anything herself, and sucks me into taking charge.

Therapist: You each feel that the other induces you into this relationship where Sol is the caretaker, and you each resent this. Do you think there is some type of need to perpetuate this form of relationship? [He explores their unconscious projective identification processes, with Sol experiencing himself as having to perform as the savior S+ for his demanding mother, and Dora experiencing Sol as the bad domineering father, O−.]

Dora: He hovers over me and doesn't give me space to breathe.

Sol: She does it to irritate me.

Therapist: Maybe both of you need the other to behave this way, so you each can continue to feel victimized by the other? [He is encouraging self-exploration rather than externalization.]

Sol: I don't know about that. Dora was supposed to have the chairs recaned, and she never got around to it. What am I to do, just let it go? She doesn't assume responsibility.

Dora: It wasn't a mutual decision. You kept badgering me to recane the chairs, until I said I'd take care of it.

Therapist: You, Dora, feel he has to take over, and you, Sol, feels she needs you to perform for her.

Dora: When we first met he admired my capability, since his ex-wife couldn't do a thing by herself. I know why she couldn't; it is easier to let him do it, since he wants things done his way. I feel like an obstinate kid—if he knows so much let him do it. I am not a passive person. He also tells his kids how to do everything and they comply, except his daughter, who wouldn't give him the right time of day.

Therapist: But Sol has needed to assume the role of caretaker to take responsibility to preserve peace since childhood. [Noting that Sol is not simply a bad person, but that he was compelled to perform for his parents to preserve peace.]

Sol: That's right, it was the one identity I had; but it put me in the middle. If I did anything for my father, my mother expressed her resentment openly; and if I did for my mother, my father showed his resentment indirectly.

Therapist: It sounds like you felt trapped and helpless; not only did you have to perform for them, but you were also punished. Do you experience Dora as both your parents? You need to take care of her, like your mother, but you are also punished by her, like your father? [He interprets Sol's double bind and transference.]

Sol: I get it both ways. I'm sure I do it, and always have done it, but Dora also fuels it. I'm comfortable in that role, and maybe I'm used to being resented and unhappy.

Therapist: Dora, Sol feels you fuel it also. Perhaps you might be responding like your mother did to your father. Your mother may have said to herself, if you [her husband] need to dominate me and put your feelings of inadequacy into me, I'll show you and behave inadequately. I'll frustrate you that way, and put my anger into you. [He interprets the trading of projective identifications by her parents, and Dora's identification with her mother's passive-aggressive vengeance.]

Sol: I don't mind doing things for Dora, so long as she doesn't punish me also, and shows me some acknowledgement.

Therapist: Sol did your mother acknowledge your doing things for her that she wanted?

Sol: No. Everything good I did for her was just expected, and I was berated for it by my father, and vice versa.

Dora: But I still am controlled by Sol and want to be free.

Sol: I feel I have to control her, she's uncontrollable with money. She knows it too, she overspends, and we are both frightened about our finances. I'm afraid she will wipe me out and then reject me. I'll be used up and abandoned like an old worn-out shoe. [He expresses fear that if he is no longer useful he will be abandoned. Giving up autonomy, and being used, guards against abandonment. Does Dora also need to be calmed and to have her impulsivity controlled by Sol?]

Therapist: Sol feels you need his controls on your spending.

Dora: Partly he's right; I can't control myself, but he is not capable of controlling me. I see him self-destruct financially in business. He has lost more money than me.

Sol: It isn't a contest of who can lose more money.

Dora: I have difficulty with money. When I feel deprived, I satisfy that emptiness by shopping.

Therapist: Do you feel guilty about that?

Dora: Yes, I'm working on that in my individual therapy. It's a compulsion, and it's a way of punishing Sol. When he is disrespectful of me, and I can't stomach what he's doing but can't stop him, I go out shopping.

Therapist: You [Dora] feel abused, helpless, and angry.

Dora: I feel treated like dirt. He doesn't talk to me with respect for my competence and intelligence. He talks down to me, is disdainful and bullying.

Therapist: Then shopping is your way of counteracting feeling demeaned, of filling yourself up and getting back at Sol.

Dora: At least I get satisfaction for myself by buying nice clothing or other things. I can shut him out of my life for a while and get back at him subconsciously. He is not really taking care of me with his little gifts, like the scissors. The way I would like to be taken care of is for him to earn a good living and be considerate.

Therapist: Both of you want more acknowledgment and consideration from each other then.

CONCLUSION OF TREATMENT

Marital therapy proceeded at a faster pace than usual, since this couple had previously had considerable individual therapy with other therapists (Dora was still in treatment), were functioning at a high level, and could be honest with themselves. Both were able to reown their projective identifications and to continue to work through their conflicts at an intrapsychic level.

Dora continued to work on her identification with her masochistic mother, who had been treated as an incompetent by her father. Dora acknowledged that, like her mother, she expressed her anger at Sol through her indecisiveness. She also dealt with her identification with her critical father, and became aware that she demeaned Sol just as she and her father had done to her mother. She then worked through her guilt toward her mother, and became less self-defeating. As she psychologically separated from her father, she stopped idealizing him. She became aware of her repressed rage at her father. Dora noted that if her father had preferred her to her mother, as if she were his mistress, and then indeed did have an affair with a woman, she distrusted him as well as men in general as unfaithful. Her vengeance toward her father found expression in her attempting to make Sol feel inadequate in comparison to her former wealthy husband, just as Dora had felt inadequate when her father found another woman and when he abandoned Dora during her illness. After working through her rage, she felt she did not need to hurt her father or her husband anymore. She mourned the lack of a real relationship with and nurturance from her father.

Sol continued to work on his guilt and his identification with his destroyed and destroying father. He became aware that his relationship with Dora represented a flip-flop, back and forth, between his internalized self and father object. He felt treated by Dora as if she were like his critical father, and in turn he treated her like his father had treated him. He was then able to work through his rage and guilt toward his exploitative and domineering father. He admitted and owned his feelings of weakness and helplessness as a child, and how he had felt used and denied personal freedom by both his parents. He had always wanted to be loved and admired, and had complied in the role of peacemaker for his parents. When he performed for one of them, he was rewarded by that parent but then punished by the other one. He first felt he was like a "lightning rod," able to divert the anger between his parents away from them and onto himself. Then, he felt, he served as a "shock absorber" to contain the anger in his family, in order to keep his parents' marriage together. He was aware that he also served as a shock absorber to contain Dora's anger at men. He hoped that he would be loved again for being the peacemaker and thus avoid abandonment. However, Dora's father had also been a peacemaker, which only made Sol the target of more of her transferential anger. Sol also misinterpreted Dora's requests or statements as demands or criticisms. He became aware that he was relating to her as though he were still the helpless child living with his critical and controlling parents. He worked through his rage at his mother, father, and Dora, which stemmed from his feeling that he had to comply and sacrifice part of himself in order to be accepted. He admitted to feelings of inadequacy with his parents, never having felt accepted or good enough for either of them. He became aware that part of him wanted Dora also to feel inadequate, so she would experience what he did in growing up. He then recognized that Dora retaliated for his doing this by spending his money. Dora's actions were her way of saying if you make me feel small and insignificant, I can spend your money and diminish you. They both recognized their defiance and vengeance toward each other, which ultimately proved to be mutually self-defeating. They both felt that during their childhoods they had had to comply to a parent for fear of abandonment, and each still felt externally controlled and without autonomy. Sol beame aware that his distancing from Dora was like a symbolic murder of her as with his father. He wiped her out, and she no longer existed. He was able to admit to rageful and murderous feelings that he would have previously found intolerable and felt too guilty to acknowledge. As they developed insight into the genesis of their behavior, they stopped acting out their conflicts, and were able to change their vengeful interaction that had been so destructive to one another. Each of them then worked through their feelings of anger and sadness, connected with separation and the loss of their therapist as treatment proceeded to termination.

14

Termination

CRITERIA FOR TERMINATION

Optimally, termination occurs with the mutual agreement of the therapist and the family that the family has been helped by the treatment, and that no further change can be expected by continuing. In short-term family therapy, termination is easier to define because the goals of treatment are more concrete. The goal may be simply symptom removal or resolution of a particular dysfunctional interaction. At times, because the therapist takes a directive stance, the family itself may wish to discontinue the treatment once these limited goals are achieved. Consciously they may idealize the therapist, but unconsciously the therapist may be experienced as a controlling persecutory bad object, who needs to be escaped from. If the limited goals of the therapist and the family coincide, termination becomes a relatively easy matter.

In analytic family therapies, the matter is more complex because of greater intimacy and more abstract goals. Ideally, termination follows the resolution of resistances and structural changes in the individual members and in the family as a group. However, the conditions necessary to reach the ideal goals for termination may not exist, due to many factors. The family may drop out of treatment, the therapist may leave, or there may be transference/countertransference blocks, and so on. If these factors cannot be changed, the therapist needs to accept the limitations and work through his or her feelings about the premature loss of the family and the incompleteness of their therapy. In this way, the negative countertransference of the therapist will not impede helping the family to separate and work through their feelings about terminating.

What are some of the resistances that need to be resolved before structural changes and termination can occur? I refer first of all to the resistances in individual therapy, before dealing with those in family treatment.

EGO RESISTANCES

These resistances consist of the ego's mechanisms of defense, which serve to avoid anxiety, danger, and displeasure. The main ones are *repression, denial,* and *projection.* In treatment, unconscious thoughts and feelings that are unacceptable or painful need to be made conscious and to be owned by the patient.

The second type of ego resistance is *transference,* which is the hallmark of all analytic forms of therapy. This process involves displacement of conflicts from past objects to present relationships, particularly that with the therapist. Transference to the therapist is encouraged to develop by the assumption of an abstinent neutral position by the therapist, who becomes a screen for the patient's projections. The therapist needs to interpret the transference at the appropriate time, so that the patient remembers, verbalizes, and emotionally reexperiences old relationships in the here and now, instead of just repeating them behaviorally without any conscious awareness.

The third type of resistance is *secondary gain.* Here the ego resists change because of gratification or relief obtained from the symptom itself. This also needs to be interpreted and worked through.

ID RESISTANCES (ACTUALLY OTHER EGO RESISTANCES)

In Freud's one paper dealing with termination (1937), "Analysis Terminable and Interminable," he considered that patients repeat their suffering out of a sense of guilt or masochism, which was due to the death instinct in the id. Most modern psychoanalysts do not adhere to the death instinct, but consider the repetition compulsion as the ego's attempt both at resisting change and at mastery. It is during the working-through process of treatment that the repetition compulsion is dealt with in order to produce change.

Adhesiveness of the libido was another id resistance that Freud (1937) noted in this same paper. Here again, most modern psychoanalysts would see this resistance as due to the rigidity of ego defenses or character structure.

SUPEREGO RESISTANCE

The superego resistance is often overlooked. Some patients resist improvement out of a need to atone for unconscious guilt. This needs to be interpreted and worked through, so that the patient does not sabotage the treatment by self-defeating behavior. An example of this was in the case of Dora and Sol in Chapter 13.

COUNTERTRANSFERENCE RESISTANCE (DUE TO THE THERAPIST)

Countertransference as a source of the therapist's making technical errors in the treatment was first noted by Sandor Ferenczi (1932a). When this is due to a subjective countertransference, it needs to be perceived through self-awareness and corrected by self-analysis. If it is due to objective countertransference, it needs to come to the conscious awareness of the therapist in order for him or her to understand empathically and interpret the internal world of object relations in the patient. Analysts such as Racker (1957), Greenson (1967), and Langs (1978) have also noted that the therapist's countertransference also influences the patient's transference and other resistances. Kohut (1977) found that the therapist's empathic failure markedly increased the patient's resistance. These are interactive processes, with the patient affecting the therapist and the therapist affecting the patient.

OBJECT RELATIONS RESISTANCES

Sandler and Joffe (1969) summarized object relations resistances as follows:

The first resistance involves threats to the patient's self-esteem and personality integrity.

The second object relations resistance involves the restructuring of the patient's internal world of objects, which is experienced as a loss and dreaded. Even though the bad internalized object was founded on a pathological basis, there is difficulty in giving it up. It involves an identity crisis, mourning the loss, and, in additon, modification of existing interpersonal relations. The concept of resisting interpersonal change fits in with family studies regarding homeostasis. The family tries to preserve its homeostatic balance of relationships even though it supports pathological functioning instead of a more adaptive systemic change.

CRITERIA FOR TERMINATION IN OBJECT RELATIONS FAMILY THERAPY

The same resistances that need to be resolved in individual therapy ideally also need to be resolved before termination of object relations family therapy. One marked difference from individual therapy transferences is that those in family therapy exist not only toward the therapist, but between each of the family members. In addition, as the Scharffs (1987) point out, in family therapy there is also a transference of the family as a whole group toward the therapist.

Ideally, the therapeutic alliance, which has helped the family members perceive and experience themselves and others through the therapist's perspective, has become internalized. The therapist has not punished or rejected them for thoughts and feelings that were experienced as too threatening or painful. Because the therapist has been able to contain and detoxify these thoughts and feelings, the family members can now recognize and tolerate them without shame or guilt. Thought and fantasy thereby become clearly differentiated from action.

Under these ideal conditions, there is less need to use such ego defenses as splitting and projective identification, to deny and put into others unacceptable aspects of the self, as a way of externalizing and controlling a problem. By not needing to parcel out aspects of the self into others, family members are permitted to have greater differentiation and autonomy. Interpreting the defenses of splitting and projective identification is essential, since it ties together the systemic, interpersonal, and intrapsychic levels of interaction. Unconscious collusive patterns of object relations in the family that are pathogenic can then be resolved, and the identified patient released from the role of scapegoat, go-between, savior, or avenger. Individuals can reown their problems, and work them through intrapsychically. This facilitates greater ego strength, since all the members can acknowledge unacceptable aspects of themselves, and integrate their own ambivalence.

The family members, having developed insight into their behavior and worked conflicts through in treatment, are able to use more responsible and conscious ways of handling issues. Their behavior is less driven by unconscious drives, affects, and fantasies, and determined more by conscious processes that take into account current reality and are more adaptive to the needs of each other.

The Scharffs (1987) mention that at termination the family can provide the contextual and centered holding for its members that is so necessary for attachment and growth. The family is able to return to or reach its appropriate developmental level, so that it fits in with the developmental needs of its members for intimacy and autonomy.

There is greater acceptance of the strengths and limitations not only of oneself, but of one's parents and family members as separate people. With the renunciation of the need to cure their parents, and of the need for them or others to make up for past deprivations, patients have less self-defeating behavior or desire for vengeance. Hand in hand with this acceptance of themselves, their parents, and other family members, resolution of the transference to the therapist occurs.

TERMINATION AS A DISTINCT PHASE

Termination is one of the most important phases of therapy, and has unique issues associated with it. It is the end of treatment when separation and loss are worked through, resulting in feelings of sadness or anger. Many times termination is not handled well by patients or therapists, because the breaking of attachments is associated with deprivation, abandonment, or death. The therapeutic relationship needs to end, which may bring out strong transferential feelings in the patients and countertransference feelings in the therapist. These tend to be less intense than in individual therapy, since the transference is diluted toward the family therapist. However, the family therapist needs to be sensitive to these issues and to work with them as they come up in treatment.

In the termination process, preexisting problems in each of the family members, of separation and individuation from the mother during early childhood and from the family during later childhood, tend to be revived and reexperienced. Even when the mother and the family later on provided good enough holding, these issues still come up at termination but there is less difficulty in separating. If, however, there was insufficient holding, or if a significant other used the person as a container for projective identification, then separation is more difficult at the termination of treatment. In this latter event, there tends to be fixation at Mahler's (1964) rapprochement subphase of separation individuation. The individuals remain symbiotically tied to an external object, instead of internalizing the mother and developing object and self-constancy. The same fixation, using Klein's (1948) developmental schema, would be the lack of progression from the paranoid-schizoid position to the depressive position. The result is a lack of integration of ambivalence and consolidation of psychic structures, as well as an inability to recognize oneself and others as separate and whole.

During the termination process, the transferences of the family members onto the therapist tend to be either that of the original infantile mother–child relationship, of objects from early childhood or from the current family, or all three. With the prospect of termination, the regression may manifest itself by feelings of anger over exploitation or abandonment, and a demand for satisfaction of unfulfilled developmental needs. These feelings can become manifest even when the family members themselves bring up the topic of termination. If the therapist agrees to termination, they may feel that he or she does not want to see them and is pushing them out the door to get rid of them. The therapist's ability to contain these angry feelings, to represent an object who is constant, nonjudgmental, and not rejecting, helps work these issues through. These problems of termination are relived in the present transference, and can be interpreted so that repressed feelings and thoughts can be expressed openly and contained without being acted out. The therapeutic alliance with the family members, and their internalization of the therapist's functioning, facilitates their looking at themselves objectively and working with the interpretation. They can view the process of termination not simply from an infantile perspective but from an adult viewpoint and thereby work through their transference. If, however, the therapist feels abandoned by the family, as if they were a rejecting mother or father, then the therapist's own countertransference reactions may be a roadblock holding up this process. The therapist may feel deprived or diminished and be angry at the family, and in subtle or overt ways interfere with the normal process of termination. Thus sensitivity to countertransferential issues and resolving them through self-analysis is essential.

The loss of the therapist as an idealized object, into whom family members could put their own infantile grandiosity, goes along with their developing autonomy. They can give up their symbiotic fusion with the therapist, who was seen as an omnipotent and protective parent. The therapist's encouragement of their developing independence and strength relieves them of fear and guilt over separation and individuation. They are not engulfed back into symbiosis, nor rejected for independent strivings by a clinging, "bad" parental object or therapist.

Resolution of the tranference toward the therapist and toward each other allows the members to move developmentally into the depressive position, so that bad internalized objects can be given up. These internalized objects could be a parent's father and/or mother, or the children's parents, who were experienced as preventing separation and individuation out of their own needs. Developmentally during infancy and childhood, separating from this parent and being autonomous was experienced as likely to result in abandonment, and to threaten self-esteem or even survival. Thus separation from this bad object, which had become internalized, is often experienced with dread and anxiety. Individuals may feel that their survival is threatened by some impending catastrophe or illness as they improve. Once this is worked through, the loss of the internalized bad persecutory object can be mourned and given up without threatening personal integrity.

Restructuring of the internal world of object relations for each of the family members can now occur, with resultant modification of their interpersonal relations. The self is experienced as separate and less dependent on external objects to sustain self-esteem and identity. Therefore each of the family members optimally will end treatment with a more coherent and autonomous self. Not only will the family members be more differentiated from one another, but they will be able to function as a group in a more intimate and adaptive fashion that meets each other's needs. Because the family members have achieved insight into their problems and have had a productive, growth-enhancing experience in marital or family therapy, they are more likely to enter individual therapy or engage in other activities to consolidate their newfound gains.

References

Abraham, K. (1911). Manic depressive states and the pregenital levels of the libido. In *Selected Papers on Psychoanalysis*. London: Hogarth Press, 1965.

Ackerman, N. W. (1958). *The Psychodynamics of Family Life*. New York: Basic Books.

Adler, G. (1980). A treatment framework for adult patients with borderline and narcissistic personality disorders. *Bulletin of the Menninger Clinic* 44:171–180.

Adler, G., and Buie, D. H. (1979). Aloneness and borderline psychopathology: the possible relevance of child development issues. *International Journal of Psycho-Analysis* 60:83–96.

Adorno, T. W., Frankel-Brunswick, E., Levinson, D. J., and Sanford, R. N. (1950). *The Authoritarian Personality*. New York: Harper & Row.

Alexander, F. (1954). Psychoanalysis and psychotherapy. *Journal of the American Psychoanalytic Association* 2:722–733.

Alger, I., and Hogan, P. (1969). Enduring effects of videotape playback experience on family and marital relationships. *American Journal of Orthopsychiatry* 39:86–98.

Amidei, N. (1986). Poor families and public policy. Paper presented at the AFTA annual meeting, Washington, DC.

Antonovsky, A., and Lerner, M. J. (1959). Negro and white youth in Elmira. In *Discrimination and Low Incomes,* ed. A. Antonovsky and L. Larwin. New York: New School for Social Research.

Arieti, S. (1962). The psychotherapeutic approach to depression. *American Journal of Psychotherapy* 16:397–406.

Arlow, J. A. (1975). Discussion of Kanzer's paper. *International Journal of Psychoanalytic Psychotherapy* 4:69–73.

Balint, M. (1979). *The Basic Fault.* New York: Brunner/Mazel.

Barry, W. A. (1970). Marriage research and conflict: an integrative review. *Psychological Bulletin* 73:41–54.

Bateson, G. (1972). *Steps to an Ecology of Mind.* New York: Ballantine.

Bateson, G., Jackson, D. D., Haley, J., and Weakland, J. H. (1956). Toward a theory of schizophrenia. *Behavioral Science* 1:251–264.

Becvar, R. J., and Becvar, D. S. (1982). *Systems Theory and Family Therapy: A Primer.* Washington, D C: University Press of America.

Berger, M. (1978). *Videotape Techniques in Psychiatric Training and Treatment.* New York: Brunner/Mazel.

Bergin, A. E. (1971). The evaluation of therapeutic outcomes. In *Handbook of Psychotherapy and Behavior Change,* ed. A. E. Bergin and S. Garfield. New York: Wiley.

Bernstein, B. (1961). Social class and linguistic development: a theory of social learning. In *Education, Economy, and Society,* ed. A. H. Halsey, J. Floud, and C. A. Anderson. Glencoe, IL: The Free Press.

⎯⎯⎯ (1962). Social class, linguistic codes, and grammatical elements. *Language Speech* 5:221–240.

Bieber, I., Dain, H. J., Dince, P. R., et al. (1962). *Homosexuality: A Psychoanalytic Study.* New York: Basic Books.

Bieber, T. B., and Bieber, I. (1968). Resistance to marriage. In *The Marriage Relationship,* ed. S. Rosenbaum and I. Alger. New York: Basic Books.

Bion, W. R. (1961). *Experience in Groups.* New York: Basic Books.

⎯⎯⎯ (1967). *Second Thoughts.* London: Heinemann.

⎯⎯⎯ (1970). *Attention and Interpretation.* London: Tavistock.

Bonime, W. (1959). The psychodynamics of neurotic depression. In *American Handbook of Psychiatry,* vol. 3, ed. S. Arieti. New York: Basic Books.

Boszormenyi-Nagy, I. (1965). A theory of relationships: experience and transaction. In *Intensive Family Therapy,* ed. I. Boszormenyi-Nagy and J. L. Framo. New York: Harper and Row.

Boszormenyi-Nagy, I., and Spark, G. M. (1973). *Invisible Loyalties.* New York: Harper and Row.

Bowen, M. (1978). *Family Therapy in Clinical Practice.* New York: Jason Aronson.

Brenner, C. (1979). Working alliance, therapeutic alliance, and transference. *Journal of the American Psychoanalytic Association (Suppl.)* 27:137–157.

Buber, M. (1958). *I and Thou.* New York: Scribners.

Burnham, D., Gladstone, A., and Gibson, R. W. (1969). *Schizophrenia and the Need-Fear Dilemma.* New York: International Universities Press.

Burton, R. V., and Whiting, J. W. M. (1961). The absent father and cross-sex identity. *Merrill Palmer Quarterly* 7:85–95.

Caligor, L. (1969). Report on Solidarity House Conference, United Automobile Workers, New York.

Clark, K. B. (1964). *Youth in the Ghetto.* New York: Orans.

Clark, K. B., and Clark, M. P. (1950). Emotional factors in racial identification and preference in Negro children. *Journal of Negro Education* 19:341–350.

Chein, I., Gerard, D. L., Lee, R. S., and Rosenfeld, E. (1964). *The Road to H.* New York: Basic Books.

Cohen, N. (1974). *Explorations in the fear of success.* Unpublished doctoral dissertation, Columbia University.

Crocetti, J., Spiro, H. R., and Siassi, I. (1971). Are the ranks closed? Attitudinal social distance and mental illness. *American Journal of Psychiatry* 127:1121–1127.

Dell, P. F. (1982). Beyond homeostasis: toward a concept of coherence. *Family Process* 21:21–41.

_____ (1986). In defense of lineal causality. *Family Process* 25: 513–521.

_____ (1986a). Why do we still call them "paradoxes"? *Family Process* 25:223–234.

Deutsch, M. (1962). Minority group and class status as related to social and personality factors in scholastic achievement. *Society for Applied Anthropology.*

Dicks, H. V. (1963). Object relations theory and marital studies. *British Journal of Medical Psychology* 36:125–129.

Emde, R. N. (1987). The role of positive emotions on development. Paper presented at Pleasure Beyond the Pleasure Principle Conference, Columbia University Center for Psychoanalytic Training and Research, New York.

Erikson, E. H. (1963). *Childhood and Society.* New York: Norton.

_____ (1964). *Insight and Responsibility.* New York: Norton.

Fairbairn, W. R. D. (1952). *Psychoanalytic Studies of the Personality.* London: Tavistock.

_____ (1954). *An Object Relations Theory of the Personality.* New York: Basic Books.

Ferenczi, S. (1920). *Further Contributions to the Theory and Technique of Psychoanalysis.* London: Hogarth Press.

_____ (1932a). *Final Contributions to the Problems and Methods of Psychoanalysis.* New York: Basic Books.

_____ (1932b). Confusion of tongues between adults and the child. Paper presented at the International Psychoanalytic Congress, Weisbaden.

Fleming, J. (1975). Some observations on object constancy in the psychoanalysis of adults. *Journal of the American Psychoanalytic Association* 23:743–760.

Foulkes, S. H. (1948). Introduction to Group-Analytic Psychotherapy. London: William Heinemann Medical Books.

Framo, J. L. (1981). The integration of marital therapy with sessions with family of origin. In *Handbook of Family Therapy,* ed. A. S. Gurman and D. P. Kniskern. New York: Brunner/Mazel.

Fraser, J. S. (1982). Structural and strategic family therapy: a basis for marriage or grounds for divorce? *Journal of Marital and Family Therapy* 8:13–22.

Freud, S. (1905a). The fragment of an analysis of a case of hysteria. *Standard Edition* 7:3–124.

_____ (1905b). Three essays on the theory of sexuality. *Standard Edition* 7:125–248.

_____ (1915). Papers on metapsychology. *Standard Edition* 14:105–260.

_____ (1920). Beyond the pleasure principle. *Standard Edition* 18:3–66.

_____ (1921). Group psychology and the analysis of the ego. *Standard Edition* 18:67–143.

_____ (1923). The ego and the id. *Standard Edition* 19:3–66.

_____ (1937). Analysis terminable and interminable. *Standard Edition* 23:216–253.

_____ (1938). Splitting of the ego in the process of defense. *Standard Edition* 23:273–278.

_____ (1940). An outline of psychoanalysis. *Standard Edition* 23:139–171.

Gill, M. M. (1982). The analysis of the transference. In *Curative Factors in Dynamic Psychotherapy,* ed. S. Slipp. New York: McGraw-Hill.

Gitelson, M. (1962). The curative factors in psychoanalysis. The first phase of psychoanalysis. *International Journal of Psycho-Analysis* 43:194–205.

Glueck, S., and Glueck, E. (1950). *Unraveling Juvenile Delinquency.* New York: Commonwealth Fund.

Gould, R. E. (1967). Dr. Strangeclass or how I stopped worrying about the theory and began treating the blue-collar worker. *American*

Journal of Orthopsychiatry 37:78–86.

Greenberg, G. S. (1977). The family interactional perspective: A study and examination of the work of Don D. Jackson. *Family Process* 16:385–412.

Greenberg, S. (1980). An experimental study of underachievement: the effects of subliminal merging and success-related stimuli on the academic performance of bright, underachieving high school students. Unpublished doctoral dissertation, New York University.

Greenson, R. R. (1967). *The Technique and Practice of Psychoanalysis.* New York: International Universities Press.

Grier, W. H., and Cobbs, P. M. (1968). *Black Rage.* New York: Basic Books.

Grotstein, J. S. (1981). *Splitting and Projective Identification.* New York: Jason Aronson.

Gunderson, J. G., and Singer, M. T. (1975). Defining borderline patients: an overview. *American Journal of Psychiatry* 132:1–10.

Gurman, A. S. (1983). Family therapy research and the "new epistemology." *Journal of Marital and Family Therapy* 9:227–234.

Haley, J. (1963). *Strategies of Psychotherapy.* New York: Grune and Stratton.

—— (1980). *Leaving Home: The Therapy of Disturbed Young People.* New York: McGraw-Hill.

Harrington, M. (1962). *The Other America.* Baltimore: Penguin.

Hartmann, H. (1964). *Essays on Ego Psychology.* New York: International Universities Press.

Heimann, P. (1950). On countertransference. *International Journal of Psycho-Analysis* 31:81–84.

Heisenberg, W. (1958). *The Physicist's Conception of Nature.* New York: Harcourt Brace.

Herz, F. M., and Rosen, E. J. (1982). Jewish families. In *Ethnicity and Family Therapy,* ed. M. McGoldrick, J. K. Pearce, and J. Giordano. New York: Guilford Press.

Herzog, E. (1966). Is there a breakdown of the Negro family? *Social Work,* January, pp. 3–10.

Hirsch, S., and Leff, J. (1971). Parental abnormalities of verbal communication in the transmission of schizophrenia. *Psychological Medicine* 1:118–127.

Hollingshead, A. B., and Redlich, F. C. (1958). *Social Class and Mental Illness.* New York: Wiley.

Horney, K. (1950). *Neurosis and Human Growth.* New York: Norton.

Jackson, D. D. (1957). The question of family homeostasis. *Psychiatric Quarterly (Suppl.)* 31:79–90.

Jacobson, E. (1964). *The Self and the Object World*. New York: International Universities Press.

James, W. (1963). *Pragmatism and Other Essays*. New York: Washington Square Press.

Janik, A., and Toulmin, S. (1973). *Wittgenstein's Vienna*. New York: Simon and Schuster.

Johnson, R. (1957). Negro reactions to minority group status. In *American Minorities,* ed. M. L. Barron. New York: Knopf.

Johnson, A. M., and Szurek, S. A. (1954). Etiology of antisocial behavior in delinquents and psychopaths. *Journal of the American Medical Association* 154:814–817.

Johnston, M., and Holzman, P. (1979). *Assessing Schizophrenic Thinking*. San Francisco: Jossey-Bass.

Kanter, D., and Neal, J. H. (1985). Integrative shifts for the theory and practice of family systems therapy. *Family Process* 24:13–30.

Kardiner, A., Karush, A., and Ovesey, L. (1959). A methodological study of Freudian theory. II: The libido theory. *Journal of Nervous and Mental Disease* 129:133–143.

Kardiner, A., and Ovesey, L. (1951). *The Mark of Oppression*. New York: Norton.

Katz, D., McLintock, C., and Sarnoff, I. (1957). The measurement of ego-defense as related to attitude change. *Journal of Personality* 25:465–474.

Keeney, B. P. (1983). *Aesthetics of Change*. New York: Guilford Press.

Kernberg, O. F. (1975). *Borderline Conditions and Pathological Narcissism*. New York: Jason Aronson.

_____ (1976). *Object Relations Theory and Clinical Psychoanalysis*. New York: Jason Aronson.

_____ (1986). Identification and its vicissitudes as observed in psychosis. *International Journal of Psycho-Analysis* 67:147–159.

Klein, M. (1934). A contribution to the pathogenesis of the manic depressive states. In *Contributions to Psychoanalysis 1921–1945*. London: Hogarth Press, 1948.

_____ (1946). Notes on some schizoid mechanisms. *International Journal of Psycho-Analysis* 27:99–110.

_____ (1948). *Contributions to Psychoanalysis, 1921–1945*. London: Hogarth Press.

_____ (1975). *Envy and Gratitude and Other Works 1946–1963*. New York: Delacorte Press.

Kohut, H. (1977). *The Restoration of the Self*. New York: International Universities Press.

Komarovsky, M. (1940). *The Unemployed Man and His Family*. New

York: Holt, Rinehart & Winston.

Kressel, K., and Slipp, S. (1975). Perceptions of marriage related to engagement in conjoint therapy. *Journal of Marriage and Family Counseling,* October, pp. 367–377.

Langner, T. S., and Michael, S. T. (1963). *Life Stress and Mental Health.* Glencoe, IL: The Free Press.

Langs, R. (1976). *The Bipersonal Field.* New York: Jason Aronson.

——— (1978). *The Listening Process.* New York: Jason Aronson.

——— (1982). Countertransference and the process of cure. In *Curative Factors in Dynamic Psychotherapy,* ed. S. Slipp. New York: McGraw-Hill.

Lachkar, J. (1985). Narcissistic/borderline couples: theoretical implications for treatment. *Dynamic Psychotherapy* 3:109–125.

Leff, J. P. (1976). Schizophrenia and sensitivity to the family environment. *Schizophrenia Bulletin* 2:566–574.

Leighton, A. H. (1959). *My Name is Legion.* New York: Basic Books.

——— (1965). Poverty and social change. *Scientific American* 212:21–27.

Lewin, K. (1935). Psycho-sociological problems of a minority group. *Character and Personality* 3:175–187.

Lewis, O. (1959). *Five Families.* New York: Basic Books.

——— (1961). *The Children of Sanchez.* New York: Random House.

——— (1966). *La Vida.* New York: Random House.

Lidz, T. A., Cornelison, A. R., Fleck, S., and Terry, D. (1957). The intrafamilial environment of schizophrenic patients. II: Marital schism and marital skew. *American Journal of Psychiatry* 114:241–248.

Linehan, E. (1979). A study of the effects of subliminal symbiotic stimulation on self-disclosure during counseling. Unpublished doctoral dissertation, St. John's University.

Lippitt, R., and White, R. K. (1958). An experimental study of leadership and group life. In *Readings in Social Psychology,* ed. E. E. Maccoby, T. M. Newcomb, and E. L. Hartley. New York: Holt, Rinehart & Winston.

Locke, H. J., and Wallace, K. M. (1959). Short marital adjustment and prediction tests: their reliability and validity. *Marriage and Family Living* 21:251–255.

Mahler, M. S. (1964). On the significance of the normal separation-individuation phase. In *Drives, Affects, and Behavior,* vol. 2, ed. M. Schur. New York: International Universities Press.

——— (1965). On early infantile psychosis: The symbiotic and autistic syndromes. *Journal of the American Academy of Child Psychiatry* 4:554–568.

Mahler, M. S., and Furer, M. (1968). *On Human Symbiosis and the Vicissitudes of Individuation.* Vol. 1. New York: International Universities Press.

Mahler, M. S., Pine, F., and Bergman, A. (1975). *The Psychological Birth of the Human Infant: Symbiosis and Individuation.* New York: Basic Books.

Martin, A. (1975). The effect of subliminal stimulation of symbiotic fantasies on weight loss in obese women receiving behavioral treatment. Unpublished doctoral dissertation, New York University.

Masterson, J. F., and Rinsley, D. B. (1975). The borderline syndrome: the role of the mother in the genesis and psychic structure of the borderline personality. *International Journal of Psycho-Analysis* 56:163–177.

Maturana, H. R. (1978). Biology of language. The epistemology of reality. In *Psychology and Biology of Language and Thought,* ed. G. A. Miller and E. Lenneberg. New York: Academic Press.

McGill, D., and Pearce, J. K. (1982). British families. In *Ethnicity and Family Therapy,* ed. M. McGoldrick, J. K. Pearce, and J. Giordano. New York: Guilford Press.

McGoldrick, M. (1982). Irish families. In *Ethnicity and Family Therapy,* ed. M. McGoldrick, J. K. Pearce, and J. Giordano. New York: Guilford Press.

Merton, R. K. (1957). Social structure and anomie. In *Social Theory and Social Structure,* ed. R. K. Merton. Glencoe, IL: The Free Press.

Milner, E. (1953). Some hypotheses concerning the influence of segregation on Negro personality development. *Psychiatry* 16:291–297.

Minuchin, S. (1964). Family structure, family language, and the puzzled therapist. Paper presented at the American Orthopsychiatric Association Annual Meeting, Chicago.

———— (1974). *Families and Family Therapy.* Cambridge MA: Harvard University Press.

Minuchin, S., Montalvo, B., Guerney, B. G., Rosman, B. L., and Schumer, F. (1967). *Families of the Slums.* New York: Basic Books.

Modell, A. H. (1976). The holding environment and the therapeutic action of psychoanalysis. *Journal of the American Psychoanalytic Association* 24:285–307.

Moynihan, D. P. (1965). *The Negro family, the case for national action.* Office of Policy Planning and Research, U.S. Department of Labor. Washington, DC: U.S. Government Printing Office.

Myers, J. K., and Roberts, B. H. (1959). *Family and Class Dynamics in Mental Illness.* New York: Wiley.

Nacht, S. (1964). Silence as an integrative factor. *International Journal of Psycho-Analysis* 45:299–308.

Neiderland, W. G. (1965). The role of the ego in the recovery of early memories. *Psychoanalytic Quarterly* 34:564–571.

Paolino, T. J., and McCrady, B. S. (1978). *Marriage and Marital Therapy: Psychoanalytic, Behavioral, and Systems Theory Perspectives.* New York: Brunner/Mazel.

Palmatier, J. (1980). The effects of subliminal symbiotic stimulation in the behavioral treatment of smoking. Unpublished doctoral dissertation, University of Montana.

Parloff, M. B. (1976). The narcissism of small differences and some big ones. *International Journal of Group Psychotherapy* 26:311–319.

Pettigrew, T. (1964). Negro American personality: why isn't more known? *Journal of Social Issues,* April, pp. 4–23.

Racker, H. (1957). The meanings and uses of countertransference. *Psychoanalytic Quarterly* 26:303–357.

Rainwater, L. (1966). Crucible of identity: the Negro lower-class family. *Daedalus, Journal of the American Academy of Arts and Sciences,* Winter, pp. 172–216.

Rinsley, D. B. (1985). Notes on the pathogenesis and nosology of borderline and narcissistic personality disorders. *Journal of the American Academy of Psychoanalysis* 13:317–328.

Rodman, H. (1968). Family and social pathology in the ghetto. *Science* 161:756–762.

Rosen, V. H. (1955). The reconstruction of a traumatic childhood event in a case of derealization. *Journal of the American Psychoanalytic Association* 3:209–221.

Rotunno, M., and McGoldrick, M. (1982). Italian families. In *Ethnicity and Family Therapy,* ed. M. McGoldrick, J. K. Pearce, and J. Giordano. New York: Guilford Press.

Ruesch, J. (1956). Communication difficulties amongst psychiatrists. *American Journal of Psychotherapy* 10:432–447.

Sager, C. J. (1976). *Marriage Contracts and Couple Therapy.* New York: Brunner/Mazel.

Sampson, H., and Weiss, J. (1977). Research on the psychoanalytic process: an overview. *The Psychotherapy Research Group,* Bulletin No. 2, March, Department of Psychiatry, Mt. Zion Hospital and Medical Center.

Sandler, J., and Joffe, W. (1969). Toward a basic psychoanalytic model. *International Journal of Psycho-Analysis* 50:79–90.

Sass, L. A., Gunderson, J. G., Singer, M. T., and Wynne, L. C. (1984). Parental communication deviance and forms of thinking in male schizophrenic offspring. *Journal of Nervous and Mental Disease*

172:513–520.

Scanzoni, J. (1967). Socialization, achievement and achievement values. *American Sociological Review* 32:449–456.

Schafer, R. (1977). The interpretation of transference and the conditions of loving. *Journal of the American Psychoanalytic Association* 25:335–362.

Scharff, D. E., and Scharff, J. S. (1987). *Object Relations Family Therapy.* Northvale, NJ: Jason Aronson.

Scheflen, A. E. (1963). Communication and regulation in psychotherapy. *Psychiatry* 2:126–136.

———— (1964). The significance of posture in communications systems. *Psychiatry* 27:316–331.

Schurtman, R. (1979). Subliminal symbiotic stimulation as an aid in the counseling of alcoholics. Unpublished doctoral dissertation, New York University.

Searles, H. (1975). The patient as therapist to his analyst. In *Tactics and Techniques in Psychoanalytic Therapy. Vol. 2: Countertransference,* ed. P. Giovacchini. New York: Jason Aronson.

Segal, H. (1964). *Introduction to the Work of Melanie Klein.* New York: Basic Books.

Selvini-Palazzoli, M. (1974). *Self Starvation: From the Intrapsychic to the Transpersonal Approach to Anorexia Nervosa.* London: Chaucer.

Selvini-Palazzoli, M., Boscolo, L., Cecchin, G., and Prata, G. (1978). *Paradox and Counterparadox.* New York: Jason Aronson.

Shands, H. C. (1971). *The War with Words.* The Hague: Mouton.

Shapiro, E. R., Zinner, J., Shapiro, R. L., and Berkowitz, D. A. (1975). The influence of family experience on borderline personality development. *International Review of Psycho-Analysis* 2:399–411.

———— (1977). The borderline ego and the working alliance: indications for family and individual treatment in adolescence. *International Journal of Psycho-Analysis* 58:77–87.

Shapiro, R. J., and Budman, S. H. (1973). Defection, termination, and continuation in family and individual therapy. *Family Process* 12:55–67.

Silverman, L. H. (1971). An experimental technique for the study of unconscious conflict. *British Journal of Medical Psychology* 44:17–25.

———— (1975). On the role of laboratory experiments in the development of the clinical theory of psychoanalysis. *International Review of Psychoanalysis* 2:43–64.

Silverman, L. H., Frank, S., and Dachinger, P. (1974). A psychoanalytic reinterpretation of the effectiveness of systematic desensitization: experimental data bearing on the role of merging fantasies. *Journal of Abnormal Psychology* 83:313–318.

Silverman, L. H., and Wolitzky, C. (1972). The effects of the subliminal stimulation of symbiotic fantasies on the defensiveness of "normal" subjects in telling TAT stories. Research Center for Mental Health. New York: New York University.

Silverman, L. H., and Wolitzky, D. L. (1982). Toward the resolution of controversial issues in psychoanalytic treatment. In *Curative Factors in Dynamic Psychotherapy,* ed. S. Slipp. New York: McGraw-Hill.

Singer, M. T. (1977). The borderline diagnosis and psychological tests: review and research. In *Borderline Personality Disorders,* ed. P. Hartocollis. New York: International Universities Press.

Slipp, S. (1969). The psychotic adolescent in the context of his family. Paper presented at the American Medical Association annual meeting, New York. Also in *The Emotionally Troubled Adolescent and the Family Physician,* ed. M. G. Kalogerakis. Springfield, IL: Charles C Thomas, 1973.

_____ (1973). The symbiotic survival pattern: a relational theory of schizophrenia. *Family Process* 12:377–398.

_____ (1976). An intrapsychic-interpersonal theory of depression. *Journal of the American Academy of Psychoanalysis* 4:389–409.

_____ (1977). Interpersonal factors in hysteria: Freud's seduction theory and the case of Dora. *Journal of the American Academy of Psychoanalysis* 5:359–376.

_____ (1980). Marital therapy for borderline personality disorders. *The American Journal of Family Therapy* 8:67–71. Also in *Practical Problems in Family Therapy,* ed. A. S. Gurman. New York: Brunner/Mazel.

_____ (1981). The conflict of power and achievement. In *Object and Self: A Developmental Approach. Essays in Honor of Edith Jacobson,* ed. S. Tuttman and C. Kaye. New York: International Universities Press.

_____ (1982). *Curative Factors in Dynamic Psychotherapy.* New York: McGraw-Hill.

_____ (1984). *Object Relations: A Dynamic Bridge Between Individual and Family Treatment.* New York: Jason Aronson.

Slipp, S., Ellis, S., and Kressel, K. (1974). Factors associated with remaining in or dropping out of conjoint family treatment. *Family Process* 13:413–426.

Slipp, S., and Kressel, K. (1978). Difficulties in family therapy evaluation. I: a comparison of insight vs. problem-solving approaches. II:

design critique and recommendations. *Family Process* 17:409–422.

_____ (1979). Does family therapy produce change? An overview of outcome studies. *Group* 3:23–34.

Slipp, S., and Nissenfeld, S. (1981). An experimental study of theories of depression. *Journal of the American Academy of Psychoanalysis* 9:583–600.

Spiegel, J. P. (1971). *Transactions: The Interplay Between Individual, Family, and Society*. New York: Science House.

Spinley, B. M. (1953). *The Deprived and the Privileged. Personality Development in English Society*. London: Routledge and Kegan Paul.

Spitz, R. A. (1965). *The First Year of Life*. New York: International Universities Press.

Srole, L., Langner, T. S., Michael, S. T., Opler, M. K., and Rennie, T. A. C. (1962). *Mental Health in the Metropolis: New York Midtown Study*. New York: McGraw-Hill.

Stanton, M. D. (1984). Fusion, compression, diversion, and the workings of paradox: A theory of therapeutic/systemic change. *Family Process* 23:135–167.

Stern, D. N. (1985). *The Interpersonal World of the Infant*. New York: Basic Books.

Stern, D. N., and Sander, L. (1980). New knowledge about the infant from current research: implications for psychoanalysis. *Journal of the American Psychoanalytic Association* 28:181–198.

Stone, M. H. (1988). *Long Term Follow-up of Borderlines: The P.I. 500*. New York: Guilford Press.

Sullivan, H. S. (1953). *The Collected Works of Harry Stack Sullivan*. New York: Norton.

Thomas, A., and Chess, S. (1980). *The Dynamics of Psychological Development*. New York: Brunner/Mazel.

Thompson, C. (1950). *Psychoanalysis: Evolution and Development*. New York: Grove Press.

Tienari, P., Sorri, A., Lahti, I., et al. (1984). *The Finnish Adoptive Family Study of Schizophrenia*. Presented at the International Symposium on the Psychotherapy of Schizophrenia, New Haven, CT.

Toman, W. (1961). *Family Constellation*. New York: Springer.

Towne, M., Messinger, S., and Sampson, H. (1962). Schizophrenia and the marital family: accommodations to symbiosis. *Family Process* 1:304–318.

VanderVeen, F. (1965). The parent's concept of the family unit and child adjustment. *Journal of Counselling Psychology* 12:196–200.

Volkan, V. (1973). Transitional fantasies in the analysis of a narcissistic personality. *Journal of the American Psychoanalytic Association* 21:351–376.

Voltaire (1949). *The Portable Voltaire,* ed. B. R. Redman. New York: Viking Press.

Willi, J. (1984). The concept of collusion: a combined systemic-psychodynamic approach to marital therapy. *Family Process* 23:177–185.

Winnicott, D. W. (1958). *Collected Papers: Through Pediatrics to Psycho-Analysis.* London: Hogarth Press.

_____ (1965). *The Maturational Process and the Facilitating Environment.* New York: International Universities Press.

Witkin, H. A., Lewis, H. B., Hertzman, M., Machover, K., Meissner, P. B., and Wysner, S. (1954). *Personality Through Perception.* New York: Harper and Row.

Wolf, A., and Schwartz, E. K. (1962). *Psychoanalysis in Groups.* New York: Grune and Stratton.

Wynne, L. C. (1986). Structure and lineality in family therapy. In *Evolving Models for Family Change: A Volume in Honor of Salvador Minuchin,* ed. H. C. Fishman and B. L. Rosman. New York: Guilford Press.

Wynne, L. C., Ryckoff, I. M., Day, J., and Hirsch, S. (1958). Pseudomutuality in the family relations of schizophrenics. *Psychiatry* 21:205–220.

Wynne, L. C., and Singer, M. T., (1963). Thought disorder and family relations of schizophrenics. *Archives of General Psychiatry* 9:199–206.

Wynne, L. C., Singer, M. T., Bartko, J., and Toohey, M. L. (1977). Schizophrenics and their families: recent research on parental communication. In *Developments in Psychiatric Research,* ed. J. M. Tanner. London: Hodder and Stoughton.

Yalom, I. D. (1970). *The Theory and Practice of Group Psychotherapy.* New York: Basic Books.

Zetzel, E. R. (1956). Current concepts of transference. *International Journal of Psycho-Analysis* 37:369–378.

Zinner, J., and Shapiro, E. R. (1974). Splitting in families of borderline adolescents. In *Borderline States in Psychiatry,* ed. J. Mack. New York: Grune and Stratton.

Index